The Origins of Woke

Civil Rights Law, Corporate America,
and the Triumph of Identity Politics

The
ORIGINS
of
WOKE

RICHARD HANANIA

BROADSIDE
BOOKS

HarperCollins books may be purchased for educational, business, or sales
promotional use. For information, please email the Special Markets Department at SPsales@harpercollins.com.

Broadside Books™ and the Broadside logo are trademarks of HarperCollins
Publishers.

FIRST EDITION

Library of Congress Cataloging-in-Publication Data
Names: Hanania, Richard, author.
Title: The origins of Woke : civil rights law, corporate America, and the tri-
    umph of identity politics / Richard Hanania.
Description: New York : HarperCollins Publishers, 2023. | Includes index.
    Identifiers: LCCN 2023013172 (print) | LCCN 2023013173 (ebook) | ISBN
    9780063237216 (hardcover) | ISBN 9780063237230 (ebook)
Subjects: LCSH: Civil rights—United States. | Corporate governance—Law
    and legislation—United States. | Corporations—Political aspects—United
    States. | Social engineering—United States. | Identity politics—United
    States. | Business and politics. | Republican Party (U.S. : 1854–)
Classification: LCC KF4749 .H345 2023 (print) | LCC KF4749 (ebook) | DDC
    342.7308/5—dc23/eng/20230608
LC record available at https://lccn.loc.gov/2023013172
LC ebook record available at https://lccn.loc.gov/2023013173

ISBN 978-0-06-323721-6

23 24 25 26 27 LBC 5 4 3 2 1

Contents

Introduction

This book is the product of more than a decade of research and thought about American politics and culture. It was only in the mid-2010s that the subject of "wokeness" came to dominate political discourse. The phenomenon seemed to start on college campuses. Within a few years, it had migrated to other institutions. Those who critique what has happened to our institutions tend to think more of style than substance, pointing to instances of crying college girls demanding safe spaces, angry students yelling at their professors over "microaggressions," and public debates litigating the definition of "woman." From this perspective, when wokeness seeps into policy, it is usually in the context of debates about standardized tests and crime prevention, but it is common to see a self-identified liberal who has an aversion to the aesthetic components of wokeness while accepting most of its policy agenda.

Having followed these issues for years, I saw what was happening differently. To me there was always something off about the mainstream liberal worldview when it came to issues of race and sex, and the role of government in preventing discrimination on certain "protected" grounds. Such goals, I thought, naturally resulted in misguided policies that were destructive in terms of personal freedom, economic growth, and even the mental health of much of the public. I had gone to law school and spent a summer interning at the Center for Individual Rights, a public interest firm that fought against overreaches in civil rights law. When I saw the rise of what most educated people call wokeness, it seemed to be only the long overdue cultural manifestation of assumptions and beliefs that have in many instances been deeply embedded in American law for over half a century.

It is not that culture and aesthetics are unimportant. People can and do legitimately debate moral standards, the purpose of art, and the nature of justice. Wokeness as a cultural phenomenon has something to say about all those things, as does the backlash to it. But what I found strange about the anti-wokeness side of the debate was that its proponents seemed oblivious to the extent to which the beliefs and practices they disliked were mandated by law. No act of Congress or federal regulation technically requires one to express the belief that differences in income between men and women are due to sexism, but expressing the opposite view as a corporation can be extremely costly, and not just because of any potential public relations backlash. In the "marketplace of ideas," the intellectual is free to be a conservative, liberal, libertarian, or anything else. The corporate executive, however, is only given one option. For so many public intellectuals and politicians to be anti-woke but indifferent to civil rights law struck me as similar to worrying about global warming but not bothering to know anything about energy policy.

Of course, something changed in the mid-2010s. But when it comes to how major institutions in the country operate, the changes have mostly been superficial, at least relative to the magnitude of those that occurred decades before. Since at least the 1970s, major corporations have been forced to be highly conscious of race and sex and on the lookout for practices and behaviors that may have a "disparate impact," which the law has considered a sign of discrimination. Since the 1980s, firms have been all but required to police the speech of their employees to prevent them from saying things that might offend women and non-whites, and since 1991 the most litigious among those workers have been able to receive punitive damages in lawsuits, whether or not they suffered career consequences. Opponents of wokeness sometimes say that "facts don't care about your feelings." But the federal judiciary does.

As the anti-woke have observed and noted, corporations today are increasingly likely to make public statements about hot-button issues and pledge support to left-wing academic ideas. Many firms hold trainings about "privilege" that strike most reasonable people as absurd. But when it comes to substantive practices regarding how they run their businesses and manage employees, there is more continuity than change.

It is not difficult to understand why the current discourse would miss all of this. The conceptual similarities between principles of civil rights law and wokeness are easy enough to explain, but the burdens that the law imposes on employers and workers tend to have indirect and complicated effects on how institutions operate and on the larger culture.

My thoughts about the relationship between wokeness and the legal system were spelled out in a June 2021 article called "Woke Institutions Is Just Civil Rights Law." I was surprised to learn just how interesting the revelations in the piece were to conservatives, and to anti-wokes more generally. Those who had never been to law school did not know much about government regulations. At the same time, those with a legal background often had a superficial understanding of the issues involved but had not read or thought too deeply about how the law has shaped the wider culture. On more than one occasion, I have been talking to a highly intelligent conservative activist who was shocked when I told him that there is an executive order mandating that all large government contractors adopt affirmative action programs. The corollary is that an executive order could—at least in theory—also end such programs. Why hasn't any Republican president even felt pressure from his base to undertake such an action, much less actually do it? Well, as it turns out, Ronald Reagan wanted to, and the story of how he was stopped, as told in chapter 6, offers interesting lessons for today's politics.

This book is of more than historical interest. As Friedrich von Hayek wrote in his preface to *The Road to Serfdom*, "When a professional student of social affairs writes a political book, his first duty is plainly to say so. This is a political book."[1] My motivation stems from my opposition to wokeness and my belief that there is a political path forward for those who would like to do something about it. Explaining what this path is involves a discussion of at least four things: the exact provisions in civil rights law that have led to wokeness; how they have influenced institutional culture; the mechanisms that can be used to change the law; and the political prospects of doing so. This last point is extremely important and makes this book unique in the extent to which it hopes to be a useful guide for activists, journalists, policymakers, and others who dislike where the culture has gone and want to do something about it.

Books arguing about public policy usually focus on the laws or regulations their authors would like enacted, while ignoring political realities. An underlying theme of this book, however, is that the marketplace of ideas is somewhat overrated. While there is a vigorous and seemingly evenly matched public debate between intellectuals on the pros and cons of wokeness, in institutions the identity-obsessed left has all the power. This is not because they have the most convincing arguments, but because for half a century laws, institutions, and structures have helped enforce their ideas about social justice. It would be an act of negligence for me to recommend that laws be changed to take away that power without a discussion about the best ways of doing so. Broad social and political developments—increasing polarization, Republican success in appointing federal judges, popular anger against wokeness as a cultural phenomenon, and the rise of right-wing media—put opponents of wokeness in a better position to effect change than they have been in decades past. A major ambition of this book is to help them realize that.

Of course, wokeness has taken on its own momentum largely independent of law. Those who are concerned should continue to create art and form private institutions, including media companies, to push back against the phenomenon. But politicians, bureaucrats, and lawyers also have a major, perhaps preeminent, role to play and should pull the levers available to them. If they do, they might be surprised by the extent of their own power. This book provides the road map to legal reform, seeing it as a necessary, even if not fully sufficient, step to ultimately remaking the culture.

The Origins of Woke

CHAPTER 1

How to Understand Wokeness

At its core, what is American politics about? In some democracies, voters are clearly divided along lines of region, ethnicity, religion, or class. Although such divides clearly exist to a certain extent in the United States, the white majority is relatively split between the two major parties, and economic circumstances are a weak predictor of political attitudes. If there is one lesson that political scientists have learned over the last several decades, it is that American voting behavior is driven by cultural and moral values rather than material interests. If you want to know how the average American voted in the last election, you're better off asking about her attitudes toward political correctness and declaring gender pronouns than about last year's income.

While Americans debate taxes and foreign policy, culture and identity issues appear to be what is truly motivating many of the nation's most prominent activists, media figures, and political leaders on both sides, along with the mass of their voters. In 2016, Republicans selected Donald Trump as their presidential nominee—despite his rejection of much of what had traditionally been the conservative agenda—because he pushed the right cultural buttons. The motto of the 2021 Conservative Political Action Conference (CPAC) was "America Uncanceled." On the other side of the political spectrum, liberal institutions have come to speak with one voice on issues of race, gender, and sexual orientation as they suppress those who dissent from the dominant worldview. A conservative speaker may be shouted down on a college campus today, but it is never for his views on the marginal tax rate or the withdrawal from Afghanistan.

While politicians and media figures on the right complain about the "cancellation" of Dr. Seuss, the use of phrases like "birthing mother," a general decline in masculinity, and the book *White Fragility* becoming a staple of corporate training programs, they have rarely presented realistic solutions to fix what is bothering them. In early 2021, the writer Ramesh Ponnuru said that when he asked Tom Cotton what he as a senator would do about the cultural trends he and other conservatives complain about, "he didn't have much of an answer."[1] Nonetheless, as Ponnuru pointed out, Republican voters want to hear their concerns over what has been called "wokeness" reflected in the words of their leaders. There appears to be little hope that those leaders can actually stem or reverse cultural trends.

Conservative politicians and activists are not alone in being unable to see the connections between culture and law. Whichever side they're on, most knowledgeable observers consider the radical cultural shift of the last few decades to be something that has occurred independently of who actually wins elections or sits atop the government. Following Lyndon Johnson's landslide victory in the wake of the Kennedy assassination, between 1968 and 2016—a span of two generations—Republicans won eight of thirteen presidential elections. Even when Democrats did come into office, it tended to be with relatively conservative candidates. Jimmy Carter's most lasting domestic influence was arguably the deregulation of industry, while Bill Clinton signed welfare reform, famously triangulated on social issues, and declared that "the era of big government is over." Yet on issues related to race, gender, and sexual orientation, the country has consistently moved left, toward institutions emphasizing classification based on identity, a results-based approach to seeking out equality between groups, and the stamping out of dissent from liberal orthodoxy.

In 1975, former Nixon aide and future presidential candidate Pat Buchanan published a book called *Conservative Votes, Liberal Victories*. Nearly half a century later, the title no less accurately summarizes the past several decades. Electoral victories have not made conservative activists and intellectuals happy or satisfied. Particularly in recent years, their rhetoric has trended toward the apocalyptic. In the run-up to 2016 Michael Anton wrote an essay called "The Flight 93 Election" for the *Claremont Review of Books*. He argued that, like the doomed passengers on that plane, conservatives had no choice but to rush the cockpit and hope they survive; a Hillary Clinton presidency was certain death. Trump won the election, yet social liberalism continued its march to the top of nearly all major institutions, even ones that we used to think of as apolitical and unlikely to ever be co-opted by one side of the culture war. Is one to conclude that, if one's concerns are primarily cultural, politics doesn't matter?

Conservatives are not alone in being angry and befuddled by what is going on. Nonpartisan moderate or liberal organizations such as the Foundation for Individual Rights and Expression (FIRE) aim to protect free speech on college campuses. Joe Rogan, one of the most popular podcasters in the country, has supported Bernie Sanders and considers himself to be on the left but is widely disliked by the liberal establishment for his positions on identity-related issues. The media talks about the libertarian leanings of Silicon Valley, and while this is to a large extent exaggerated, the tech industry has produced a disproportionately large number of anti-woke public figures, including Marc Andreessen, Elon Musk, and Peter Thiel. Clearly there is overlap between the concerns of the conservative movement and those outside of it. The behemoth they mutually oppose looks like a house of sand when one considers its intellectual merits but seems unbeatable. It appears to have no center but constantly self-radicalizes, seizing new territory with barely any resistance.

How should we understand wokeness, this force that has come to dominate our politics and culture? Is it really worth worrying about, or is the entire debate nothing but a distraction from larger issues facing humanity? Where did wokeness come from, and how can we get rid of it? The main arguments of this book are radical, but founded on facts that are largely beyond dispute. These facts have been missed, in part, because of education polarization: Republicans have become the less educated party, making them less likely to make direct connections between their cultural concerns and government policy, even when the two are related.

Most Americans subscribe to the idea that their government treats them as individuals. In this view, while the state sometimes interferes in private affairs in order to address cases of explicit discrimination, it mostly subscribes to color-blind ideals. To conservatives, the focus on individualism is a source of pride in the American system. Liberals sometimes argue for more race-consciousness in making policy, as if they are advocating a novel approach to solving inequality. With few exceptions, there has been a general inability or unwillingness to accept the fact that what we call wokeness has been facilitated and encouraged by concrete actions undertaken by the federal government. Not only that, but race- and sex-consciousness are embedded in almost everything that Washington does, and it forces the rest of the country to behave similarly through how it regulates businesses, state and local governments, universities, and other institutions.

The idea that wokeness has something to do with law has lately been associated most prominently with the conservative writer Christopher Caldwell. In *The Age of Entitlement* (2020), he argued that the only way to undo the damaging cultural developments that have emerged in recent decades would be through repealing the Civil Rights Act of 1964.[2] Yet, as will be shown in later chapters, not legislation but mostly the innovations in civil rights law that came out of the federal bureaucracy and the courts have brought us to this point.

What Is Wokeness?

For the purposes of this book, we can say that wokeness has three central pillars.

1. The belief that disparities equal discrimination: Practically any disparity that appears to favor men over women, or whites over non-whites, is caused by some combination of past and present discrimination. Disparities that favor women over men or non-whites

over whites are either ignored or celebrated. This includes not only material outcomes like differences in income or representation in high-status professions but "disparities in thought," or stereotypes about different groups.

2. Speech restrictions: In the interest of overcoming such problematic disparities, speech needs to be restricted, particularly speech that suggests that they are caused by factors other than discrimination or that stereotypes are true.

3. Human resources (HR) bureaucracy: In the interest of overcoming disparities and regulating speech, a full-time bureaucracy is needed to enforce correct thought and action.

The first and second components are key to whether an individual or idea is woke. If a person believes that discrimination is the primary cause of disparities but not that there should be speech restrictions to enforce that idea, we generally just call them a liberal instead of woke. We likewise do not use the term to describe someone who favors speech restrictions but only in the form of banning blasphemy and pornography—they are a religious fundamentalist. The third part involves how wokeness is enforced at an institutional level. It therefore does not refer to any particular person's belief or the content of an ideology, but in practical terms the woke do usually support bureaucracies as necessary to enforce their views.

These three pillars are the core of wokeness and sufficient for the purposes of this book, although much more can obviously be said. For example, the ideology has a standard way to divide people based on race, hence unnatural categories like "Asian American Pacific Islander" and "Hispanic." Often, in the interest of overcoming disparities, wokeness attacks the measurement or standard it holds responsible—hence the war on standardized tests, or even the broader concept of merit. Moreover, the crusade to overcome gender stereotypes has morphed into a questioning of the biological reality of sex, although this principle sits uneasily beside the requirement that the stated identity of a trans-identifying individual is to be taken as an objective fact. Though sexual orientation and gender identity have become increasingly important to wokeness, it is still an open question how long-lasting these debates will be. Controversies over wokeness as related to race and gender issues can be traced to the "PC wars" of the 1980s and 1990s and, before that, to the Nixonian backlash to the turmoil of the 1960s in the aftermath of Johnson's Great Society programs. Meanwhile, LGBT issues are relatively new, and although they are increasingly important to contemporary wokeness, I will mostly set them aside to focus on the core of what has been a long-standing debate in American society.

Each of the three pillars above can be traced to specific government policies. While Congress banned "discrimination" based on certain protected categories in the Civil Rights Act of 1964, it never defined the term. That was done later, mostly through executive actions, the unelected bureaucracy, and the courts. Together, these actors decided that discrimination did not have to be explicit, or even conscious, and that it was a sin committed not against individuals but against "classes" of people entitled to pursue class action remedies. It consisted of practices having a disparate impact on a protected group, potentially creating legal liability regardless of intent. And affirmative action was not only not banned by the CRA but for all practical purposes required by it. The doctrine of the "hostile work environment" made comments that were rude, condescending, or mean a matter not only of hurt feelings but of potential tort or regulatory liability if they had racial or sexual connotations.

Title IX, which as a matter of statutory text simply banned discrimination in government-funded educational institutions and programs, has been used to micromanage the sex lives of college students. The Civil Rights Act of 1991, which allowed punitive damages for certain lawsuits, created financial incentives for individuals to develop extremely thin skins when it came to sensitive issues. And because all of this has been inherently ambiguous about exactly what is or isn't allowed, we have seen the rise of the human resources profession, along with its more recent offshoot, the diversity, equity, and inclusion (DEI) industry, in order to track and enforce the rules. Government got into the business of social engineering, while outsourcing much of the enforcement of its mandates and regulations to the private sector.

While the 1964 Civil Rights Act itself was a popular bill passed by Congress and signed by the president, therefore giving it democratic legitimacy, later innovations mostly came from decisions made by and negotiations between the courts, big business, and the federal bureaucracy. Most of the time, these innovations ignored, or even contradicted, the plain text of the 1964 law and the original intent of those who wrote and voted for it. With a few exceptions, like the Civil Rights Act of 1991, a bureaucratic and legal elite made most of the major decisions regarding what discrimination actually meant, whether the state should be in the business of regulating dating and humor in the workplace, and whether and how major institutions classify people according to ancestry. All the while, the general public was at most dimly aware of what was happening. To borrow an old economic metaphor, the state has been the "invisible hand" molding and shaping institutions toward the collection of values that we now identify with the far left.

While many liberals have expressed concern over cultural trends and neither side of the political spectrum is monolithic, political realities ensure that if any politicians adopt the suggestions put forth in this book in the coming years, they will be Republicans. I take into account political realities not only by explaining how exactly the trends documented in this book can be reversed, but why doing so is probably easier than most observers would think. Just as it took generations to go from a world of the Civil Rights Act, with its promise of color-blindness, to one in which social engineering and discrimination against whites and men is almost universally accepted in major institutions, undoing the cultural damage of the past few decades will take a very long time. Nonetheless, the legal and policy changes that need to be enacted can begin today, and in most cases do not even require new legislation.

The Myth of the Marketplace of Ideas

Cycles of outrage over institutional wokeness have a certain rhythm. Conservatives and centrists might notice, for example, that Google has a training program based on critical race theory, or that a Harvard anthropology professor is facing an absurd sexual harassment allegation.[3] Stories like this, along with countless others, are treated as signs of the triumph of certain ideas. Few will point out that Google is a government contractor, and that contractors are regularly required by the Department of Labor to institute new race and gender training programs.[4] Harvard is similarly under the thumb of federal bureaucrats; in 2014, it reached a settlement with the Department of Education that expanded its Title IX bureaucracy and mandated the lowest possible standard for establishing sexual harassment and assault.[5] While the federal regulation of universities, unlike the regulation of contractors, has been extensively covered in the media, there is usually enough of a time delay between when new requirements are instituted and when their results are felt that few make the connection between them. When every employer in the country has to pay a Social Security tax, we understand that they all take the same steps because the federal government requires them to. Yet when major institutions throughout the country all start taking the exact same positions on matters of race and sex, there is a tendency to treat each one of them as making an independent decision. Civil rights law is not as precise as Social Security requirements, but its rules are no less binding.

In many cases, their lack of precision can make them more consequential by creating uncertainty and a chilling effect on speech and conduct throughout American life.

Intellectuals tend to put a great deal of faith in the importance of ideas. If something has gone wrong, it is often said to be because society decided to listen to Philosopher A instead of Philosopher B. It is therefore unsurprising that opponents of wokeness will often trace its rise to individuals like Karl Marx, Michel Foucault, Herbert Marcuse, or—in the case of the really intellectually ambitious—Martin Luther. If only the United States had rejected the ideas of a few European intellectuals instead of letting them "march through the institutions," or all of Christendom was still under the jurisdiction of the pope, none of this would have happened. Similarly, those who call themselves classical liberals, often from within academy, talk about society moving away from the principles of tolerance and free speech as if it is simply a matter of individuals exchanging one philosophy for another.

For example, in *The Diversity Myth*, originally published in 1995, David Sacks and Peter Thiel saw the switch from the classics to so-called multicultural education at Stanford as a microcosm of what was happening to higher education and the rest of society. More recently Helen Pluckrose and James Lindsay argue that social justice ideology can be traced to postmodern philosophy, which at first "developed in relatively obscure corners of academia" and now "has spread to other parts of the academy, into activism, throughout bureaucracies, and to the heart of primary, secondary, and post-secondary education."[6] They contend that postmodernism "co-opted the notion of social justice from the civil rights movements and other liberal and progressive theories," and that this began "just as legal equality had largely been achieved." When discussing the negative societal effects of the Frankfurt School, Pluckrose and Lindsay echo socially conservative thinkers like Pat Buchanan and Michael Lind, who conceptualize their opponents as "cultural Marxists." Professor Paul Gottfried finds roots that are even deeper, arguing that political correctness is a kind of "secular theocracy" and emphasizing the "fit between the current state of Protestant Germanic religious consciousness and the politics of guilt."[7]

A historical perspective, however, provides many reasons to doubt theories that blame any particular philosophy or religion for what has happened. Wokeness resembles civil rights law more than it does Protestantism or the writings of any postmodern philosopher, and we can look at the historical and legal record to understand the motivations of those who made that law. Pluckrose and Lindsay are mistaken when they say that legal equality was achieved in the 1960s. Within just a few years after the passing of the Civil Rights Act, the government was mandating that employers divide people by race and sex, giving preference to supposedly disadvantaged groups, and even drawing congressional districts in ways that legitimized tribalism, under the assumption that the right to vote wasn't enough, and that American citizens of certain backgrounds could only be adequately represented by members of their own race.[8] A particular problem for the idea that wokeness came from the university is the fact that identity politics had to originally be forced upon much of higher education by Washington, with the Department of Health, Education, and Welfare originally coercing schools like Columbia and UC Berkeley to adopt quota-based faculty hiring during the early 1970s.[9] The government mandates came first, and the ideology later.

This shouldn't be too surprising. We understand the primacy of politics over ideology when we read about the histories of other countries. After a communist regime takes power and we see a rise in pro-communist rhetoric coming from the government and the rest of society, we accept that what has happened is that most people are apolitical most of the time and will express support for the values and ideas least likely to get them into trouble. It is not that one side has triumphed in the marketplace of ideas.

To understand why Russia was communist in 1960, it is more useful to study 1917 and the years immediately after than it is to look at the doctrines of the Russian Orthodox Church and the culture of eighteenth-century peasants. Of course, a new regime will inspire true believers in the dominant ideology throughout the system. At the same time, we understand that removing the influence of harmful ideas is primarily a political project, one that depends on a small group of individuals changing the nature of the regime they live under. It is not a matter of winning a debate within the larger society and hoping that more people start to act differently based on new convictions and without their incentives to do so having been changed.

Long before wokeness was a cultural phenomenon, it was law. Just because the post–civil rights regime in the US has been less overtly authoritarian than other official state ideologies does not mean it has not been effective in reshaping society. The secret to its success is in its hidden, indirect nature. Rather than having a government that loudly and boldly proclaims a certain set of beliefs and then goes and locks up dissenters, civil rights law involves constantly nudging institutions in the direction of being obsessed with identity and suppressing speech, all while it speaks in the language of freedom and nondiscrimination. Enforcement is not carried out by the state itself, but mostly outsourced to trial lawyers and the human resources industry, at the expense of private institutions, which end up absorbing much of the cost of and backlash to political correctness. The fact that there is occasion to write this book—that American conservatives and moderates can at the same time be obsessed with wokeness and have so little understanding of where it comes from—is a testament to the success of civil rights law in remaking society while being able to obscure what it has been doing.

Arguably, it would have been difficult to design a more effective system of social engineering, one aiming to change matters as fundamental as how men and women date and appropriate standards of interracial communication, at least in a democracy. It is tempting to believe that it was actually designed in the sense that there was a small group of individuals who created the laws that we now live under, all the while foreseeing their downstream effects on society. This would be a mistake. In tracing the development of civil rights law over time, we can see that it was not created by philosophically inclined liberals who were reading Marcuse and Gramsci. The historical record is clear on this point. The members of Congress who voted for the Civil Rights Act believed that they were dismantling a caste system in the South that was sustained by intentional and conscious private and state-backed discrimination. They did not see the bill as a way to remake American society, redistribute wealth, or destroy capitalism.

From there, politicians and government bureaucrats in institutions like the Equal Employment Opportunity Commission (EEOC) and the Department of Labor, usually under pressure to produce tangible results, undertook a long-term project to get around the plain text of the law and ultimately try to achieve equality of outcome, first for blacks and later for other minorities and women.[10] Sometimes their motivations were extremely idiosyncratic, as when President Nixon tried to sell congressional Republicans on racial quotas in order to create friction within the Democratic coalition between the civil rights lobby and organized labor.[11] Other times they were engaged in more normal political behavior, which meant seeking votes or responding to pressure from well-organized interest groups.

At each point in the process, actors were constrained by political, legal, and bureaucratic factors. This forced even the most zealous advocates to compromise, sometimes in ways that appeared to weaken civil rights law but ultimately made it a more effective tool of social engineering. For example, many liberals within the federal bureaucracy wanted to impose racial quotas on industry, which contradicted the plain text and original intent of the Civil Rights Act. They instead had to settle for standards like disparate impact, which said that any hiring practice that had a disproportionately negative effect on minorities or women was presumptively illegal.

While this interpretation of the law was no more legally defensible, the Supreme Court ultimately signed off on it. Rather than employers being allowed simply to fill a quota and otherwise forget about race and sex, they had to navigate a world in which almost everything that they said or did could potentially get them into trouble. This made the more centrist approach to civil rights law seemingly less heavy-handed but culturally more important, as employers had to rethink every aspect of their relationship with their employees and the wider public. The irony is that if the left had achieved more of a total victory in the 1960s and 1970s and had been able to mandate racial quotas, there may have been less of a need to remake the American workplace.

The development of laws surrounding workplace speech can be understood in a similar way. One could imagine a government regulation that simply banned employees from dating coworkers or made it against the law to say certain words. Such a course would have been politically difficult and likely struck down as unconstitutional. Instead, the law says that such conduct can violate civil rights law and be considered harassment if it is "severe and pervasive." Nothing is explicitly allowed, or prohibited. Employers have little choice but to be extremely cautious, while creating bureaucracies and processes that signal to judges and regulators that they take the issue of workplace harassment seriously.

Perhaps the clearest example of an intellectual concept being used as a post-hoc justification for a political compromise that was historically contingent can be seen in the rise of the idea of "diversity." Throughout most of the 1960s and 1970s, Americans debated whether there should be racial preferences for black Americans. Conservatives argued that the law should be color-blind, while liberals wanted racial balancing in order to undo the effects of past discrimination. In *University of California v. Bakke* (1978), the Supreme Court was bitterly divided on the issue. Four justices would have allowed the quota system at the Medical School of the University of California at Davis to stand, while four others would have simply struck it down. The case thus ultimately came down to the opinion of Justice Lewis F. Powell Jr., who held that while quotas were illegal, the Fourteenth Amendment did allow government institutions to consider race in the interest of seeking a diverse student body.

Because it ultimately decided the case, Powell's opinion was the most influential on the Court, but it was also the least coherent. The four liberal justices pointed out that a system that gives bonus points based on race operates in pretty much the same way as a quota system, the only real difference being that the former is less honest and therefore more politically palatable. The Powell view—that it was acceptable to consider race as one factor in order to achieve diversity, but quotas were illegal—was confirmed by majorities in the *Gratz v. Bollinger* and *Grutter v. Bollinger* cases twenty-five years later. Once again, there was more intellectual honesty on both the right and the left than there was in the center. Chief Justice William Rehnquist, in a dissent signed on to by other conservatives in *Grutter*, provided data proving that the University of Michigan was engaging in racial balancing. Justice Ruth Bader Ginsburg, in her dissent in *Gratz*, wrote of the strangeness of banning quotas but being able to reach the same ends "through winks, nods, and disguises."

Despite the ad hoc nature of the diversity rationale and the logical incoherence of the position that considering race is acceptable but quotas are not, we can see how Justice Powell's opinion in *Bakke* became official ideology throughout American elite institutions. Peter Wood, in *Diversity: The Invention of a Concept*, searches major newspapers and court decisions before *Bakke* and finds almost no mention of the benefits of diversity in higher education.[12] The University of California did not even put much emphasis on diversity in the arguments it presented to the Supreme Court, and the idea was barely mentioned in the original opinion of the California Supreme Court.

In the years after the decision, all this changes. The number of newspaper articles mentioning diversity in higher education goes from a trickle to a flood, as it becomes the standard justification for affirmative action policies. We can see the invention of a concept in real time. While "diversity" is certainly an idea, it is not one that can claim any kind of intellectual depth or historical pedigree. It was basically the creation of one judge acting out of either political timidity or intellectual laziness.

At its root, the original push for quotas was based on sympathy for the situation of African Americans as they began to advocate for equal rights, white guilt over their plight, and a desire to make things better. Before the Civil Rights Act, the entirety of the civil rights lobby was united in consistently calling for racially neutral anti-discrimination laws.[13] Soon, however, there was a realization among elite institutions that, under a color-blind system of college admissions, there might not be many more blacks in positions of power and authority than there were before the Civil Rights Act.

Political norms and legal standards emerged in the context of years of violent inner-city riots, and major American institutions saw racial preferences as a way to calm the residents of urban centers that seemed to be slipping into anarchy. Perhaps the two best historians of the period in question are in agreement on this point. In *The Civil Rights Era: Origins and Development of National Policy, 1960–1972*, Hugh Davis Graham convincingly argues that—in contrast to the pleasant-sounding conventional wisdom that violence usually hurts a cause—it was inner-city riots that originally convinced policymakers in Washington to go beyond color-blindness and adopt policies like affirmative action and minority set-asides in order to buy social peace.[14] The sociologist John Skrentny agrees, seeing affirmative action as a kind of "crisis management" during a period of mass violence, and shows how moderate black leadership was pushed aside through pressure from below in favor of a new generation of activists interested in using intimidation to bend institutions.[15] Some of Tom Wolfe's works, particularly *Mau-Mauing the Flak Catchers*, serve to dramatize parts of this dynamic.

Whether policies like affirmative action and minority set-asides are actually useful in achieving social peace is beside the point; self-styled "community leaders" often do a good job of convincing politicians and bureaucrats that they are. We saw something like this happen in the aftermath of the death of George Floyd, where the more communities rioted, the more convinced institutions became that they had to listen to activists who could claim to speak for them.

The historical record reveals that wokeness can be understood as a series of political compromises. Some, like the *Bakke* decision, while intellectually incoherent, are sufficiently successful in obscuring what is being done that the political salience of the relevant policy is lowered. This means diversity initiatives but not quotas, and vague sexual harassment laws but not direct prohibitions on speech or conduct, which would be more of an explicit repudiation of traditional American freedoms. Instead of policies with clear justifications, guidance, and goals, the law comes to act as a sort of ethical scold that is responsive to mass panics and evolving ideas about nondiscrimination and equality that can be easily incorporated into the current system without gaining approval through the democratic process.

Universities adopting quota systems that they justified as necessary to redress historical wrongs done to blacks, for example, would at least have had a limited cultural effect, as affirmative action has in other countries where it is practiced. In contrast, anchoring affirmative action in the rationale of "diversity" required the creation of a new and largely incoherent official ideology that has been used to justify crusades against "inequity" and constant management of the thoughts and behaviors of students and faculty. Only after this process is complete and the initial rationale is set—in this case by judicial fiat—do we see the intellectual justifications, as when universities started citing supposed empirical evidence for the benefits of diversity in the years after the *Bakke* decision.[16]

In addition to the historical record, there is another reason to doubt that wokeness is the product of philosophical currents with deep roots in American history or Western culture. As critics point out, many of the opinions educated people feel coerced to accept are not even consistent, let alone representative of any particular philosophy. Whenever there is a lucrative profession that attracts a disproportionate number of men, the only socially acceptable—in some cases, the only legally permissible—view is that women are being discriminated against, if they happen to find themselves in the field, or are somehow discouraged from entering the field in the first place. Entire academic disciplines are built around the idea that differences between men and women are based on social conditioning.[17] What are we to make, then, of the sudden triumph of the view that trans identity is an immutable characteristic, meaning that individuals born with XY chromosomes can "know" that they are women, often by citing evidence like a desire to wear dresses and play with dolls as a child? At the same time, when a biological female feels the urge to do those exact same things, we look for social, rather than genetic, causes of said behavior.

Similarly, we can understand that sex was included in the Civil Rights Act as a protected category for very strange and idiosyncratic reasons, placed in the bill through the machinations of a southern segregationist in the hopes of killing it. Nonetheless, within a few years, feminist activists were pushing for the executive branch to take the prohibition on sex discrimination as seriously as it took discrimination against blacks. Now as then, feminist activists have tended to be disproportionately career-focused, meaning they were the ones who determined the kind of "womanhood" that the law would cultivate and protect. To some, blank-slate notions of gender were appealing, as such ideas validated their own choices and inclinations. The fact that feminist and LGBT dogma contradict each other is a problem for logicians and political philosophers but not for the law or the psychology of true believers. Wokeness is rooted in neither a blank-slate view of human nature nor genetic determinism. It can force individuals to adopt one perspective on one issue and the opposite on another, as when a reporter for the *Daily Caller* asked members of the Congressional Black Caucus why men tended to be arrested for crimes at higher rates than women, and two of them cited biological realities and group differences in behavior.[18]

Gender ideology is only the most absurd and extreme example of the contradictions of wokeness. It inspires a backlash because it reaches a point where the reigning ideology goes too far even for "Havel's greengrocer," a stand-in for the average citizen who does what he is told so as to be able to live a quiet life as long as he can maintain some dignity.[19] Yet we find parallel absurdities in how we think about and classify people according to race; bureaucratic processes and decisions made mostly in the 1960s and 1970s determined which groups were protected and which were not, and narrative and law have been built around those rules ever since. Why should relatively well-off Cubans get government advantages and privileges over Cajuns? A Yemeni immigrant is considered white by the federal government, yet a pure-blooded Spaniard can be a "disadvantaged minority." One might say that any classification system is going to have its flaws, but the state must make choices in this area for the purpose of seeking social justice. Yet that doesn't explain the problems with the larger narrative that American society is built to advantage whites, given that there are people of over a dozen non-European ethnic backgrounds that have a higher annual income than the white population.[20] Note that when whites do better than another group, it is taken as prima facie evidence of injustice. Someone who picks up a book by a left-wing thinker such as Ibram X. Kendi expecting even a nontrivial attempt to justify any of this is bound to be disappointed.[21]

The ideas associated with wokeness did not win in a marketplace of ideas. In many cases, it almost gives them too much credit to even consider them ideas in the first place. All of the contradictions noted above can be explained by understanding wokeness as the name we give to a collection of beliefs that one must hold for legal and psychosocial reasons, without any mechanism to ensure logical consistency built into the system. We do not look for logical consistency in an act of Congress that we know was the product of logrolling, compromise, and debate between various factions. The creation of a cultural phenomenon is even more complicated than a piece of federal legislation, and how it is lived and experienced is even less likely to have a close relationship with any philosophical text.

Like an act of Congress, wokeness can similarly be seen as a "logrolled" set of cultural beliefs. Individuals and organizations that claim to speak for some identity group complain and make certain demands for explicit recognition and support. Political barriers prevent them from getting all of what they want, but politicians, bureaucrats, and institutions find ways to pacify them without inspiring too much of a backlash by making what is happening too clear or explicit. This involves speech restrictions in the name of vague goals like "managing diversity" or "protecting safety," which lead to the creation of large bureaucracies within institutions with open-ended and moralistic missions. Like a complex congressional bill that is the product of negotiations, the end result is not what any individual would have wanted.

Important Phenomena Can Have Trivial Causes

This means that the whole project of seeking a grand philosophical explanation for wokeness relies on a conceptual mistake, likely rooted in the need of intellectuals to exaggerate their importance. One is today supposed to believe a list of things about race, gender, and sexual orientation that are consistent with one another in some ways but not others. Although I defined wokeness in terms of three pillars—disparities equal discrimination, speech controls, and HR bureaucracy—these beliefs and practices should be seen less as a philosophical doctrine with its own impeccable inner logic than as a political program that has emerged from a combination of factors such as interest group lobbying, mass emotional sentiment, and bureaucrats seeking to increase their power.

Understanding the role of the state can explain much of what is puzzling about wokeness as a cultural phenomenon. When there were growing concerns about racism against Chinese Americans in the midst of the Covid-19 pandemic, why did we speak about hatred against "Asian Americans and Pacific Islanders," given that there did not appear to be any attacks against Samoans? Why do we worry about disparities in arrests and school achievement between "Hispanics" and "whites" but not between Swedes and Italians or Puerto Ricans and Arabs? Why, despite a war on terror that led to the victimization of Muslims both at home and abroad, do we see so little organized political activity among Muslim Americans relative to politicians and activists who identify with artificial categories like Hispanics and AAPI?

The wokeness-as-law perspective can help one understand all of this and much else.

The question of whether wokeness is understood more as a political or philosophical phenomenon is of more than historical interest. How we answer it determines how one pushes back. If it is a matter of philosophy and belief, then the answer is more books, articles, essays, and scientific studies debunking the beliefs that form the basis of identity politics and political correctness. In other words, keep employing the same strategy that opponents of earlier and more contemporary forms of wokeness have used since at least the 1970s, when disillusioned former liberals who came to be known as "neoconservatives" began to write about the failures of the Great Society. Their work continues today on social media and in online publications such as *Quillette*, which has one foot in academia and few connections to the American right. If, however, this book is correct, and wokeness should be understood as a matter of government power, then the political entrepreneur is more important than the essayist. That is, unless the latter can produce work that serves as a catalyst for effective activism, as this book aspires to do.

In addition to its role in stroking the egos of intellectuals, the temptation to believe wokeness has deep philosophical roots likely stems from the need to believe that if the consequences of a phenomenon are serious, then its causes must be too. And critics of wokeness are indeed correct that the phenomenon is everywhere, and has important implications for society. Institutions no one had ever considered political before now speak with one voice in swearing fealty to woke values. Prominent figures in areas as diverse as knitting, weightlifting, and video games have faced major controversies related to issues of race and gender. David Rozado, Zach Goldberg, and others have documented the "Great Awokening" in the media. Beginning around 2011, we see a major increase in terms related to race, gender, sexual orientation, and left-wing ideas about the causes of group differences like "systemic racism."[22] While it is difficult to know what changed around that time, the start of the Great Awokening did coincide with Twitter taking off, which suggests a plausible connection. In America, almost every major institution now proclaims a belief in its duty to close disparities between certain groups. A sample of 999 university job listings in 2021 found that 34 percent of those at elite schools required a "diversity statement," and 78 percent mentioned "diversity."[23] When the Supreme Court considered the issue of affirmative action in higher education in 2015, it received amicus briefs signed by dozens of Fortune 500 companies, with none taking the other side of the issue.[24]

Some of the cultural changes that people complain about can seem small and petty, as when conservative media spent the early part of 2021 in a frenzy over the "degendering" of Mr. Potato Head. Yet other developments are much more serious and have deep implications for American politics and civic life. The entire concept of merit—whether measured through standardized tests or other forms of academic achievement—is treated with suspicion, as schools close down gifted programs and more universities drop SAT requirements, putting increasing emphasis on subjective measures like extracurriculars that have even worse class and political biases than the practices being eliminated.

In 2020, the University of California system, the largest in the country, decided to do away with its standardized testing requirement for undergraduates, over the recommendations of its own panel created to study the issue.[25] The math curriculum of that state is similarly being remade to take into account "equity" concerns. Between 1990 and 2020, the abstracts of successful National Science Foundation grant applications with highly politicized terms having to do with identity issues, like "gender" and "inclusion," increased from 3 percent to 30 percent.[26] While there are often nonpoliticized uses of these kinds of terms, this cannot explain such a massive rise. In 2013, half of NASA's graduating class of astronauts was female, a fact that the New York Times compared favorably to the record of China, where women astronauts remain rare.[27] While there may be some women able to meet the same standards as men, it strains credulity to believe that, given the gender gap in math and science proficiency, a meritocratic system would produce a perfect equality of outcomes.

At almost every level of society, then, from elementary schools to the most elite universities and professions, the United States has seen a move away from merit and toward systems and processes that seek to achieve representational parity between groups. Wokeness also increasingly infects public health and safety. The public health profession was discredited among wide swaths of the population when much of the community recommended lockdowns during the Covid-19 pandemic but made an exception for protests against racism. When safe and effective vaccines later became available, the US became an outlier among developed states in the number of its elderly citizens who did not want to take one.[28] While it is difficult to make a direct connection between the politicization of public health and anti-vax sentiment, elites have given credibility to those who would reject even sound medical advice. The year 2020 also saw the largest single-year increase in homicide in over a century, as concerns over systemic racism and the microscopically small number of police shootings of unarmed black men came to dominate our political discourse.[29] Just as with the discussion around Covid-19, mainstream media accounts of the increase in murder have been deformed by a political narrative. Despite the fact that a similar rise in homicide did not occur in other nations that were also suffering from the pandemic, the media sought to place the blame on disruptions related to Covid-19 instead of the Black Lives Matter movement.[30]

Politics and Culture Are Not Separate

Andrew Breitbart, the late media entrepreneur whose eponymous website has become massively influential on the political right, helped popularize the adage that "politics is downstream from culture." Many opponents of wokeness have taken this phrase to heart. Of course there is nothing wrong with creating art, media, and other private institutions that reflect conservative values. Nonetheless, a reliance on the Breitbart doctrine can also lead to political passivity.

"Culture versus politics" is a false dichotomy. At the state, local, and national levels, government spent about 47 percent of GDP in 2020, and it regulates the workplace in an endless number of ways, both obvious and subtle. Most children attend government schools five days a week for at least twelve years, and many spend more waking hours with state employees than with their own parents. The state is so intertwined with the rest of life that it makes little sense to treat culture and politics as separate forces in a modern society. They exist in a self-reinforcing cycle, and any movement strong enough to conquer nearly all elite institutions, as wokeness has, surely has had both working in its favor.

By way of analogy, imagine a historian trying to understand whether "politics" or "culture" was more important in explaining how Christianity triumphed over Rome. Even as it was occasionally oppressed by the authorities, the religion began to expand not long after the death of Christ. This provided the background that led to the conversion of the Emperor Constantine in 312 AD and the Edict of Milan (313), which gave the faith official legal protection. Eventually, state legitimacy throughout Europe came to be based on Christianity, and rival faiths were extinguished through the use of government force.

To draw a simple explanation that seeks to understand Christianization as a matter of culture or politics would be misguided. For a faith to come to dominate a continent, it needed both on its side, and the results did not unfold through a dialectical process of logic but depended on historically contingent factors. In later centuries, there were countries where state power was hostile to Christianity, such as China and Japan, and in those places Christianity did not gain a foothold, let alone penetrate deep into society. Yet state power is not a magic bullet, and when the Emperor Julian sought to restore religious eclecticism to Rome in the middle of the fourth century, it was too late, as Christianity continued to advance and ensured that the days of paganism were numbered.

We only need to look at the current state of the law and its historical development to understand the extent to which the American government manages social relations. Every major corporation must keep statistics on race and sex, and the process of classification itself creates mental categories and influences thought. Businesses must display "EEO Is the Law" posters, which tell the world that an employer both practices affirmative action and does not discriminate based on race. Citizens are thus socialized to engage in doublethink, not question official dogma on sensitive issues, and walk on eggshells when faced with the demands of noisy activists within institutions, no matter how unreasonable they might be. Human resources, as the extended arm of the state, plays the role of enforcer. Government legitimizes certain identities as a basis for political organization while delegitimizing others, makes highly contentious and largely absurd ideas about the causes of disparities between groups official doctrine, and punishes those who believe differently or would build institutions that take an alternative view. Culture has its own independent force, but the state has since the 1960s been putting its thumb on the scale.

The Civil Rights Act of 1991 was the last piece of legislation that made a major difference in the kinds of trade-offs institutions face when deciding how to police speech and behavior, and its signing roughly corresponds with the rise of political correctness as a dominant force in American culture. In addition to showing that the basics of wokeness have been baked into the legal system for decades, this book argues that the regulatory regime we live under has provided the suprastructure through which broader cultural changes have taken place.

To understand how static laws can be causes of changes in a dynamic culture, think of a country that privileges a certain religion over others. The state decides what counts as correct doctrine, forces institutions and private organizations to take religion into account in promotion and hiring decisions, enforces anti-blasphemy laws, and provides direct and indirect subsidies to certain churches and not others. Even under such a regime, religiosity among the general public can fluctuate over time. This does not mean that the state is irrelevant; during periods in which religiosity is on the rise, we can still reasonably say that the legal regime is in part responsible. We would be especially likely to give credence to this view if heightened religiosity takes the form of adherence to doctrinal tenets that justify state power.

Overview

This book is both a work of history and a practical guide to politics. Others have argued that no matter what the roots of group disparities are, government programs to fix them are likely to backfire and make things worse.[31] This book goes further than most in its perspective on how disastrous the downstream effects of policies meant to reduce inequality between designated groups have been.

The first unique contribution of this work is in explaining how we got to our current cultural moment, through a focus on legal structures and practical politics rather than philosophy. The opening chapters of the book provide a history of the law and show how government regulations have changed American practices and institutions. Some Americans celebrate the triumph of left-wing ideas on race and gender once relegated to the fringes of the academy, while others denounce it. Yet each side has an interest in understanding how we got here, and the historical and legal analysis provided can hopefully be of benefit to all intelligent readers, regardless of political orientation.

Second, this book seeks to provide a plan for how those opposed to wokeness can reverse its effects. The story of how we moved from the Civil Rights Act of 1964, a bill that is on its face race-neutral and only concerned with explicit discrimination, to practically all major institutions being dominated by wokeness, is one of path dependency and unintended consequences. This provides those on the right with practical steps they can take to return to a world in which they at least have a chance in the culture wars. It offers a path back toward a society that places more emphasis on merit and free speech, and less on achieving equality between groups. It shows how, by changing or repealing a few laws, one can foster diversity across institutions, instead of using race- and sex-consciousness to promote diversity within institutions, which ironically leads to their homogenization.

How would the policy recommendations argued for in this book ultimately change the culture, away from politicized institutions and a focus on disparities in outcomes, and toward objective standards of merit and an ideal of equal treatment? What would the downstream effects be on the larger society? While it would be naive to think that reversing the excesses of civil rights law would change the culture overnight, what our politics can do is give less control to left-wing bureaucrats and allow markets and individual preferences to have more of a say in how institutions evolve.

For established institutions that have gone all in on the new faith, particularly colleges and universities, there are likely limits to what can be done. Coca-Cola and Microsoft will continue to be woke, and government policy is unlikely to make much of a difference. The hope is that the next generation of successful entrepreneurs and the institutions they build are molded in a legal environment that is more politically neutral. We see hints of what may come in the rise of corporations, like Coinbase, Substack, and Basecamp, that are explicitly disavowing political activism, even in the absence of any changes in civil rights law. There will be no V-Day in the war on wokeness; rather, those outraged by current trends should try to change laws today in the hopes of creating a new society decades down the line, perhaps well after the political and cultural battles of the present are forgotten.

Table 1 on the following page summarizes the main doctrines that underpin wokeness, explaining where they came from, their practical effects, and how they can be undone. Unless the reader has a legal background, not much of it will be comprehensible now. Nonetheless, including the table here can provide a framework and reference point for understanding the rest of the book. Moreover, even if the reader puts the book down after reading the introduction and chapter 1, they will have at least seen the "cheat sheet" and hopefully absorbed something about the argument.

Table 1 is not meant to be all-exhaustive. To describe all the ways in which government uses race, gender, and sexuality to encourage certain identities and discourage others, restrict speech, discriminate between its citizens, and interfere in private affairs would require volumes of legal analysis. In 1995, when Sen. Bob Dole asked the Congressional Research Service for a report on federal programs that use racial and ethnic criteria, it came back with 160 of them.[32] This book focuses on the most important doctrines that have been used for the purposes of social engineering, and encourages those who are anti-woke to prioritize new laws, regulations, and judicial decisions that can have the most far-reaching impact on undoing the damage.

Wokeness in its current form was not explicitly created at the top and forced on every firm; rather, anti-discrimination laws as invented and interpreted by bureaucrats, lawyers, and judges created incentives

Table 1. Characteristics of the main doctrines of wokeness as law (nonexhaustive list) and legal mechanisms for reform

Doctrine	Legal Basis	Description	Enforcement	Effects	How to Undo
Affirmative action in government contracting and government employment	Executive orders, particularly EO 11246 (contracting) and EO 11478 (federal government)	Forces federal agencies and contractors and subcontractors of a certain size to adopt affirmative action programs, other forms of race- and sex-consciousness	Office of Federal Contract Compliance Programs (OFCCP) in Department of Labor, other agencies	Applies to almost a third of US workforce, mandatory race- and sex-consciousness, "soft quotas" with vague standards and arbitrary government power, rise of HR	Amend EO 11246 and EO 11478 to ban affirmative action instead of requiring it, similar action with state contracting, courts declaring current interpretations unconstitutional
Disparate impact (private sector)	Title VII of Civil Rights Act of 1964 (CRA), *Griggs v. Duke Power Company* (1971), CRA of 1991	For all employers of a certain size, any practice that has a "disparate impact" on a certain group is presumptively illegal	Equal Employment Opportunity Commission (EEOC), private lawsuits	Similar to affirmative action requirements, but even more arbitrary enforcement since everything has a disparate impact	Court decision that disparate impact doctrine violates Equal Protection Clause by requiring discrimination
Disparate impact (government funding)	Title VI of CRA, Title IX (1972), of questionable legality (*Alexander v. Sandoval*, 2001), but continues nonetheless	Institutions receiving federal funding cannot discriminate, interpreted to mean disparate impact as with Title VII	Throughout the executive branch, particularly Civil Rights Division of the Department of Justice (CRD) and Office for Civil Rights in the Department of Education (OCR)	Similar to disparate impact in private sector, anti-merit and bureaucratization in education and state and local government; makes fighting crime and school discipline more difficult	Court decision that Title VI of CRA requires intentional discrimination; executive branch reinterpreting law to be consistent with original intent
Anti-harassment law (private sector)	Title VII of CRA	Bans conduct "severe or pervasive" enough based on a protected category	EEOC, private lawsuits	Corporate HR policies that have "zero tolerance" for anything potentially offensive, sanitization of the workplace	Declare aspects unconstitutional as infringements of First Amendment by in effect outlawing private speech
Anti-harassment law, parity in women's sports (education)	Title VI of CRA, Title IX (1972)	Institutions receiving federal funding cannot discriminate, used for social engineering in education	Throughout the executive branch, but particularly OCR	University bureaucratization, regulation of speech and social life	Reining in OCR, court decisions against its interpretation of Title IX

that had the practical effect of stamping out diversity across institutions, which have been shaped within a particular cultural and legal environment. People don't change their politics much as they grow older, which means that public opinion often shifts largely due to generational turnover.[33] The development of dominant attitudes and patterns of behavior among institutions likely works in a similar way. Yet there is institutional turnover. Only 38 percent of Fortune 500 companies in 1995 were still on the list by 2016, with an average of fourteen new firms per year.[34] Moreover, the rate of turnover appears to be accelerating, with S&P 500 companies in 1965 having had more staying power than those from 2012.

Opposing wokeness cannot just be about changing institutions today. Inertia is simply too strong of a force. Our major corporations came of age in a legal environment in which bureaucrats and courts were on the constant lookout for racism and sexism, and they built an entire section of their workforce in order to address such concerns. Those hired, and all those who have benefited from the resulting system, are unlikely to go anywhere. In the last few years, conservatives have begun to realize that they are fighting for the minds of future generations as they've mobilized around issues related to school curricula, particularly the teaching of critical race theory and new ideas about gender and sexual orientation. As Tanner Greer points out, "culture wars are long wars." Millennials may be lost to conservatives, along with Generation Z, but the college graduates of 2030 and beyond might not be.[35] Institutions must be thought of in the same way. Undoing the excesses of civil rights law is not the ultimate solution to wokeness. Rather, it should be seen as the first step toward evening the playing field so the real game can begin.

CHAPTER 2

Lies, Damned Lies, and Civil Rights Law

On February 8, 1964, as Congress debated what would become the Civil Rights Act, Rep. Howard Smith (D-VA) introduced an amendment to the bill. As proposed, the law prohibited discrimination based on race, color, religion, and national origin in employment. In an attempt to kill the bill, Rep. Smith proposed including sex as a protected category. In explaining why, he claimed to have received a letter from "a lady" who was upset that the country had too many women relative to men, meaning that many "spinsters," he said she'd written, were deprived of "the 'right' of every female to have a husband." Amid laughter, he assured the House of Representatives that "she has her statistics, which is the reason why I am reading it to you, because this is serious."[1]

Despite Rep. Smith's intentions, the amendment passed, as did the Civil Rights Act. In its early years, the newly formed EEOC had no idea what to do with the ban on sex discrimination, a concept that seemed fanciful in the mid-1960s. Its first executive director in 1966 called the provision a "fluke" that was "conceived out of wedlock," asserting that "men are entitled to female secretaries."[2] The EEOC was initially unsure whether the Civil Rights Act even prohibited protective legislation at the state level, which banned women from certain professions or limited their hours.[3] But due to pressure both from within and outside government, things soon began to change radically, and by the early 1970s, feminism in something resembling its current form had triumphed within the federal bureaucracy. In 2020, the ban on sex discrimination—passed at a time when homosexuality and transgenderism were widely believed to be forms of social deviance—was relied on by the Supreme Court in *Bostock v. Clayton County* to rule that discrimination based on sexual orientation or gender identity was also prohibited. The story of how sex discrimination became illegal, and how the definition of "discrimination" changed over time, tells us something fundamental about how the American system works.

In the simplified version of constitutional law presented to schoolchildren, Congress passes bills, the executive branch enforces them, and courts interpret the law. But in the hands of bureaucrats, executive agencies, and judges, the text can take on a life of its own.

This is the story of civil rights law. It is likely that few, if any, members of Congress at the time would have believed that the bill signed by President Johnson would ultimately force police departments to lower their physical fitness standards to accommodate women, much less make employers subscribe to theories about the malleability and subjectivity of gender that had yet to be invented. What is called civil rights law today has little to do with the values and beliefs of American society in 1964. The debate that culminated in the CRA was about the misfortunes of black people in the South, and even that resulted in a compromise that mandated equal treatment in the private and public sectors.

No one in American society thought that Congress was in the process of creating an open-ended and indefinite commitment to achieving equality between various groups. Between 1940 and 1972, the *New York Times* reported on 3,800 demonstrations in favor of civil rights, of which 95 percent were in relation to discrimination against African Americans.[4] One analysis shows sixty-nine instances of representatives for black organizations testifying before Congress in civil rights hearings between 1940 and 1972, compared to two for all other races, and nine for any national origins group.[5] When President Johnson signed the Civil Rights Act, he only mentioned discrimination based on race and color. The first annual report from the EEOC, released in 1966, stated plainly that "the chief thrust of the statute was, of course, aimed at discrimination against the Negro."[6]

The federal government has not only interpreted the CRA in ways that Congress could not have foreseen. In some ways, its interpretations have directly contradicted what legislators promised and agreed to. In his opening statement in the debate over the bill, Sen. Hubert Humphrey told fellow legislators that there was no chance that it would lead to reverse discrimination.[7]

> That bugaboo has been brought up a dozen times: but it is nonexistent. In fact, the very opposite is true. Title VII prohibits discrimination. In effect, it says that race, religion, and national origin are not to be used as the basis for hiring and firing.

Further emphasizing the point, the future vice president told a skeptical colleague that if he could find "any language which provides that an employer will have to hire on the basis of percentage or quota related to color . . . I will start eating the pages." Yet Congress wasn't satisfied with such assurances. So the following text was also added to the bill:

> Nothing contained in this title shall be interpreted to require any [employer or labor union] to grant preferential treatment to any individual or to any group because of the race, color, religion, sex, or national origin of such individual or group on account of an imbalance which may exist . . .

The text of the document and the legislative history agree on this point. Yet ultimately none of this would matter, and it would be used to justify proportional hiring by race and sex. In 1968, Clifford Alexander, the director of the EEOC, declared, "Our most valid standard is in numbers . . . The only accomplishment is when we look at all those numbers and see a vast improvement in the picture."[8] A few years later, a Labor Department official would explain requirements for government contractors by saying that "affirmative action is anything you have to do to get results."[9]

Congress would pass other bills, including the Equal Employment Opportunity Act (EEOA) of 1972 and the Civil Rights Act of 1991, that would be more friendly to race-conscious remedies for past discrimination. But it never explicitly endorsed the main innovations of civil rights law. The Supreme Court—engaging in the kind of sophistry that has become all too common when judges mistake what they want the law to be for what the law says—has at times taken the fact that Congress hasn't overruled bureaucratic and judicial innovations as an endorsement of them. This ignores the status quo bias built into most systems, including our own. On several issues, Congress could not have been clearer about what was or wasn't allowed in 1964, but ultimately text on paper passed by two large and divided legislative bodies has proved no match for the machinations of permanently placed bureaucrats and judges.

We can think of civil rights law as existing on three levels, which can be analogized to the different ways a religion develops and is practiced. The first is the text of legislation itself, which can be seen as the holy book. While technically it is the highest authority one can appeal to, religious books are often vague and self-contradictory. They are not updated to account for changes in the real world. Even when a participant in an argument appears to lose a debate based on the "plain text" of holy writ, they can always appeal to the "spirit" of a relevant doctrine.

At the second level is the priestly class that interprets the faith. Unlike the original authors of the text, these individuals are aware of and respond to later historical and cultural circumstances, and have wide discretion in interpretation. In civil rights law, these are most prominently civil rights lawyers, bureaucrats, and judges. But there are additional interpreters of the law, including those within the executive branch, and at lower levels, individuals like HR professionals, school administrators, and others who might be considered part of the "managerial class." This is where one finds the major innovations in civil rights law.

Finally, there is the community of religious believers who, by relying on the priestly class, interpret the faith in ways consistent with pragmatism and local conditions. This can be analogized to folk understanding of what the state of the law is. For example, about a quarter of Americans believe that hate speech is illegal, which is not technically true; but it can be seen as an understandable mistake, given the state of anti-harassment law.[10]

The Civil Rights Act of 1964 was the culmination of a moral struggle that had helped define the United States since its founding. Debates over slavery almost derailed the adoption of the Constitution and led to a series of compromises among the founding generation: the three-fifths rule; a prohibition on Congress banning the slave trade until 1808; and the Fugitive Slave Clause of the Constitution. After the Civil War, the main question of American politics centered around what to do with newly emancipated slaves. Reconstruction, an attempt to use federal power to force racial equality onto the old Confederacy, ended in the aftermath of the election of 1876, through a congressional compromise that elevated Rutherford B. Hayes to the presidency. After that, questions centered around the relationship between black Americans and the rest of society were generally treated as settled and a relatively minor issue until the 1950s.

What changed in the mid-twentieth century? It would be surprising if the rise of television did not play a role, as it both nationalized politics and provided footage that increased sympathy for the plight of black southerners. In 1950, only 9 percent of American homes had a television. This number rose to 65 percent in 1955, and 87 percent in 1960.[11] In the words of historian Rick Perlstein, writing on the power of the broadcast networks, "TV news styled itself a moral center of American civic life . . . It was *their* footage of Bull Connor's fire hoses in Birmingham that catalyzed the Civil Rights Act of 1964, *their* footage at the Edmund Pettus Bridge that brought about the Voting Rights Act of 1965."[12]

With the passage of these laws and others during the Johnson administration, most Americans believed their elected officials were responding to a specific problem in one area of the country. They were not convinced of the need for an open-ended commitment that would struggle to remove every statistically detectable form of inequality between blacks and whites, much less whites and other groups, or men and women. Nonetheless, in the words of Nathan Glazer, soon after Congress prohibited discrimination based on race, color, religion, or national origin, "we then began an extensive effort to record the race, color, and (some) national origins of just about every student and employee and recipient of government benefits or services in the nation;

to require public and private employers to undertake action to benefit given groups; and school systems to assign their children on the basis of their race, color, and (some) national origins."[3] This is not what the country signed up for, and it certainly did not believe that government had been given a mandate to regulate humor and dating, nor reach into the subconscious thoughts and desires of its citizenry to cure them of their hidden biases.

This chapter addresses the four great innovations in civil rights law: federally mandated affirmative action, disparate impact, harassment law, and Title IX as a tool to regulate education. Ultimately, these doctrines have led to arbitrary government power. Their requirements are tangible enough to force institutions to be obsessed with race and sex, while either being vague enough to rarely give clear guidance regarding what is allowed or forbidden, or, in the case of Title IX, micromanaging the professional and personal lives of students and those employed by schools and universities. In the case of disparate impact, the doctrine makes practically everything potentially illegal. It gives government discretion as to what to go after, making it the skeleton key of the identity-obsessed left. All of this can help one understand the subject of the next chapter, which discusses how these doctrines have given rise to bureaucracies that suppress speech, regulate conduct, and enforce adherence to left-wing beliefs about the sources of inequality between groups.

Affirmative Action for Contractors

In theory, executive orders, which are signed by the president, are federal directives on how an existing law will be interpreted and enforced. In practice, they often make law, just as judicial decisions do. The executive branch has long used its contracting power to regulate business in ways that would require legislation if applied to non-contractors. Congress appropriates money, but the executive branch, by necessity, must sign and enforce the contracts to carry out government functions, and this has given the latter leverage over the private sector.

The first modern EO on equal opportunity in federal contracting was signed by President Roosevelt in June 1941, just months before the

US entered the Second World War. It banned discrimination by federal agencies, along with unions and companies engaged in war-related work. Shortly after taking office, President Kennedy in EO 10925 required government contractors with business beyond a minimum threshold to "take affirmative action" to ensure nondiscrimination in employment with regard to "race, color, religion, or national origin," and created the President's Committee on Equal Employment Opportunity. The year after the CRA was passed, President Johnson signed EO 11246, which, as amended throughout the years, has become the basis of the modern affirmative action in contracting regime. It created what would come to be called the Office of Federal Contract Compliance Programs (OFCCP), located within the Labor Department. In 1967, Johnson added "sex" to its prohibited categories, and Obama included "sexual orientation" and "gender identity" in 2014.

While Johnson originally signed EO 11246, it was the Nixon administration that ironically created the affirmative action regime we see today, over the resistance of a bipartisan coalition in Congress. Under the Labor Department, the administration began by forcing affirmative action on construction workers, first in Philadelphia, and then nationwide. This was followed up in 1971 by Revised Order No. 4, which expanded the regulations beyond the construction industry to all contractors and subcontractors doing business with the government beyond a minimum threshold, forcing them to adopt goals and timetables whenever women or minorities were shown to be "underutilized" relative to the relevant labor pool.[14]

The ultimate authority of the executive branch to legally mandate affirmative action among contractors is unclear. A 1969 memo from Attorney General John Mitchell mentioned the Civil Rights Act but mostly relied on the president's constitutional authority.[15] A decade later, the Supreme Court mentioned two other statutes as potential sources of executive power in this area.[16] While it may seem strange to non-lawyers that there is such a high degree of uncertainty about the legal justification for regulations that have done so much to remake the American workplace, this is only one of the many contradictions and paradoxes inherent in decades of making law through obscure regulatory procedures, subject not to democratic processes but only judicial review, and often not even that.

Nonetheless, while its legal basis is murky, there is much less doubt about the reach of EO 11246 and its successor documents. Because of the extent to which government spends money and involves itself in the economy, its ability to regulate contractors has always been a major source of leverage. Employers required to have an affirmative action program must include all of their facilities, employees, and operations in the plan, even if the government contracts in question represent only a small portion of their business. Moreover, the biggest employers in the private sector are more likely than most other businesses to have federal contracts; about a third of Fortune 500 companies did so in 2015.[17] Today, about a quarter of the American workforce is employed by a government contractor.[18] It is important to note that, pursuant to EO 11478 of 1969, affirmative action also exists within the federal government itself, which employs another 6 percent of the workforce.

Under affirmative action guidelines as applied to government contractors, it is no exaggeration to say that businesses are forced to be obsessed with race and sex. Long before people noticed that identity-related issues had consumed American universities, something resembling modern wokeness had already been forced on big business. Affirmative action is required for every employer with fifty employees that does at least $50,000 worth of business a year with the federal government, and every subcontractor with at least $10,000 in business. Government regulations specify that a "central premise underlying affirmative action is that, absent discrimination, over time a contractor's workforce, generally, will reflect the gender, racial and ethnic profile of the labor pools from which the contractor recruits and selects."[19] If a contractor falls short in any particular area, it must take "practical steps" to make up for its deficiency.

The employer is required to participate in a detailed process of identity-based classification and analysis. Middle managers for construction companies and retail store owners become social scientists. First, employers are forced to create an "organizational profile," defined as "a detailed graphical or tabular chart, text, spreadsheet or similar presentation of the contractor's organizational structure." The contractor must break his business down into "organizational units," and record the race, gender, and ethnicity of the supervisor of each one. Within each unit, the business must record the number of males and females of each of the following groups: blacks, Hispanics, Asians/ Pacific Islanders, and American Indians/Alaskan Natives. Race and sex are to be determined by self-identification, with the employer prohibited from overruling an individual's selection, although visual classification is acceptable under certain conditions.[20] The next step is engaging in a "workforce analysis," which divides the employees of a company by job title. Those with titles that are similar in terms of work and pay are combined into "job groups."

This initial work is required to get to the "job group analysis." This means comparing the number of women and minorities in each job group to their estimated availability in the population. And how does one determine availability? By coming up with a number for the "percentage of minorities or women with requisite skills in the reasonable recruitment area." When a particular demographic is underrepresented in a job group, the employer must create "placement goals" to correct its deficiency.

This system is bizarre in several respects. Instead of the government mandating a number of women and minorities to be hired in a given job, it leaves the employer to engage in a series of subjective analyses and set goals and timetables for itself. The contractor has discretion regarding how it classifies its employees into job groups and to some extent how it decides to place them with regard to the four "minority groups." The "availability analysis" itself is particularly absurd, as it would be a challenge for a team of social scientists to determine how many women and minorities in a particular area are qualified for each job category. How business owners and corporations should be reasonably expected to do so is never adequately explained. One is advised to consult "census data, data from local job service offices, and data from colleges or other training institutions." The contractor is warned, however, that it cannot define "reasonable recruitment area" in a way "to have the effect of excluding minorities or women."

Every aspect of employers' analysis is reviewable by government bureaucrats. For the same reason that a contractor can always get around affirmative action requirements, the government can always find grounds to apply pressure on a business. From the contractor's perspective, all they can know for certain is that they must go through the motions, and that hiring and promoting more minorities and women will be less likely to get them in trouble.

At the same time, businesses are told that "quotas are expressly forbidden." Incredibly, we are to believe that placement goals as they are intended to be used "do not create set-asides for specific groups, nor are they intended to achieve proportional representation or equal results." Somehow, sentences like this are found in the exact same regulations requiring placement goals based on nothing more than disparities in representation. Quite simply, businesses need to classify their employees, and in many cases engage in reverse discrimination, though they are prohibited from being too explicit about it. As Edward C. Sylvester, the first director (1965–1968) of what became the OFCCP, said in a statement to businessmen, "Affirmative action is anything you have to do to get results. But this does not necessarily include preferential treatment. The key word here is 'results.'"[21] "Results" but not "quotas." This presumes that there is always a way to get results by neutral and objective methods, an idea that there has never been the slightest bit of evidence for, which is of course why government regulations mandate that businesses take into account race and sex in the first place. Politicians have played the same game. As one historian wrote about the thirty-seventh president, "The affirmative action measures Nixon adopted were goals; those he rejected were quotas."[22]

Places of business must broadcast this doublethink to the world, announcing themselves as "equal opportunity employers," which means that decisions are made without discriminating based on protected categories. No reader should make the mistake of believing that the detailed and dense nature of Labor Department regulations means that they are logically coherent or adhere to basic principles of the rule of law. Rather, they make a soft quota system politically and legally palatable while giving regulators arbitrary power over business as they pretend to restrain themselves.

The result is not simply that the contractor works toward numerical goals and treats some employees differently than others. To do business with the federal government, one must participate in rituals that both legitimize the goals of the state while hiding the nature of the project. Among the requirements placed on employers is one to make someone in the organization responsible for the affirmative action program. Every individual in the workforce, and even applicants, are to be recorded and classified according to sex and government race categories. Each business must be aware of the racial dynamics in its own community, forcing the private sector into the dishonest project of creating identity-obsessed institutions that simultaneously champion equal treatment.

Sociologists and anthropologists have noted the role that ritual plays in legitimizing religious, social, and political orders. Some definitions even focus on ritual as the defining feature of religion, as opposed to what individuals truly believe. Government contract compliance serves this purpose when it forces the private sector to express agreement with and act on the basis of left-wing beliefs about the ubiquity of discrimination and its role in causing group disparities. Wokeness starts to look deeply rooted in the beliefs of individuals and therefore indestructible as every elite institution appears to be speaking with the same voice, or even using the same exact words and phrases that the government forces them to repeat in order to remain in good standing.

In Vaclav Havel's famous story about the greengrocer that mouths communist propaganda, a shop owner displays an official message to communicate to the world that he is the type of person who wants to live a quiet life and be left alone.[23] But the message cannot explicitly state this, for his sense of dignity will not allow him to publicly announce his cowardice to the world. The obfuscatory nature of affirmative action regulations plays a similar role. Americans believe in equal opportunity and treating people as individuals. Few Americans want to devote their lives to institutions that openly discriminate against their fellow citizens. Instead of making individuals refute widely held principles and directly face the fact that they must adopt identity-based preferences in order to receive government contracts, individuals who run private institutions are forced to be obsessed with race and sex, but in the name of nondiscrimination.

Disparate Impact: Everything Is Illegal

While the authority of the executive branch to force affirmative action onto government contractors continues to rest on an uncertain premise, the doctrine of disparate impact claims to be based on the Civil Rights Act of 1964. This principle ensures that even private businesses without government contracts must embrace an identity-based view of the world. The history of the disparate impact doctrine is illuminating in showing the extent to which government bureaucracies and judges can ignore the law in pursuit of a political agenda.

What has become civil rights law bears little resemblance to the act that Congress passed in 1964. Nondiscrimination was to apply to public accommodations (Title II), public facilities (Title III), public education (Title IV), public assistance programs (Title VI), and employment (Title VII).[24] The last of these provisions, in Section 703, makes it illegal

1. to fail or refuse to hire or to discharge any individual, or otherwise to discriminate against any individual with respect to his compensation, terms, conditions, or privileges of employment, because of such individual's race, color, religion, sex, or national origin;

2. to limit, segregate, or classify his employees in any way which would deprive or tend to deprive any individual of employment opportunities or otherwise adversely affect his status as an employee because of [same protected categories].

The act itself never defines "discrimination." But the historical record is about as clear as it can possibly be regarding what the authors of the bill meant. Time and again, members of Congress foresaw the possibility that Title VII could be used to push for a disparate impact standard or equality of outcomes, and it is difficult to imagine how they could have made themselves clearer that such interpretations were forbidden.

Seeing the extent to which Congress was explicit about the bill it was passing, and how judges and bureaucrats would ignore its wishes anyway, raises serious questions about who ultimately has the power to make law under our system of government.

At various points throughout the debate over the Civil Rights Act, critics of the bill expressed concern that it might do *x*. In response, supporters of the bill would say, "no, it won't do *x*," and the two sides would agree to a compromise that involved entering a clause into the bill in effect saying that "*x* is prohibited." Usually within a decade, the EEOC and the federal courts would do *x* anyway.

According to Herman Belz, "Provisions of Title VII that were thought to have a clear and unequivocal meaning in the debate on the Civil Rights Act were redefined by the plaintiffs' bar and the judiciary at will."[25] For example, the law included a provision that protected seniority systems that had existed before the bill was passed, meaning that the new law was not supposed to be retrospective, but simply stop discrimination in the future. Within a few years, old collective bargaining agreements were being thrown out on the grounds that they froze patterns of racial inequality in place. The most harmful interpretation of the Civil Rights Act, however, would ultimately be the disparate impact standard. As the bill was being debated, an anti-discrimination state commission in Illinois held Motorola to be acting in an unfair manner because it gave an aptitude test that disproportionately screened out blacks. The result in Washington was outrage across the political spectrum. Sen. John Tower (R-TX) was therefore able to insert Section 703(h) into Title VII. This provision allowed employers to make use of "any professionally developed ability test," as long as it was not "designed, intended, or used" to discriminate.[26]

The testing provision was only a specific articulation of a more general principle. Members of Congress were unanimous in saying that quotas were discriminatory and that preferential treatment, even of the "reverse discrimination" kind, was not allowed, and therefore of course not mandatory. Hubert Humphrey's promise to eat the bill if it required quotas is perhaps the most famous of the assurances given. But others were just as clear. In April 1964, Sen. Joseph P. Clark (D-PA) and Sen.

Clifford P. Case (R-NJ), the floor managers of the bill, submitted a joint memorandum to clarify that there would be no reverse discrimination or disparate impact standard. Not only would Title VII not require racial balancing, but it would explicitly forbid it. Even if there were a job qualification where, "because of differences in background and education," some groups performed better than others, Title VII would do nothing to make it illegal. According to the memorandum, "an employer may set his qualifications as high as he likes . . . and he may hire, assign, and promote on the basis of test performance." Sen. Harrison A. Williams (D-NJ) put it even more bluntly when he declared that "an employer with only white employees could continue to have only the best qualified persons even if they were all white."[27]

Despite all this, in 1968, the EEOC commissioner would say that "our most valid standard is numbers . . . The only accomplishment is when we look at all those numbers and see a vast improvement in the picture."[28] The Supreme Court sanctioned this approach in *Griggs v. Duke Power Co.* (1971), which ruled that intelligence tests on which blacks scored lower than whites could not be used in hiring without creating a presumption that the employer was discriminating based on race. The new doctrine of disparate impact did not require any discriminatory intent on the part of a firm. As long as something the firm did benefited one group at the expense of another, it could potentially face legal liability. The *Griggs* decision allowed for an employer to defend itself by pointing to "business necessity." In practice, however, the EEOC took this to mean that employers would have to engage in expensive validation procedures for a test to be allowed, and the agency put up other hurdles, such as requiring that tests be shown to be predictive for every particular minority group, every single job within an organization, and for the same job across different institutions.[29] A Department of Justice (DOJ) memorandum in 1976 noted that the rules had made practically every employer that used tests potentially noncompliant, and businesses were therefore engaging in numerical hiring to achieve racial balance. Observers made the reasonable assumption that the goal of EEOC regulations was to make standardized tests as difficult as possible to use, in order to push employers toward hiring and promotion procedures that were geared toward achieving high enough levels of representation for women and minorities.

The outrageousness of *Griggs* can be seen in the fact that even those who have supported preferential treatment for blacks have acknowledged that there is little support for their favored policy in either the text of the Civil Rights Act or the congressional record. The EEOC itself urged the NAACP not to appeal its limited victory in the Fourth Circuit in *Griggs* because the test in question was of the exact type the statute sought to protect in 1964.[30] Just two years before the decision, the EEOC had published an official history in which it admitted that the common understanding of Title VII was that discrimination required intent on the part of the employer. Once its preferred interpretation of the law was reviewed by the judiciary, it predicted that "the Commission and the courts will be in disagreement." Nonetheless, the year after *Griggs*, the Equal Employment Opportunity Act brought state and local employment under the power of the EEOC, thus applying the disparate impact standard in those contexts too. The law also consolidated anti-discrimination efforts within the federal government in that same body.[31]

Ironically, by being concerned with unintentional discrimination against certain "protected" groups, disparate impact doctrine requires intentional discrimination against others. An employer who wants to use intelligence tests to hire is potentially barred from doing so because whites could do too well. He must make a conscious decision to pick a hiring practice that guarantees fewer white people, in order to avoid one that has a disparate impact against blacks. *Griggs*, therefore, diverges from the original intent of the Civil Rights Act in two ways, both expanding the definition of what counts as "discrimination" when it comes to women and minorities, and by necessity therefore giving whites and men less protection than Congress thought it was providing them.

When faced with undeniable evidence in the plain text of the law and historical record, judges have appealed to the higher purpose of the statute. By passing the Civil Rights Act, Congress meant to help black people, so the "purpose" of the law can supposedly allow disparate treatment by race in order to achieve equal results. An unusually honest opinion was the concurrence by Justice Harry Blackmun in *United Steelworkers v. Weber* (1979). In that case, the Labor Department had forced a quota system onto a contractor and the labor union it worked with, requiring that half of new positions in a program to train skilled craftsmen go to blacks. A white employee filed a class action lawsuit on the grounds that he and others of his race had been discriminated against under Title VII.

The case thus forced the Supreme Court to address the contradiction between affirmative action requirements placed on government contractors, which were explicitly geared toward achieving racial balance, and the Civil Rights Act, which prohibited racial discrimination against individuals. Justice Blackmun signed on to the 5–2 decision authorizing reverse discrimination even though, in his concurrence, he agreed with the dissent that "the Congress that passed Title VII probably thought it was adopting a principle of nondiscrimination that would apply to blacks and whites alike." Nonetheless, he decided that allowing preferences in favor of blacks—in this case with government encouragement through the Labor Department—should be allowed for reasons he called "practical and equitable."

If this sounds like a judge making up the law to fit his own political preference, that is because that is exactly what it is. At the very least, Justice Blackmun should be credited for his candor. But to appeal to the purpose of a statute to contradict its plain text is to nullify the bargain that Congress ultimately arrived at. Yes, the Civil Rights Act was meant to improve the condition of black people. But that goal was to be balanced against concerns of individual liberty, economic freedom, federalism, and the principle that nobody—including whites—should be discriminated against on account of their race.

Laws are not supposed to be blank checks for courts and bureaucrats to seek out their preferred policy outcomes. Alfred Blumrosen, an official who worked for the EEOC in its early days, wrote with unusual candor about how the agency sought to get around the plain meaning of the law, as he and his allies preferred to see civil rights statutes more as broad "charters for equality" than explicit rules about what government can and cannot do.[32]

In a narrow sense, *Griggs* was about written tests used in the private sector. However, the disparate impact doctrine also applies to government employment, government-funded institutions, and practices other than written exams. Title VI bans discrimination under any program that receives financial assistance from the federal government. In *Alexander v. Sandoval* (2001), the Court ruled that Title VI banned international discrimination, yet left open the question of whether it also prohibits disparate impact, while also holding that it did not create a private cause of action in the latter kind of case. What this means in practice is that the disparate impact standard in federally funded institutions is—while legally controversial and perhaps soon to be found inconsistent with the Civil Rights Act—enforced through the federal bureaucracy, though not through private lawsuits, like Title VII usually is. Grant recipients under Title VI include agencies of state and local governments and practically all schools and universities. Given what was done with Title VII, it is not surprising to learn that Title VI has made disparate impact a standard woven into private institutions and American governance at all levels.

This is why the Obama administration went out of its way to harass schools about punishment gaps between white and black students, explicitly telling administrators that race-neutral policies could have a disparate impact and therefore be illegal.[33] In 1974, the Supreme Court deferred to the Office for Civil Rights (OCR) in finding that not providing bilingual education to children of immigrants was a violation of Title VI, although later Supreme Court decisions made it difficult to enforce this invented right.[34] One result of applying Title VII to government employment has been that states and localities hiring police, firefighters, and correctional officers are now forced to lower physical standards in order to be able to hire more women. Even literacy tests for teachers have been the subject of civil rights lawsuits.[35]

Gail Heriot, a law professor and a member of the US Commission on Civil Rights (USCCR), has offered to donate $10,000 to the charity of choice of anyone who can find a single employment criterion that does not have a disparate impact on some group.[36] She hasn't had to pay up, and never will, since we find group differences with regard to practically any trait, behavior, or exam subject to measurement. It is no exaggeration to say, in her words, that disparate impact "makes almost everything presumptively illegal." The EEOC now adopts the four-fifths, or 80 percent, rule, which says that if one group's promotion or hiring rate is below four-fifths that of another, it will be taken as evidence of disparate impact. If that includes virtually everything, then which practices are likely to place extra scrutiny on an employer, government department, or federal grant recipient? There is no good answer to be found in law, and we are left with a system in which courts and the federal bureaucracy have arbitrary power over how institutions function and behave.

Harassment Law

Since disparate impact already covers just about everything, one might suspect that any other doctrine would be unnecessary for civil rights enforcement. Nonetheless, harassment law—built on the idea that Title VII is violated when women or minorities are made to feel uncomfortable at work—has developed to ensure that business owners must have their own speech restricted, and also police their employees under federal law. The first major court case to recognize a cause of racial harassment was *Rogers v. Equal Employment Opportunity Commission* (1971), decided by the Fifth Circuit Court of Appeals. A Hispanic woman in Texas working for an optometrist claimed, among other things, that her employer used different colors of ink to take the appointments of black and white patients. The employer resisted this particular part of the resulting EEOC inquiry on the grounds that it had nothing to do with an allegation made under Title VII; at most, the practice would indicate discrimination against patients, which was not under the jurisdiction of the body.

By a 2–1 decision, the Fifth Circuit disagreed. The opinion, by Judge Irving L. Goldberg, held that discrimination against black customers could contribute to an environment in which a Hispanic employee could feel discriminated against. The court discerned in the statutory language of the Civil Rights Act "a Congressional intention to define discrimination in the broadest possible terms," which showed an acknowledgment "that constant change is the order of our day and that the seemingly reasonable practices of the present can easily become the injustices of the morrow." A mere seven years after the signing of the bill, this now meant that the law mandated the elimination of "working environments so heavily polluted with discrimination as to destroy completely the emotional and psychological stability of minority group workers."

As with everything in civil rights law, courts and bureaucrats were quicker to act to expand the definition of "harassment" based on race than they were for sex. When it came to preventing the harassment of women, they started with the most egregious and least sympathetic conduct before then moving on and eventually reaching a point where there was practically no limit to what kinds of behavior or speech were forbidden. In early sex discrimination cases, courts found that a boss could demand sexual favors from his subordinates without violating the Civil Rights Act, based on the logic that it was the physical attraction to an employee or applicant, not her sex per se, that motivated the conduct.[37]

This changed with the 1977 case of *Barnes v. Castle*. A female employee working for the EPA claimed that her supervisor repeatedly propositioned and eventually fired her for rejecting his advances. The DC Circuit ruled that this was a violation of the law: "but for her womanhood, from aught that appears, her participation in sexual activity would never have been solicited." The degree to which one has to stretch the meaning of Title VII to find this result is shown in footnote 55 of the opinion: there the Court says that if a supervisor or employer is bisexual, insisting on sexual favors does not qualify as sexual harassment under the logic of the decision. Left unanswered is whether it would violate civil rights law if the bisexual employer was attracted to, say, thin women but only fat men, thus treating the sexes differently.

Had this been as far as the courts and federal bureaucracy were willing to go, there may have been little to complain about, no matter how badly reasoned we consider such interpretations of the law. Yet simply forbidding the demanding of sexual favors, like only attacking intentional discrimination, did not go far enough for those motivated by profit and self-righteousness and operating far outside of the view of democratic processes. In 1979, law professor Catharine MacKinnon published *Sexual Harassment of Working Women*. This work helped publicize the term "sexual harassment," which in the early 1970s appeared in around one in 50 million n-grams (two-word phrases, in this case), according to the Google Ngram viewer. By its peak in the mid-1990s, it was at about one in every 200,000.

Only in 1986, in *Meritor Savings Bank v. Vinson*, did the Supreme Court sign off on the idea that speech or conduct could contribute to a "hostile work environment" that potentially violated the law, even if there was no tangible harm to the victim. Other innovations followed: sexual harassment cases could be filed as class actions (*Jenson v. Eveleth Taconite Co.*, Eighth Circuit, 1997); employers could be held responsible for the actions of their employees, not just themselves (*Faragher v. City of Boca Raton*, 1998; and *Burlington Industries, Inc. v. Ellerth*, 1998); and offensive language and pornography can constitute a hostile workplace, even if not targeted at any particular employee (*Reeves v. C. H. Robinson Worldwide, Inc.*, Eleventh Circuit, 2010). We have therefore moved from bans on explicit discrimination to practically any behavior or speech potentially offensive to women.

In determining exactly which conduct is prohibited, courts have decided that behavior is a violation of Title VII when it is "severe or pervasive" enough to create a "hostile or abusive work environment" based on a protected category, with a "reasonable person" standard for deciding which conduct qualifies.[38] As UCLA law professor Eugene Volokh points out, there is no exception for speech that is protected by the First Amendment, including religious, social, and political viewpoints. Even speech outside the workplace can contribute to a hostile work environment. Volokh lists a large number of court cases and bureaucratic decisions at the state and federal levels that have found in constitutionally protected speech evidence of a hostile work environment: signs with the phrase "Men Working"; "draftsman" and "foreman" as job titles; pictures of Ayatollah Khomeini and a burning American flag in a cubicle; an ad campaign using samurai, Kabuki, and sumo wrestling to refer to Japanese competition; jokes of a sexual nature not targeted at any particular person; misogynistic rap music; and circulating offensive jokes and an employer praising a subordinate for doing so.

Although the doctrine of hostile work environment does not make

isolated remarks or actions illegal, Volokh points out that the only plausible way for employers to be sure they are following the law is to restrict
speech that could potentially be used as evidence of discrimination.
Imagine a manager hearing about a single incident in which a worker is
offended. Based on the guidance provided by regulators and the courts,
such an action is not necessarily against the law in isolation, but is potentially illegal if it is part of a larger pattern. How can an employer thus
create a rule that tells employees that they have the right to speak freely
on controversial topics or display certain imagery, but only if other employees are not engaging in similar conduct beyond a certain undefined
threshold? An anti-harassment training program that said "you can only
make off-color jokes if others have not also made off-color jokes" creates
an impossible standard, one that requires workers to monitor not only
their own speech but everyone else's to even begin to know what is allowed or prohibited. The only reasonable approach is to ban any actions,
words, or behaviors that might offend anyone.

The EEOC, largely staffed by liberal ideologues, has, as in the case of
disparate impact, pushed the definition of "harassment" as far as courts
have allowed them to take it. According to its website meant to provide
guidance to employers, offensive conduct may include "offensive jokes,"
"insults or put-downs," "ridicule or mockery," or "offensive objects or
pictures."[39] Moreover, the harasser does not need to be the victim's supervisor; he could even be "an agent of the employer, a co-worker, or a
non-employee." Following the standard articulated in *Rogers*, a person
can be a victim of harassment without their being the individual targeted by the offensive conduct. Jokes between two parties can result in a
lawsuit from a third. It is little wonder that human resource professionals tend to recommend a zero tolerance approach to offensive speech.

One can see a real-world application of civil rights law in the case of
James Damore, the Google engineer who was fired in 2017 for suggest-
ing that female underrepresentation in certain technical fields might
be due to sex differences in personality and preferences. Damore was
part of a lawsuit against the company, filed partly on the grounds that
he faced discrimination as a white male and for his conservative views,
as California makes politically based discrimination illegal. Eventually,

he settled with the company, though many legal commentators argued that Google needed to fire Damore to avoid creating a discriminatory environment for women. While the civil suit against Google was settled, a lawyer for National Labor Relations Board relied on EEOC guidance to conclude that Damore's speech was not protected, and Google was not discriminating against whites and men because his memo expressed belief in stereotypes about women.[40] It is unlikely that the management of Google was sympathetic to Damore's viewpoint, but the important thing to realize is that even if they were, civil rights law probably made firing him the right business decision.

Title IX: Sports and Sexuality

As originally written, Title VI of the Civil Rights Act, unlike Title VII, did not ban discrimination on account of sex. That change came with the Education Amendments of 1972, which included a provision in Title IX stating that "no person in the United States shall, on the basis of sex, be excluded from participation in, be denied the benefits of, or be subjected to discrimination under any education program or activity receiving Federal financial assistance." Few people noticed at the time, and Nixon's signing statement made no mention of what was to become one of the most consequential legal changes of his presidency. But the law opened the door to social engineering throughout schools and universities, and while one can fault other civil rights doctrines for being vague, under Title IX the Office for Civil Rights has promulgated rules and regulations in painstaking detail.

Under American law, Congress passes statutes, and agencies make "rules" interpreting them. These rules are made through a highly formalized process that, under the Administrative Procedure Act (APA), involves a "notice and comment" period in which the public can submit feedback regarding what a particular agency is proposing. Of course, even rules don't cover every possible ambiguity in interpretation, so agencies sometimes also make statements that clarify rules. Importantly, this is not supposed to be a way to make substantive changes to underlying law.

Women's rights advocates saw a straightforward analogy between race and sex discrimination. Shortly after Title IX was passed, however, it became clear that there were important fundamental differences between the two concepts. In 1974 and 1976, Congress added Title IX exemptions that allowed for different living facilities for men and women, and for fraternities and sororities; scholarships for beauty pageants; the Boy Scouts; and father-son and mother-daughter events.[41] As women made rapid gains in education, Title IX began to bizarrely focus more and more on sports, an area in which men have always shown more interest. The law came to in effect require something approaching equality, or making progress toward equality, in athletic participation. Its other major effect has been to make the federal government regulate the sex lives of college students.

The process through which we got from the text of Title IX to a federal government obsessed with sports and sex in college is hardly believable in a country that prides itself on the rule of law. In every society that has ever existed, men have shown more interest in athletic competition than women, and the wider society has been more interested in seeing athletic contests between men than between women, which is unsurprising given higher levels of male athletic performance and aggression.[42] Thus a natural interpretation of Title IX as applied to sports would simply say that colleges and universities needed to provide men and women similar opportunities in ways that take into account the differences between them. In fact, this would have been a completely reasonable interpretation of the 1975 rules promulgated by OCR—then part of the Department of Health, Education, and Welfare—which stated that schools needed to "effectively accommodate the interests and abilities of both sexes."[43]

As political scientist R. Shep Melnick writes, this was officially the last time that the federal government made a major change to Title IX, as OCR has simply been issuing "clarifications" to the text of Title IX and its 1975 rules ever since.[44] The most important of these came in 1979, when OCR issued a "three-part test" to determine whether schools were discriminating against women in the field of athletics. In 1993 and 1996, the First Circuit issued two opinions in *Cohen v. Brown University* that strengthened that test and, in effect, required that the demographics of the varsity athlete population resemble that of the university as a whole. Other circuits followed, and in 1996 OCR issued another "clarification," endorsing the *Cohen* standard. Melnick calls this "leapfrogging," the process of "courts and agencies each taking a step beyond the other, expanding regulation without seeming to innovate."[45] When Quinnipiac University was sued in 2010, "the district court relied heavily on OCR's 1996 'clarification' of its 1979 'interpretation' of its 1975 regulations." Congress has acknowledged that statutory text is often insufficient to provide complete guidance as to how an agency should fulfill its mission, which is why it created the rule-making process specified in the APA. To ignore that process in order to create substantial changes in the law subverts the entire system, but OCR has gotten away with it when the courts have let it.

Simply requiring equality in the number of varsity athletes has not settled the issue, however. Courts and government bureaucrats have found themselves in the position of ruling on the merits of various sports. In the Quinnipiac case, it was determined that "competitive cheering and tumbling" did not count for the purposes of Title IX, so the school had to reinstate the women's volleyball team.[46] When faced with clear evidence that women are less interested in sports than men, regulators and judges have responded that this is due to sex stereotyping, and that civil rights law requires schools and universities to make men and women more psychologically similar. For this reason, social engineers have shown a distinct hostility to counting cheerleading as a sport, as well as refusing to countenance less competitive and all-consuming models of female athletic involvement, including one that as of 1972 was represented by the Association for Intercollegiate Athletics for Women (AIAW)—an organization that could have been the female version of the NCAA had federal regulators and judges not imposed the model of the male organization on both sexes.[47] There is nothing in the text of Title IX that mentions sports, and women outnumbering men in student government, music, and other kinds of extracurricular activities has never bothered OCR or the federal judiciary.[48]

Just as civil rights law in employment imposes soft quotas to get around the fact that some groups have more productive workers than others, so too colleges and universities have had to deal with the hard fact that men are more interested in athletics by cutting male sports and padding their numbers of female athletes through methods such as including on lists those who never attend practices or games and double- or triple-counting participants.[49] One common loophole even allows schools to count male practice players on women's teams as female athletes.[50] Title IX has been particularly good for women's rowing, a sport there is little demand for but that has rules that can be manipulated in order to artificially inflate the number of participants.[51] Women's rowing was at the center of the USC admissions scandal that led to the indictment and eventual jailing of two Hollywood actresses in 2019, an event that captured the attention of the public as a story about wealth and privilege. Few noticed the absurdity of being able to get into college by pretending to play a sport that might cease to exist if not for a 1972 law.

As bizarre as the saga of Title IX in sports has been, the federal government here looks prudent and restrained when we examine how the same law has come to be used to impose a radical understanding of heterosexual relations on higher education. As with the field of college athletics, OCR has avoided following both the plain text of the law and the official rule-making process as the avenue through which to make major policy changes. In the 1990s, it started to inch toward importing harassment law as it developed under Title VII into Title IX regulations to regulate social life at schools and universities.[52] After the Supreme Court made clear that it would look skeptically on any attempts to "transfer" harassment law from the context of employment to education, OCR began to ignore Title VII.

In the first decades of Title IX, the law did not even address peer-to-peer harassment but required schools to create grievance procedures to determine whether institutions themselves were discriminating.[53] It was only in 1997 that OCR put out guidance that created an affirmative duty to stop sexual harassment, and on the last day of the Clinton administration it issued a thirty-seven-page document that detailed how schools should handle categories of harassment. New innovations allowed for subjectivity in deciding which conduct was prohibited and lowered the standard for how pervasive or serious actions had to be in order to constitute a violation of Title IX.[54]

The Clinton rules were held in abeyance and went unenforced under the Bush administration but came back with a vengeance and were expanded under Obama. Harvard Law professors (and husband and wife) Jacob Gersen and Jeannie Suk have written about the resulting regulation and bureaucratization of sex, focusing on universities as both a microcosm and an extreme example of this particular effect of civil rights law.[55] The Obama administration ushered in grievance procedures to address incidents in which one student had allegedly committed an offense against another. In 2011, OCR released a "Dear Colleague" letter that forbade universities from requiring "clear and convincing" proof of sexual misconduct before punishing a student, imposing a watered-down "preponderance of the evidence" standard instead.[56]

The administration also showed how elastic the concept of "discrimination" could be. A White House task force created a model survey that defined "sexual violence" as including everything from unwanted remarks about a person's physical appearance to rape.[57] This document helped provide the basis for assessments on campus climate carried out by colleges and universities across the country, and ultimately led to headlines that alleged astronomically high levels of sexual violence on college campuses. The Obama-era regulations also resulted in kangaroo courts in which convictions of men accused of sexual assault were all but assured, even for alleged conduct that was by all accounts legal.

The Department of Education under Obama also put a large emphasis on shaping the beliefs, actions, and behaviors of students and university employees. Melnick notes that "no word is repeated more frequently in OCR guidance documents than 'training.'"[58] In a forty-six-page document called "Questions and Answers on Title IX and Sexual Violence" released by OCR in 2014, "train" and other forms of the word appear eighty times.[59] While the documents themselves lack specificity as to what "training" actually means, when OCR has reached settlements with universities accused of discrimination, it has been willing to specify exactly what it wants, which usually involves teaching that men systematically oppress women and adopting expansive definitions of what constitutes sexual harassment and assault.

A specialized bureaucracy has been needed in order to address these issues. The Obama administration recommended that schools employ a full-time Title IX coordinator who could act independently, reporting not to an administrative body but directly to "senior leadership, such as the district superintendent or the college or university president."[60] A section in one document titled "Visibility of Title IX Coordinators" notes an obligation to distribute the contact information of such officials on a school's "website and in various publications."[61] They were to be "appropriately trained," with a recommendation that schools see OCR's regional offices for technical assistance in the process.

In addition to guidelines released under Title IX, the Violence Against Women Reauthorization Act of 2013 required schools and universities to produce "a statement of policy" with regard to what they were doing to "prevent domestic violence, dating violence, sexual assault, and stalking."[62] The Department of Education interpreted this to mean that schools would need to adopt policies that "foster healthy, mutually respectful relationships and sexuality, encourage safe bystander intervention, and seek to change behavior and social norms in healthy and safe directions."[63] In subsequent years, universities would start to require "affirmative," if not "enthusiastic," consent for sexual behavior; define assault to include sexual acts performed in any situation where drugs or alcohol were involved; and even suggest lines and jokes students could use to make sure that their partner was sufficiently eager to engage in sexual relations.

As Gersen and Suk write, "Under the rubric of preventing sexual violence, school mini-bureaucracies within federal bureaucratic oversight are engaged in a normative program of good-sex education, couched in views about good relationships in which that good sex should be had."[64] Title IX was also used by the Obama administration to enforce trans ideology, requiring schools to let children use bathrooms and locker rooms consistent with their "gender identity" rather than their biological sex.

None of this went through the notice and comment procedure required for enacting substantive government regulations. Rather, the Dear Colleague letters sent out by the Obama administration, while not binding as a matter of law, were treated as such. They provided the basis on which OCR entered into agreements with individual universities to take specific measures to address sexual violence. To strip funding from a university under Title IX requires a hearing explaining exactly which obligations the institution failed to live up to.[65] Yet no university undertook any legal or administrative challenge to the Obama-era regulations. In part this appears to be due to ideological sympathy, but another factor may be that, unlike private businesses, universities do not actually mind increasing bureaucratic costs, since they will be passed on to their students or the taxpayer.

When OCR guidelines were challenged in court, the Title IX tribunals of the Obama era were rebuked in dozens of cases, with the documents that created them finally being withdrawn during the Trump administration.[66] The universities could have challenged the regulations and would likely have won, but there was less of an appetite to do so than there would have been in the private sector. The bathroom policy did not even require a Dear Colleague letter, as it involved an email from OCR to a transgender activist interpreting previous Dear Colleague letters to ban discrimination based on "gender identity and the failure to conform to stereotypical notions of masculinity or femininity."[67]

The Trump administration came into office determined to roll back the Obama-era innovations. The new secretary of education, Betsy DeVos, declared in September 2017 that "the era of 'rule by letter' is over."[68] The OCR website lists nine letters released by the Obama administration and withdrawn under Trump, including the 2011 letter on sexual violence, the 2014 Q&A on the topic, and the 2015 statement on the obligations a school has regarding its Title IX coordinator, all mentioned above.[69] Nonetheless, even under the Trump administration, schools were still operating under settlement agreements signed with OCR, investigations continued, and Title IX offices within universities that were created and strengthened during the Obama years maintained their institutional power.[70]

In this way, guidelines entitled to no legal or judicial deference and released without the use of official rule-making authority had major cultural effects on schools and universities that would not be erased with a change in administration. Granting more power to social regulators has proved easier than taking it away, particularly in a university setting where many administrators and bureaucrats are sympathetic to feminist causes. In June 2022, the Biden administration announced that it would effectively seek to institute many of the Obama policies withdrawn under Trump, but this time by going through APA rule-making.[71] This will presumably make it more time-consuming and difficult for future administrations to move away from a federal policy of engaging in social engineering in schools and on university campuses.

In another worrying development, in July 2022, a Maryland federal district court ruled that Title IX even applies to private schools that do not get federal funding, on the theory that being exempt from taxation means that an institution is receiving a subsidy.[72] If such an idea were to get traction, it would remove the most common "escape hatch" parents previously had for avoiding civil rights regulations in how they educate their children. It would also threaten the institutional model of Hillsdale College, which refuses even to take financial aid for its students because it does not want to comply with federal regulations. Conservative power in the judiciary limits the damage that this idea can do on a wider scale, as it only applies to Maryland, and any school that wanted to take the issue to the Supreme Court would almost certainly win. But the decision serves as a reminder of what liberals would do if they had more power, and the importance of Republicans achieving the political victories necessary to maintain a high level of representation on the courts.

The Skeleton Key of the Left

From the text of the original 1964 statute, one would think that civil rights law protects whites and men as much as it does minorities and women. In reality, however, because it is vague and prohibits almost everything, bureaucrats and judges have a great deal of discretion with regard to who gets punished and for what. The Supreme Court has explicitly rejected for over three decades the idea that one can have different standards for discrimination against "protected" and "unprotected" groups, yet that is precisely what we find.[73]

This is part of a larger pattern, in which across a wide variety of areas we find that civil rights law allows or mandates preferential treatment for minorities and women as long as the nature and extent of the discrimination are sufficiently obscured.

For example, affirmative action practiced by state institutions potentially runs afoul of the Fourteenth Amendment, which prohibits discrimination based on race, and Title VI, which prohibits federal funding to entities that practice discrimination, a category that includes almost all private universities. As we've seen, nondiscrimination is interpreted to require race-consciousness and affirmative action in private-sector employment. The question for university admissions is whether it bans such practices under Title VI or the Fourteenth Amendment's Equal Protection Clause. As with EEOC and OFCCP standards, Supreme Court decisions have consistently found that race can be used as a factor in admission but that quotas are illegal.

In practice, universities use a barely veiled quota system, and liberal judges and government bureaucrats have looked the other way. The last major Supreme Court decisions on the topic were handed down in 2003, in *Gratz* and *Grutter*. The first of these addressed the University of Michigan undergraduate admissions program, which automatically awarded extra points to every applicant from an "underrepresented minority" background. This was ruled illegal because of its mechanistic nature, as it did not consider applicants as individuals. However, in *Grutter*, the Supreme Court upheld the University of Michigan Law School admission process, which considered race but in a more "holistic" way that sought to achieve a "critical mass" of underrepresented minority students.

Chief Justice Rehnquist wrote a dissent signed by four conservative justices. They argued that "critical mass" was indistinguishable from a quota. For each admissions cycle between 1995 and 2000, the University of Michigan Law School admitted a similar number of African American, Latino, and Native American students. Every year they apparently needed approximately one hundred African Americans, fifty Hispanics, and fifteen Native Americans to meet this standard, with

African Americans consistently needing lower scores than the other two minority groups. The law school "*never* offered any race-specific arguments explaining why significantly more individuals from one underrepresented minority group are needed in order to achieve 'critical mass' or further student body diversity" (emphasis in the original). This pattern made it clear that the "alleged goal of 'critical mass' is simply a sham." Moreover, in any given year, the percentage of the student body admitted from each of the three groups closely matched the percentage of applicants from each of those groups. Only an unofficial quota system seeking racial balance explains those admissions patterns.

As the Asian American population has grown in recent decades, universities have faced a new dilemma. What to do about a minority group that overperforms on admissions criteria? They responded similarly to how they have responded when faced with underperforming minorities: with unofficial quotas that they justified on other grounds. In 1993, 20.3 percent of the Harvard incoming class was Asian. But between 1990 and 2011, the number of Asians between the ages of eighteen and twenty-one in the United States doubled, while the numbers admitted to Ivy League universities stayed the same: between 15 and 20 percent of admitted students every year in every school.[74] When Harvard was sued for this, it defended itself by arguing that the school took into account intangible characteristics like "likability" and "courage." Strangely enough, Asians, the group with the highest test scores, were found by Harvard to have the worst personalities, while groups with the lowest test scores had the best.[75] As this book goes to press, the consolidated cases of *Students for Fair Admissions v. Harvard* and *Students for Fair Admissions v. University of North Carolina* are before the Supreme Court, and by now there may have been enough conservative justices appointed for this charade, or at least the legal sanction of it, to end.

Up to this point, affirmative action jurisprudence has given liberal institutions and supporters of identity politics the best of all worlds. They can use quotas to achieve balance, as long as they do not say that they are using quotas, thereby staying within the letter of the law while also obscuring what they are doing to avoid the uncomfortable truths and political backlash that would present themselves if they made racial discrimination explicit. This is primarily the fault of moderate rather than liberal judges, as the latter have shown themselves willing to uphold explicit quotas. While the current system of mandatory but implicit discrimination has proved to be ideal for those on the identity-obsessed left, it wasn't designed by them. It is the result of a compromise arrived at to please moderates who are too timid to support either colorblindness or explicit discrimination against whites, Asians, and men.

Explicit quotas are preferable to the current system in that they could potentially place limits on discrimination, leave more room for merit, and provide clarity on what is and isn't allowed. They would also be simpler to administer, lead to less bureaucracy, and not require ideological litmus tests in the form of "diversity statements," which increasingly are required in university hiring. What we have instead is a system where civil rights law serves as the skeleton key of the left. As mentioned, courts and bureaucrats treat cognitive tests with suspicion, but they have generally ignored college degree requirements despite their having, similarly, a disparate impact. As of 2019, among those twenty-five and older, 40 percent of whites had a bachelor's degree or higher, compared to 52 percent of Asians, 26 percent of blacks, and 19 percent of Hispanics. Clearly any employer that requires a BA or postgraduate degree could be accused of engaging in a practice that has a disparate impact on the latter two groups under the four-fifths rule. Unlike with cognitive tests, though, employers have seldom, if ever, gotten in trouble for requiring college degrees, even when the kind of credential necessary to be hired or promoted has no connection to the profession in question. All of this despite a large literature showing IQ tests to be predictive of job performance, and no evidence that college degrees predict performance when underlying cognitive traits are accounted for.[76]

In response to the Covid-19 pandemic, many public schools closed for long periods, and others remained open but with mask requirements. Data shows that "learning loss" from school closures hit poor and minority students the hardest.[77] Yet this has not created any issues surrounding disparate impact. Meanwhile, the Biden Justice Department has gone after state bans on mask mandates on the grounds that they might create special dangers for disabled students and deny them a right to an education.[78]

What can explain such inconsistencies? It would be naive to attribute them to any neutral interpretation of the law. Someone who carefully read reports on the current state of the law but was unfamiliar with what positions conservatives and liberals took on Covid-19 would not have guessed that civil rights law would consider bans on mask mandates, but not school closures, as potential violations. Meanwhile, someone who knew nothing of the law but was a close observer of American politics would have been able to predict exactly what happened. Had conservatives been the ones more in favor of preventative measures against Covid-19, civil rights law, overwhelmingly applied and interpreted by liberals, would likely have considered mask mandates and school closures problematic for their disproportionately negative effects on the educational and social development of minority children.

Under the standards of disparate impact and anti-harassment, the EEOC has gone after private businesses for using criminal background checks; word-of-mouth hiring; and enforcing different dress codes for male and female cocktail servers.[79] The most absurd prosecutions do occasionally get thrown out if they get to court, but challenging a government agency or defending a practice is an expensive and time-consuming endeavor for what is usually an uncertain result, and most employers would rather fold on the issue in question or, if necessary, find a new line of work. Settlements are often cheaper than fighting a charge in court; hence most prosecutions do not make it that far. Similarly, the OFCCP and other agencies applying the policies it has created are tasked with regulating contractors that are trying to create or maintain profitable relationships with the government while avoiding litigation.

If it seems that our culture has built an elaborate ranking system of races, genders, and "traumas," it is because our legal system did it first.

Affirmative action in contracting, disparate impact standards, harassment law, and Title IX social engineering are the four main mechanisms of civil rights law that have had the most far-reaching effects on American institutions. But the anti-discrimination principle is found elsewhere, and has expanded beyond issues of race and sex. Protecting "voting rights" has come to mean not treating individuals the same but banning any practice that has the effect of causing fewer non-whites to vote, and even drawing districts in ways that "dilute" minority voting power, thus legitimizing the idea that democracy itself should be a racial spoils system.[80] The federal government and certain states and localities have minority set-asides in contracting. The disparate impact doctrine has been used to go after so-called housing discrimination, with predictable effects on free speech and civil liberties.[81] Real estate agents are often told not to mention the quality of schools or the crime rate in an area lest they signal a racist preference, and even terms like "great view" and "walk-up" have been cited as potentially trying to exclude blind people and those in wheelchairs.[82]

In the years since the Americans with Disabilities Act (ADA) of 1990 came into effect, the EEOC has come to focus more on accusations of discrimination against those with medical conditions. Congress has also made age discrimination illegal, first in employment in 1967 and then, in 1975, in programs receiving government assistance. Crusades against age and disability discrimination have many of the same problems as those that target differential treatment based on race and sex—they have led to costly litigation, a decline in individual and institutional freedom, and absurd interpretations grounded in the disparate impact doctrine. Brains naturally deteriorate as they get older, meaning that the principle that one should not discriminate against the elderly is at war with the principle of merit, particularly in fields that rely on higher levels of cognitive performance. It is therefore unsurprising that tech companies like IBM, Oracle, and Google have been legally targeted in recent years.[83] A common charge against corporations is that they prefer young employees because they are cheaper, which is a strange thing for the legal system to concern itself with, given that there is widespread recognition of increasing generational wealth inequalities that advantage older Americans.

Age is at least easy enough to define; what counts as a "disability" is constantly in dispute, particularly when it comes to psychological conditions without clear physiological markers. An entire area of law has developed, for instance, focusing on issues such as when and under what conditions employers must accommodate alcoholism. Questions in this regard include what separates an individual who drinks too much from one who has a "disease" that makes him eligible for civil rights protections and at the same time more difficult to fire.[84]

In 1992, about 1 percent of EEOC charges, meaning formal accusations brought to its attention, were for discrimination based on disability. By 2021, that had risen to 37 percent.[85] The Americans with Disabilities Act adds yet another cost to doing business. It increases the power of social engineers within the federal bureaucracy to decide questions that should, in a free society, be dealt with by individuals and private institutions. As Justice Antonin Scalia pointed out in a biting 2001 dissent in a case in which a professional golfer successfully sued the PGA because it would not accommodate his need for a cart during the game, "It has been rendered the solemn duty of the Supreme Court of the United States, laid upon it by Congress in pursuance of the Federal Government's power '[t]o regulate Commerce with foreign Nations, and among the several States,' U. S. Const., Art. I, § 8, cl. 3, to decide What Is Golf."[86]

Finally, there is Section 1981, which was part of the Civil Rights Act of 1866. It guaranteed the ability to make and enforce contracts without being discriminated against based on race. In 1968 the Supreme Court decided that this provision banned discrimination in the sale or rental of property.[87] The fact that it took a century for the law to be thus applied is an indication that this may have been another instance of the Warren Court straying from the original meaning of a statute to achieve its political objective. Section 1981 has been used in the employment context, being less expansive than Title VII in only applying to racial discrimination and requiring intent, which precludes any disparate impact cases. At the same time, it has no caps on punitive damages and a longer statute of limitations. Overall, it has proved less influential than Title VII, although by providing potential windfalls to successful plaintiffs it likely does distort workplace environments and the hiring process.

Volumes on how the American government regulates and constructs identity are waiting to be composed. Nonetheless, the four doctrines highlighted in this chapter are those most responsible for what we can call wokeness—defined by its obsessions with race and sex—being embedded in law. There is perhaps a book to be written about the contribution of the Americans with Disabilities Act to our growing mental health problems, or how laws against age discrimination contribute to generational inequality and technological stagnation. One hopes that the arguments made here, against unaccountable government power used for purposes of social engineering and stamping out supposed discrimination, can be applied more broadly to a wider range of political issues.

Although no court or bureaucrat would put it in such terms, the practical consequence of civil rights law is to create the most blatant double standards based on whether one belongs to a protected or unprotected class. For those in a protected class, all speech and conduct of employers will be examined for the possibility that it creates unintentional bias. For those who are unprotected, explicit discrimination—as long as it's not too explicit in the form of, for example, official quotas—is not only allowed but required. Moreover, while free speech exists in theory under civil rights law, in practice it often does not, as human resources offices clamp down on ideas, jokes, and opinions that bureaucrats and judges may find offensive because no individual controls the patterns of behavior within any particular institution.

The distinctions between wokeness as culture and wokeness as law begin to break down when we think about the interaction between the two. An American employer is a private actor but also someone whose ideas about his role in society and professional obligations are shaped by the government regulations he lives under. A bureaucrat in the OFCCP is a government agent but also an active participant in shaping the cultures of corporations. Drawing the line between law and culture becomes even more difficult when we consider the bureaucracies that have grown within private institutions in response to civil rights law. A Title IX coordinator who believes that the United States is a white supremacist patriarchy is not only a symbol of the ideological extremism of the American university but a product of federal regulations.

Two of the central tenets of wokeness identified in the first chapter—disparities are caused by discrimination, and speech must be restricted to help overcome those disparities—are not listed as official state doctrine in any legal textbook. In practice, for over half a century, employers and educational establishments have been forced to act as if they are. The third pillar of wokeness, that is, the new bureaucratic class that has risen in order to enforce the doctrines of the faith, is the subject of the next chapter.

CHAPTER 3

The Standardization of the American Workplace and University

When most people think about what types of people are affiliated with universities, they usually think of professors and students. That impression is dated, as higher education has been taken over by professional managers who neither teach nor do research. Yale currently has about as many administrators and managers as it does students.[1] Many new employees have job titles that did not exist only a few decades before. As of 2020, Ohio State University employed 132 administrators with "diversity" or "equity" in their job titles at the cost of $13.4 million.[2]

What has happened in academia has only been an extreme example of a more general bureaucratization of American life. It was not always like this. In November 1971, Columbia University president William J. McGill wrote an open letter in which he lamented that, due to affirmative action regulations, "We are no longer in all respects an independent private university."[3] The Department of Health, Education, and Welfare was threatening to cut off federal funding unless the university provided employment data based on race and sex and timetables for hiring minorities. President McGill wrote that Columbia had a decentralized form of administration, in which individual departments were allowed to act independently. The university simply did not have the administrative capabilities to comply with new mandates coming from Washington, which required painstaking record keeping to prove that the institution was not discriminating against women and minorities. President McGill pointed out that bureaucratic bloat "will add to our burdens and our costs but we have been told that if we wish to continue to have federal resources, that is what we must do. Accordingly, we must do it."

Decades later, universities were once again struggling with the federal government, this time over its micromanaging of athletics under Title IX. At one point the president of Brown University asked how was it that schools were "free to cut libraries and academic departments, but not athletics."[4] Eventually, after losing in a series of court cases in the 1990s, as with affirmative action decades before, higher education came to identify with and support the costly regulations it once rallied against. Though universities today represent the ideological extreme, they were not always this way, and one should understand their transformation over time as a product of government intervention.

In the case of higher education, we can most easily trace the rise of bureaucracy to civil rights law. Yet colleges and universities have simply moved in step with trends that have also affected American business since the 1960s, and the underlying mechanisms at work appear to be the same. Civil rights law has led to an expansive human resources industry in the private and public sectors for three reasons. First, the law is vague: while it requires soft quotas and speech restrictions to a certain degree, an employer can never be sure just which aspects of hiring, promotion, and firing must take into account race, sex, and other protected identities, and precisely how; exactly which speech is banned; and what a firm's obligations are in monitoring workers and enforcing speech codes.

None of this would matter all that much if civil rights law wasn't also self-financing, the second reason for the existence of a robust human resources industry. Unlike in other areas of law, successful litigants can get attorney's fees for lawsuits. The practice of awarding punitive damages, codified in the CRA of 1991, has further contributed to an incentive problem in which employers face penalties for running afoul of the law that are disproportionate to the tangible harms caused.

Finally, there is the "best practices" doctrine, through which an institution can defend itself by showing that it is behaving in accordance with industry norms. Employers must pay attention not only to what judges and bureaucrats think but to the things that other corporations are doing to address discrimination. This creates an arms race, which helps explain why practices that once seemed absurd can become common.

Figure 3.1 shows the number of individuals working in human resources in the United States by year, excluding military employment:

Figure 3.1.

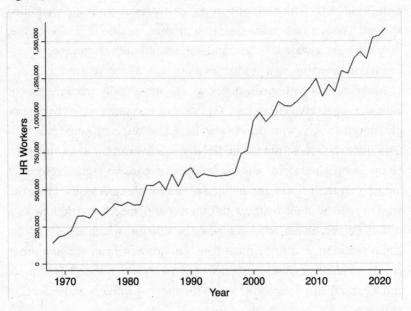

Number of Americans working in human resources, 1968–2021 (non-military). (Sources: Current Population Survey from IPUMS-CPS, University of Minnesota, www.ipums.org; FRED, https://fred.stlouisfed.org/series/LNU01000000.)

In the 1950s, human resources as a job category barely existed; fewer than 100,000 people were employed in any particular year.[5] By 1968, the number had risen to 140,000. It reached over 1.5 million in 2021. Because overall numbers may give a misleading picture due to population growth, Figure 3.2 shows the percentage of the workforce employed in human resources by year, from 1968 to 2021, overall and broken down by sex.

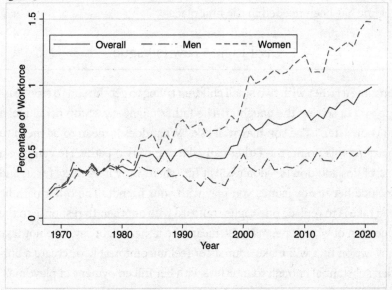

Human resources as a percentage of the entire workforce, 1968–2021. (Source: Current Population Survey from IPUMS-CPS, University of Minnesota, www .ipums.org.)

The results show the creation of an entire industry. In 1968, only 1 in 558 American workers were employed in human resources. By 2021, that number had risen to 1 in 102, including 1 in 184 men and 1 in 68 women. In his 1941 book *The Managerial Revolution*, James Burnham argued that the world was witnessing a shift from a system where capitalists comprised the ruling class to one in which they were being replaced by a managerial elite that controlled the means of production.

Yet while the rise of some kind of managerial elite was perhaps inevitable due to increasing technological and economic complexity, there was nothing inevitable about a portion of this class taking on social engineering as a career. This was a unique result of the characteristics of the American civil rights regime. Has this improved business efficiency and ameliorated problems inherent in having different kinds of people work together? Many in the human resources sector would certainly say so, but if they are correct, it raises the question of why the civil rights regime has been needed in the first place.

Civil Rights Law Is Vague

Imagine a father with two small children trying to get the son to stop teasing and upsetting the daughter. The father might say, "Stop being mean to your sister." The son may well ask, "What does it mean to be mean to her?" At this point, the father can take one of two paths. He can give a list of dos and don'ts—don't yell at her, share a toy if she asks for it, and include her in any games you play with your friends. The other path he can take is to replace one vague standard with another. In response to the question of what it means to be mean, the father might say, "Do not take any action that will make your sister feel uncomfortable or create a burden substantial enough to interfere with her full enjoyment of playtime."

Three effects here are worthy of note. First, the son still faces uncertainty in how to behave. Arguably, the definition of "being mean" is more confusing than the original phrase itself, not least because the father is using words that the son might not understand. If the father simply said "don't be mean," he and the son would quibble over the meaning of one word. By trying to be more specific about what it means to be "mean," one now can quibble over several phrases, like "substantial" and "full enjoyment of playtime." The father has pretended to provide a more exact standard, while if anything doing the opposite.

The second effect of the father's approach is that the son is on notice that the rules can change at any moment. What does not make his sister uncomfortable today might do so as she grows a bit older. Finally, the father has sent a signal that he has a broad interpretation of what it means to be mean. The son does not have exact guidance on how to behave, but he now at least knows that anything he does is potentially objectionable. The option of mostly forgetting about his sister and simply not going out of his way to make her feel bad is off the table. If he's going to listen to his father, he needs to incorporate her interests and feelings into most of what he does.

There's a reason we don't raise children like this. But vagueness wrapped in jargon is the great trick of civil rights law. This is particularly true with regard to the concept of harassment. Judges and bureaucrats could have had a standard that said "don't do anything racist or sexist." That would be an arbitrary standard, but adding more words has the effect of only making the rule look more exact and precise, while in effect doing no such thing. Not to "discriminate" under Title VII now means not to engage in sexual harassment, which in the words of the Supreme Court means avoiding conduct that is "sufficiently severe or pervasive 'to alter the conditions of [the victim's] employment and create an abusive working environment.'"[6]

Civil rights law "clarifies" what statutes mean with words that are at least as vague as the original definition, with the added problem that they refer to concepts that are too complicated for most people to understand without specialized training. But what such standards do make clear is that there are few limits on what practices, speech, or actions a court or bureaucrat might find objectionable. In the end, the father giving his son guidance in our example is saying, "I'll know it when I see it." The practitioners of civil rights law have done the same thing: those with an interest in and ideological commitment to applying the broadest possible definitions of terms like "discrimination" set the rules for the rest of us.

The "pervasiveness" requirement naturally leads to the adoption of zero tolerance policies in corporate America. The law is clear that "isolated" statements or actions cannot give rise to a cause of action, but there is no way for an employer to adopt a rule that says dirty jokes are only allowed if the total number of dirty jokes stays below some undefined threshold. The EEOC therefore naturally tells businesses to "avoid race-based or culturally offensive humor or pranks. When in doubt, leave it outside the workplace."[7]

Is vagueness an inevitable feature of modern law? Perhaps to a certain extent, as no legislation can give exact guidance for every possible situation, and this is the reason we have lawyers, judges, and bureaucrats in the first place. Yet a comparative perspective shows the extent to which the American system is unique in the vagueness of its legislative guidance. The idea that the powers of the federal government are limited is a fundamental principle of American law, but applying that principle can lead to some counterintuitive results. In their 1998 paper "The Strength of a Weak State: The Rights Revolution and the Rise of Human Resources Management Divisions," the sociologists Frank Dobbin and John Sutton show how across various areas of law, the American government regulates in an indirect way, which paradoxically leads to more bureaucracy.[8] A traditionally "strong" state can issue mandates that are clear, do not undergo transformations over time through judicial and bureaucratic procedures, are enforced through one part of the national government, and are of uncontested legitimacy. The government of France is held up as an example of a strong state, one that has been able to create a quota for hiring handicapped employees and has laws regarding employment that are stable and enforced exclusively through the Ministry of Labor.

In contrast, the American state is "weak." It does not mandate quotas; in fact, it explicitly bans them. Instead, government contractors have "goals" and "timetables" they set themselves, and all large employers must be on the lookout for "disparate impact" in a world where everything has a disparate impact. Enforcement is also highly decentralized. In the private sector, an employer may face negative consequences through a lawsuit filed by a private party, an investigation through the EEOC, or, if they have a federal contract, via the Department of Labor or the agency that the firm is directly dealing with. Firms may also face pressures at the state or local level. Public institutions such as schools similarly can face individual lawsuits or investigations and threats that funding from Washington will be cut off.

A Self-Financing System

Decades-old federal statutes create massive penalties for violations of civil rights law, giving them a unique role in our legal system. Although Congress has regularly passed statutes since the 1960s designed to provoke private lawsuits that will help enforce federal regulatory policy, a series of laws and court decisions have stacked the deck in favor of plaintiffs in this particular area.[9]

Under the "American Rule" that is the default in civil cases, each side in a lawsuit pays for its own legal representation regardless of who wins. The Civil Rights Act of 1964, however, in Section 706(k), says that in a Title VII suit, "the court, in its discretion, may allow the prevailing party, other than the [EEOC] or the United States, a reasonable attorney's fee."[10] Congress later passed the Civil Rights Attorney's Fees Award Act of 1976, which applied the same rule to practically all other kinds of civil rights cases, including Title VI and Title IX.[11]

The deal struck in 1964 as written could have had the effect of both allowing indigent plaintiffs to find legal representation and deterring frivolous lawsuits. Nonetheless, the Supreme Court, in *Christiansburg Garment Co. v. EEOC* (1978), interpreted Section 706(k) to mean that the default rule under Title VII was that successful plaintiffs should get attorney's fees and successful defendants could not, unless there were unusual circumstances. As with *Griggs* and other cases, a carefully constructed legislative bargain designed to balance a trade-off between combating anti-discrimination and other concerns was thrown out in favor of more aggressive enforcement.

Some countries have a "loser pays" system as the default, and the Civil Rights Act appeared to follow their lead in this area of the law. Due to *Christiansburg*, however, we now have an asymmetry in which plaintiffs have a right to recover attorney's fees if they win, but defendants must swallow the costs of defending themselves even when courts have determined they have done nothing wrong. The important Ninth Circuit has gone even further than that. In *Skaff v. Meridien North Am. Beverly Hills, LLC* (2007), a disabled man sued a hotel for lack of accessibility. Even though the two sides reached a settlement, the appellate court ruled that the plaintiff could still pursue legal fees under the Americans with Disabilities Act and California law. In the end, the plaintiff, who had before filed twenty-one similar cases in California, was awarded $15,000 in the settlement, but his lawyer sought $118,000 from the hotel for working on the case.

The CRA of 1991 explicitly allows for punitive damages under both Title VII and the Americans with Disabilities Act, which is, like the allowance of attorney's fees, extremely rare for any area of law.[12] That is, plaintiffs are allowed to receive money beyond what is necessary to reasonably compensate them for any harm they have suffered. In addition to certainty, a key part of a well-functioning legal system is proportionality. For this reason, many countries—for instance, Germany and Japan—do not award punitive damages at all. They are usually found in common law countries, however, such as the UK and Australia. In the United States, punitive damages in most areas of law are usually determined on a state-by-state basis, while under civil rights law a right to receive such damages exists under a federal statute.

This has led to outrageous results, with lawyers and plaintiffs receiving windfalls for conduct that is radically disproportionate to any harm suffered. While the Civil Rights Act of 1991 caps punitive and nonpecuniary damages at $300,000 per individual for major companies, the judiciary's acceptance of class action lawsuits in civil rights cases—once again, contravening legislative intent—in effect turned what had been an individual right not to be discriminated against into a group right. This created massive potential liability.[13]

Title VII cases are often tried in the media, where the slightest hint of racism could potentially bring plaintiffs out of the woodwork and destroy the reputation of a company before a lawsuit even gets to trial. The deeper the pockets of an institution, the more likely it is to be targeted. A January 2019 report revealed that 99 percent of Fortune 500 companies had made payments to at least one plaintiff in a harassment or discrimination lawsuit since 2000.[14] As of 2019, the companies that have paid the most in disclosed settlements are Bank of America ($210 million), Coca-Cola ($200 million), Novartis ($183 million), Morgan Stanley ($150 million), and Abercrombie & Fitch ($90 million). The fact that nearly every Fortune 500 company has been targeted indicates that this is not a matter of a few bad actors. Rather, courts will inevitably find instances of discrimination no matter what is happening, given the nature of harassment law and the disparate impact doctrine.

A 2021 verdict shows how conduct that should be settled by private parties—or at most result in compensatory damages—can lead to crushing penalties for a corporation. In 2015 and 2016, a black father and son named Owen Diaz and Demetric Di-az [*sic*] worked at a Tesla plant. They sued the company for racial discrimination, with the father's claims alone making it to trial.[15] The case was based on California state law and Section 1981. Racial slurs were used in the presence of Diaz, and he saw racist graffiti on a bathroom wall. It appears that the workers allegedly responsible were mostly or all minorities themselves, and each time an allegation could be verified, the employee was punished.

Tesla claimed that they had taken enough steps to address the concerns of Diaz, and also that he was a temp worker and not their employee, so the company was not responsible for protecting him from discrimination anyway. A jury disagreed, and awarded the plaintiff $137 million, an amount that the judge reduced to $15 million.[16] In response to the verdict, Tesla released a statement pointing out that witnesses confirmed that the slurs were used in a friendly manner, usually by African American employees, and without hostile intent. Questions such as whether there can be such a thing as the friendly use of racial slurs and the parameters of what kind of flirtation is acceptable were once settled by private parties. Now they are matters of federal law.

Suits that end with such a large payoff to one individual are rare, but the aggregate effect of civil rights law is to fund a certain kind of legal and political activism that depends on the belief that racism and sexism are pervasive factors in American life. While Bank of America, for example, has paid hundreds of millions of dollars over the last two decades in settling civil rights cases, such costs are easily absorbable by a corporation that makes billions in net income each quarter. The problem, again, is that the machine is self-financing, and it has become normal practice for corporations, as part of their settlements, to take on new responsibilities and funnel money to civil rights lawyers and activists.

In July 2020 the Department of Justice reached a settlement with Bank of America over its old policy of refusing loans to adults under legal guardianships or conservatorships as a violation of the Fair Housing Act.[17] The DOJ estimated that the bank would need to pay $300,000 in total to victims, but the settlement also "requires the Bank to maintain the new, non-discriminatory loan underwriting policies," "train its employees on the new policies," and "monitor its loan processing and underwriting activities to ensure compliance with the Fair Housing Act." No cost estimates are given for such activities, but they are a normal part of civil rights settlements.

A study of all class action settlements in the federal courts between 2006 and 2007 found that while 89 percent of all class actions resulted in cash relief, and less than a quarter included declaratory or injunctive relief, for civil rights class action settlements, the numbers were 49 percent and 75 percent.[18] In other words, compared to other types of legal settlements in class action cases, civil rights defendants are more likely to be required to take on indirect burdens. An analysis from 1980 found that OFCCP regulations had increased the labor and capital costs of federal contractors by 6.5 percent, which according to a 1993 estimate from *Forbes* magazine would amount to 1.7 percent of GNP.[19] This does not even include the costs of EEOC compliance.

Moreover, the money that is paid in lawsuits and settlements, while being small in terms of how much profit large corporations make, can be enough to keep the civil rights industry going. When Coca-Cola agreed to a $192 million settlement in 2000 over allegations of discriminating against black employees, $20 million of that went to legal fees.[20] The company was also required to appoint a seven-member task force to supervise its human resource and hiring practices for four years. Under the Obama administration, it was normal practice for the Justice Department to reach settlements with corporations that required them to pay money to left-wing activist groups, therefore providing funding to the administration's political allies without having to go through Congress.[21] Civil rights law implements a relatively small tax on corporations that has a massive effect in terms of creating an entire industry of lawyers, activists, and human resources professionals.

Due to both legal rules set up in this area and the wide range of individuals who can potentially be plaintiffs, the crusade against "discrimination" is more profitable than seeking to correct other supposed injustices. President Calvin Coolidge famously said that "the chief business of the American people is business." Today, one might say that the main business of the federal courts is social engineering. If an individual believes they have a claim against an employer, they can file a case with the EEOC.[22] After 180 days or after the EEOC has completed its investigation, the individual can ask for a Notice of Right to Sue regardless of whether the agency found reasonable cause.

In the mid-1970s, there were only about five thousand EEOC charges of discrimination a year. By 2010, there were close to one hundred thousand, a number that has dropped to around sixty to seventy thousand in the last few years.[23] In other words, as the US population increased by about half, we saw a twentyfold increase in discrimination complaints. In 2020, there were about 1.5 million businesses in the US with at least fifteen or more employees, the threshold to be covered under Title VII of the Civil Rights Act and the ADA. With sixty-seven thousand charges filed, that is about one for every twenty-two businesses each year. It is important to note that one individual can file more than one charge against the same firm, and, because civil rights law is a business, the risks to large employers are surely higher than for small ones. Nonetheless, any business of sufficient size faces a substantial risk of an EEOC complaint being filed against it each year, with the odds being a near certainty for the biggest employers with the largest number of workers over a long enough period. Even if many of these claims are legitimate, one has to wonder whether allowing freedom of association is not preferable to practically making the federal government the human resources department of all large firms.

Figure 3.3 shows the number of civil rights civil cases filed in federal court, both in total and as a percentage of all civil lawsuits, from 1967 to 2020.[24] This includes those that require filing a charge with the EEOC first and those that do not.

We see a massive increase, going from a few thousand a year before 1970 to a high of over 43,000 in 2019. From the early 1990s up to 2019,

Figure 3.3

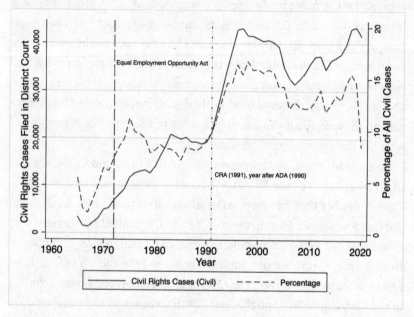

Civil rights civil cases filed in district court, and percentage of all civil cases that are civil rights cases, 1967–2020.

civil rights cases represented between 10 and 16 percent of all civil cases filed in federal court.

The number of cases had plateaued until the Americans with Disabilities Act of 1990 and the Civil Rights Act of 1991, the latter of which made changes related to the burden of proof in discrimination cases and, as mentioned before, created punitive damages under Title VII. A look at charges filed with the EEOC tells a similar story. In the final quarter of 1991, harassment charges made to the commission were up 71 percent from the same period the year before, and those numbers would continue to climb over the next twenty years.[25] As the civil rights industry appeared to begin reaching the limits of its expansion, perhaps due to the priorities of the Reagan administration, the Americans with Disabilities Act and the Civil Rights Act of 1991 breathed new life into it.

Figure 3.4 shows employment lawsuits filed from 1970 to 2020, and

Figure 3.4

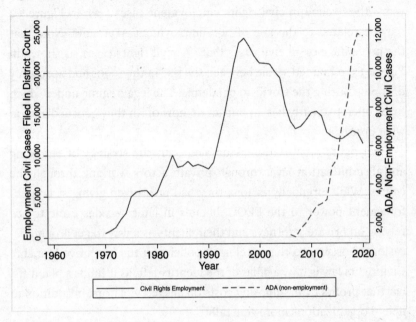

ADA cases beginning in 2006, when the federal government began to count them, up until 2020.

We see the same pattern in civil rights employment cases that we see in all civil rights cases. The number increased sharply after the EEOA of 1972, then plateaued in the 1980s, before taking off again in the 1990s. The effect of the ADA seems to have been delayed, only exploding in the late 2000s. Although we have no data on such cases pre-2006, it appears that there were very few ADA suits before that year. George W. Bush then signed the plaintiff-friendly ADA Amendments Act of 2008, after which we saw a precipitous rise.

It is more difficult to explain the drop in civil rights employment cases after the late 1990s, but one might consider the possibility that, because caps on punitive damages for employment claims have stayed constant, while dropping in real terms due to inflation, lawsuits in this area are all the time becoming less potentially lucrative.[26] Moreover, given that the supply of civil rights lawyers cannot rise in direct proportion to the number of opportunities created by federal law—due to the relative stability of the number of graduating law students each year—the decline in civil rights employment cases seen in Figure 3.4 may be related to the rise of non-employment ADA suits. Note that the percentage of all civil cases that are civil rights cases, as shown in Figure 3.3, remained stable between the rise in the 1990s and 2019, only dropping during the Covid-19 pandemic. The legal regime under which firms operate clearly has an impact on how often they get sued and on what grounds.

Civil rights organizations stumbled onto the strategy of enforcing anti-discrimination laws through private actors working through the courts. While originally in 1964 they had prioritized giving strong enforcement power to the EEOC, liberals in later decades came to see relying on private attorneys and their clients as a way to get around occasional hostility to their preferred policies in the executive branch.[27] Civil rights law is now a pillar of the identity left, as it funds a plaintiffs' bar that profits from imposing costs on alleged violators, in addition to liberal organizations more generally.

The fact that around 10–20 percent of all civil cases filed in federal court in recent years relate to discrimination of some kind should lead even those unconcerned with the implications for economic growth or freedom of association to realize that society might be overinvesting in fighting this particular harm. Of all the issues our legal system could be addressing, it is interesting that so much effort and attention is now directed at a kind of private cause of action that was not even recognized as part of the legal system until recent decades. Not that long ago, a fundamental principle of Anglo-American legal thought was that the remedy to discrimination practiced by a private party was to take one's business or labor elsewhere. That is still the default when an individual is wronged in a noncriminal manner on any basis other than some "protected" status. While centuries of mistreatment of black Americans have been used to justify a more activist government that now has powers that go beyond historical limits, the anti-discrimination principle has expanded to create two kinds of private ill-treatment based on a myriad of different kinds of identity, without anyone giving much thought as to why this should have been done.

The "Best Practices" Doctrine

Game theorists have shown how rational actors can make decisions that, while sensible for individuals, make everyone worse off. For example, if nations have no way to verify how much other states are investing in their military, one can easily end up with an arms race that no one wants. No matter what the other side is doing, each country can have an incentive to spend more to keep up with potential adversaries, even if everyone would be better off if they all disarmed instead. Civil rights law, through its vagueness, works in a similar way. Each corporation has an incentive to seem "less discriminatory" than others, which in effect means adopting fads out of academia or the HR industry and having to engage in ever more blatant forms of reverse discrimination.

The "best practices" approach has been indirectly endorsed by the judiciary. In two cases decided in 1998, the Supreme Court created an affirmative defense for sexual harassment claims, based on an employer exercising "reasonable care to prevent and correct promptly" any offending conduct and an employee unreasonably failing to use available opportunities to address the problem. As a result, lawyers and HR professionals explicitly tell businesses that having a bureaucratized complaint process can protect them from lawsuits. While the Supreme Court has said that an anti-harassment policy is not needed in every case, courts are virtually unanimous in finding that not having one precludes an affirmative defense to harassment.[28] That is not to say that an anti-harassment policy is sufficient to beat back a discrimination claim. Courts have looked favorably on additional steps that can be taken, including anti-harassment training and reprimanding supposed harassers and separating them from their alleged victims.[29] Under such circumstances, HR and DEI professionals have been able to sell their services as a good business investment, and can reasonably tell firms that they might be in trouble if they don't do at least as much as other employers to prevent harassment.

This natural tendency of civil rights law to devolve into a "woke arms race" has been given official sanction by the OFCCP and the EEOC, which are often ready to go as far as the judiciary will allow them to.

The OFCCP explicitly issues regulations based on the "best practices" of leading firms.[30] As of late 2021, it advises government contractors to set up outreach programs with Historically Black Colleges and Universities, have a social media presence, develop relationships with race-conscious organizations, and "encourage the creation of forum groups, e.g. African-American, Hispanic, AAPI, and conduct meetings with each group to discuss recruitment, outreach, mentoring, diversity, inclusion, and development programs."[31]

While these are not official mandates, the government has made clear that adopting the conservative belief in race-blindness makes an institution legally suspect. The EEOC similarly calls for "regular, interactive training tailored to the audience and the organization."[32] Nonetheless, it says that no body of regulation can cover every conceivable circumstance. This means that "at best, 'best practices' are best guesses."[33] In order to guide them, employers have come to rely on the HR profession due to its supposed expertise in such matters, or at least its ability to make courts and regulators think that a firm takes discrimination seriously.

A clear example of a principle that sounds good to outsiders but creates difficulties in practice is that of non-retaliation.[34] Under Title VII, an employer cannot punish a worker for filing a discrimination complaint. As of 2019, the majority of charges filed with the EEOC had a retaliation component.[35] An easy and natural way to deal with a difficult personnel situation is to separate the parties who are having a dispute. Yet if that is perceived as "retaliation" in any way—even if the original accusation itself lacks merit—the employer may be guilty of committing a Title VII violation. Thus employers must take all accusations of discrimination seriously, no matter how frivolous. If the firm decides to separate the two individuals having a dispute by, for example, moving one of them to a different department, or even firing one of the parties, it better be the alleged perpetrator.

Civil rights law creates protection for an employee against suffering retaliation for making an accusation of discrimination, but no protection for those falsely accused. This provides yet another example of how granting rights to a "protected" individual often involves violating those of one who is "unprotected." Employers, however, are usually more concerned with making money and preventing lawsuits than acting in accordance with idealized standards of justice, so they comply with what are unofficial mandates given the current state of the law. Completely innocent parties might be fired, if only to remedy difficult situations, and this is true even if an employer knows that an allegation being made would not hold up in court.

The growth of the diversity industry in the 1980s and 1990s coincided with political pushback to affirmative action. When put in the difficult position of being required to discriminate against white men by federal law while also—because the law maintains the pretense of protecting all groups equally—facing the possibility of reverse discrimination lawsuits, corporate America retreated into euphemisms and obfuscation. The diversity industry was self-consciously an outgrowth of the affirmative action industry, originally created to ensure compliance with federal mandates.[36] Courts and federal bureaucrats are rarely good social scientists, so practices become common without any evidence that they necessarily work.

As the sociologist Musa al-Gharbi has shown, corporations have adopted programs without any reason to think that they might improve their stated goals of achieving diversity and inclusion, and sometimes even in spite of evidence that they may backfire.[37] For example, the Implicit Association Test remains popular despite serious doubts about its validity, while diversity training can demoralize members of a minority group and increase biased behavior.[38] Given the haphazard ways in which civil rights law relies on vague standards and decisions made by government agents without a direct stake in the real world results of any intervention, it is easy to see why there is often an uncertain, weak, or even negative relationship between efforts made and the results that actors in the system purport to care about.

Even in the absence of government mandates, employers have a natural incentive to provide an environment in which workers achieve maximum productivity. This involves managing different personalities, and conflicts that may arise due to discriminatory treatment or unwanted sexual advances. The diversity industry has sold its services as necessary for improving efficiency. If they are right, there is no reason for the law to take an interest in personnel matters; the government usually doesn't have to force businesses to do things that are in their own financial interest. Civil rights law, however, has not caused employers to be more inclined to successfully manage interpersonal relations based on real world signals regarding what works. Instead, they are encouraged to find ways to convince bureaucrats, and potentially judges and juries, that they are good people who take discrimination seriously. Those are not the same thing. "Woke capital," which often refers to corporations taking left-wing stances on identity-related issues, is a natural response to a system that rewards this kind of virtue signaling.

It is difficult to exaggerate how ill-equipped lawyers, courts, and government administrators are to judge what makes for effective personnel management. The replication crisis in psychology has shown how challenging it is even for social scientists who dedicate their lives to understanding social phenomena to arrive at well-founded conclusions about the topics they study, particularly when it comes to shaping human behavior. In contrast to mandates coming from courts and bureaucrats, labor markets can give real-time feedback about what creates the best workplace environment. Employers are not necessarily good social scientists either, but they at least have the right incentives to figure things out and are directly familiar with what is happening in their own workplaces. It is unsurprising that government monitoring of the decisions they make has led to a proliferation of expensive, wasteful, and in some cases counterproductive practices.

Bureaucratic Bloat and Institutional Homogenization

The legal system has created vague rules covering practically all aspects of human interaction, making it profitable to bring suits alleging discriminatory treatment and very expensive for institutions to fall on the wrong side of the law. Even if the direct costs of lawsuits and settlement are manageable for major firms, the legal and bureaucratic structures that have been built based on civil rights law can cost a great deal in terms of larger payrolls, actions taken to avoid bad press that can draw the attention of bureaucrats and trial lawyers, and less control over hiring and promotions. The results have been a self-reinforcing system, in which entire business models in the legal and human resources professions depend on maintaining vague standards that must be complied with. Private businesses are not imagining things when they take precautions against lawsuits by restricting employee speech, enacting diversity and sexual harassment training, and engaging in explicit—but not too explicit—reverse discrimination. This last is in order to avoid even the possibility of having been found to unintentionally discriminate against protected groups.

The overall effect of civil rights law has been a great homogenization of corporate practice. As of 1970, less than 5 percent of corporations in one survey had an affirmative action officer, compared to about a quarter by 1986. While in 1956, fewer than a third had personnel offices, that number more than doubled over the next three decades.[39] Across that same period, grievance procedures for non-union employees went from rare to completely normalized, the practice existing among less than 10 percent of surveyed employers across most of the 1960s and about half by the middle of the 1980s.[40] The use of job descriptions saw an even more massive jump, from 22 percent in 1956 to 80 percent in 1985, a rise that was mirrored by an increase in performance evaluations. Other practices and tools used more frequently in private employment since the Civil Rights Act include disciplinary hearings, employment tests, job postings, salary classifications, job ladders, the centralization of hiring, and promotion and discharge guidelines.[41]

This great standardization in employment and hiring came about as firms sought to safeguard themselves against charges of arbitrary bias. If one hires and fires based on established rules and procedures that are widely accepted in an industry, one is less likely to be accused of discrimination. Everyone adopts similar procedures not because they work to achieve fair treatment or economic efficiency but because they minimize the risks of costly lawsuits and government interventions. And firms have come to rely on the same lawyers and HR professionals for advice on how to run their businesses.

Civil rights law meanwhile works as a kind of "force multiplier" for disgruntled employees, enabling them to make certain kinds of complaints, and allowing them to change institutions from the inside.[42] The same company that might not think twice about disciplining workers for making unfounded or exaggerated claims about other aspects of its business can have its hands tied if the allegations being made contain even a hint of a charge of racism or sexism. As mentioned before, civil rights law bans "retaliation" against an employee even if the underlying complaint is ultimately without merit. When Sen. Tom Cotton wrote an article in the *New York Times* in the summer of 2020 calling on the military to be sent to deal with rioters in major American cities, the opinion editor of the paper eventually resigned after employees waged a campaign against him that included sending out identical tweets saying that the piece put black staff in danger.[43] Had they claimed a grievance based on some other, "non-protected" identity, there would not have been the specter of legal liability for the article, nor would the controversy have invoked the grievance procedures and norms already established to deal with racial issues.

If a major newspaper being influenced in its staffing and editorial choices by civil rights law seems too absurd to contemplate, consider that Felicia Sonmez, a reporter for the *Washington Post*, sued her employer on the grounds that it was discriminatory to take her off #MeToo stories after she talked about her own alleged sexual assault. Although her suit was dismissed in 2022, newspapers are no different than other employers in responding to incentives.[44] Sonmez was eventually fired by the *Washington Post* in 2022 for weeks of publicly attacking coworkers on Twitter. It is reasonable to wonder the extent to which the employer's hesitancy to part ways with her was based on the incentives created by civil rights law and their downstream cultural effects.[45]

Before the 1960s, markets were the system through which American businesses decided what worked and what didn't in the realm of hiring, promotions, and employment. It was imperfect but at least provided some mechanism for driving improvements in methods, as those making the decisions were the ones who faced the consequences of their results. The benefits of fighting discrimination through increased bureaucracy, and they appear to be slight, must be balanced against the costs of putting a stop to innovation in personnel management. The genius of capitalism is that one does not need to make a judgment about any particular business practice but can remain agnostic about what works and let the market decide. Social science has proved a poor substitute for market forces, being subject to fads, politicization, and wishful thinking on the part of those who can afford to be wrong because they are making decisions about practices in areas without having a direct stake in the relevant outcomes.

IQ tests are among the most reliable measurements we have in psychometrics but are of questionable legality. Practices based on junk science—diversity training, the Myers-Briggs Type Indicator, the Implicit Association Test—have waxed and waned in popularity.[46] Lawyers, bureaucrats, and judges have been more comfortable with a cargo cult version of psychometrics than with the real thing, which might reveal uncomfortable truths about the relative performances of different groups. The result is a wasteful system that hurts productivity and mostly benefits human resource professionals, trial lawyers, and the rest of the class that has a stake in managing compliance with the law rather than achieving fairness or economic growth. Of course, even though IQ tests do provide a good measure of ability and are a cost-effective way to judge job applicants, it is almost certain that mandating them across the board would not be good government policy, even if it would be better than banning them. No government is smart enough to know what kinds of practices make sense for each particular institution. The more discrimination there is against a particular group, the more advantages there are to hiring members of that class, which provides one example of how markets are dynamic and oriented to solving problems in ways that government is not.[47]

One today needs bureaucracy to manage all aspects of interpersonal relations, and bureaucracy itself to be managed by more bureaucracy. Hence the explosion in HR personnel since the 1960s. Bureaucratic bloat has been bad enough in the private sector. When it comes to government and educational establishments that are heavily regulated and funded by the state, the results in many cases have been even more extreme. Between 1951 and 1970, money spent on federal categorical grants—those made to state and local governments covering everything from schooling to policing to improving water systems—went from $2.3 billion to $23 billion.[48] In 1962, there were only 162 categorical grant programs, a number that increased to 530 by 1970.

Even as of 1969, there were few strings attached to this kind of funding. That began to change as a consequence of the ways in which the Nixon and Ford administrations used Title VI to push for social engineering at the state and local levels, a use of government power that would have been all but unthinkable to the members of Congress who voted for the Civil Rights Act. In July 1994, Attorney General Janet Reno sent a memorandum to all departments and agencies that provide federal assistance instructing them to make use of the disparate impact standard to the greatest extent possible, a directive that represented a break with previous administrations.[49]

Relying on taxpayers for funding, instead of market forces, government institutions have little incentive to curtail spending on initiatives and jobs that do not lead to productivity gains. This is especially apparent in schools. Data from the Department of Education shows that while the number of K–12 teachers in the US increased by 8 percent from 2000 to 2017, the number of administrators increased by 75 percent.[50] At the level of higher education, there has been a steady increase in administrative costs since the beginning of the civil rights era, a trend that has accelerated in recent decades. In the 1980s, administrative costs per student increased by 46 percent.[51] Even by the early 1990s, leading universities had slightly more administrators than teachers or researchers, and the gap has widened since.[52] Looking at just full-time staff, between 1993 and 2007 the rate of new jobs for administrators grew at about four times the rate as for those working on research, teaching, or providing student services.

While this cannot all be attributed to civil rights law, the historical record is clear that administrative bloat results from federal money that comes with strings attached. The federal relations director of the Association of American Universities once put forward what he called "administrative clone theory," in which every new form of federal spending comes with a new federal office to administer the money, and then "clones" of the department are created at each university.[53] The reason administrators keep deciding to spend more money on administration is because they can; given that administrators rather than faculty exercise ultimate control over budgets, it is spending on their own jobs and privileges that we should expect to increase.

The growth of the Title IX bureaucracy during the Obama administration, discussed in the previous chapter, provides a clear example of the effects of more micro-level regulations. As of 2016, more than two hundred colleges and universities faced a Title IX investigation by the federal government over the handling of sexual assault allegations, an increase from fifty-five two years earlier.[54] No statute, of course, ever made sexual assault the responsibility of university administrators; practically everywhere else in society it is a concern for police and the courts. But under the Obama administration, in order to be able to meet newfound responsibilities placed on them four decades after the original passing of Title IX, universities started scrambling to hire "lawyers, investigators, case workers, survivor advocates, peer counselors, workshop leaders and other officials to deal with increasing numbers of [sexual assault] complaints."[55] At UC Berkeley, Title IX spending increased by about $2 million between 2013 and 2016 alone. Around this time, Yale had thirty faculty and staff members working on Title IX efforts and Harvard had fifty Title IX coordinators. In September 2017, the Trump administration withdrew the Obama-era sexual assault policies, and although there does not appear to be any data on whether the Title IX bureaucracy is shrinking, there is at least little evidence that it is still growing.

Division of Labor

Many conservatives have come to see "woke capital" as their enemy, as if those who spend a large portion of their waking hours selling goods and services are also prioritizing political activism. Most of the time, however, business leaders have their hands full simply doing their own jobs. The division of labor is a key feature of modern economies. As society becomes more complex, the more specialized the workforce becomes. In the 1950s, the field of human resources barely existed. Over the next decades, it would grow into a massive community, today comprising around 1 percent of the workforce. While many professions do their work out in the open, HR, and more recently the DEI complex, are working mostly behind the scenes to shape the rules and regulations that we all live under. If one dislikes modern architecture, one blames architects. If police brutality is a problem, then cops are more directly responsible than any other group. Likewise, if one is angry at the way interpersonal relations are governed in modern society, blame must first and foremost be attributed to government agencies that regulate them, along with the spinoff HR and DEI industries that prosper as a result.

The division of labor is usually a good thing. How a plane is flown should be determined by the pilot, not through the democratic process, as in the case of a famous *New Yorker* cartoon showing the passengers taking a vote. Yet human relationships are different. Rules and norms regarding humor, sex, and intergroup relations are rooted in human nature, history, culture, and the aggregate preferences and decisions of individuals acting in their own capacities. As long as the power of the state itself is not used to discriminate against certain groups, such matters should be left to private parties.

No science or field of expertise has the knowledge or wisdom to determine how men and women should flirt or which words should be forbidden in a workplace because they might hurt someone's feelings. No matter how well intentioned, once the government opened the door to concepts such as a "hostile work environment" and "disparate impact," there was no natural limit to the reach and power of full-time social engineers. While this class may see itself as representing the will of the community, or evolving norms, that is a myth, and the views, sensitivities, and prejudices of a small minority of the population shape how everyone is allowed to behave.

Once we understand wokeness in these terms, it focuses the attention of those who would like to defeat it. Referring to warfare, Frederick the Great once said, "He who defends everything defends nothing." One may alter the quotation and make it no less true: "He who fights everything fights nothing." Conservatives have blamed wokeness on entities as diverse as capitalists, the education system, recently arrived immigrants, financiers, Hollywood, the United Nations, "globalists," the mainstream media, the Muslim Brotherhood, *Al-Jazeera*, the upper-middle class, and the Chinese Communist Party. Some of these supposed villains are more deserving of blame than others. But such a scattershot approach, while it makes for good TV or talk radio content, provides little to focus or guide a political movement. Like the general who is given the task of defending everything, a movement faced with an endless list of powerful oppressors is likely to either stretch its forces so thin that they are overwhelmed or decide that it is trying to do the impossible and give up.

While wokeness as a cultural phenomenon does not have a single cause, the fight against it must narrow its focus. One must ask what a political movement can realistically do and how it can be most effective. With that framework in mind, the natural point of attack is civil rights law. In the US, the government does not have the power to dismantle the human resources and DEI professions through brute force. What opponents of wokeness can do, however, is fight broad and vague standards of "discrimination" through courts, legislatures, and the executive branch and at the federal and state levels. That also means concentrating on the class that has made it its specialty to manage human relations. To act otherwise is to get upset at the state of modern architecture and ignore architects to focus on the critics who praise their work or the system they are a part of.

While it may be theoretically interesting to take a broader view of the context in which the architects of wokeness perform their work, in the end a successful movement puts most of its energy toward fighting the group directly responsible for the problem it seeks to solve. Seeing wokeness as a kind of "class warfare" is generally correct, but the class in question is not capitalists, corporations, rich people, or managers more generally but the managers of human relations. That implies, first and foremost, going after rules that make civil rights litigation lucrative to plaintiffs and threatening to firms, in addition to checking the power of OCR, OFCCP, EEOC, and, when possible, the HR and DEI industries.

CHAPTER 4

Government as the Creator of New Races and Genders

In the early to mid-1950s, *I Love Lucy* was the highest-rated TV show in the United States. It centered around the life of Ricky Ricardo (Desi Arnaz) and his wife, Lucy (Lucille Ball). Ricky ran a nightclub, and his heavy Cuban accent, especially when he became upset at his wife's hi-jinks, was a source of much of the comedy of the show. Despite CBS executives' fears, Americans did not think it objectionable that the most popular show in the country featured what some might have considered an "interracial marriage." It was only in *Loving v. Virginia*, decided in 1967, that the Supreme Court would invalidate anti-miscegenation laws in the last sixteen states that still had them. Yet an American public that, in much of the country at least, supported laws to maintain the purity of the white race regularly welcomed Lucy and Ricky into their homes without giving the issue of race much thought.

In this, they were taking the lead of their government. On the 1950 Census, the racial options were "White," "Negro," "American Indian," "Japanese," "Chinese," "Filipino," and "Other." As late as the 1960s, Mexican American activists rejected the idea that they should be labeled non-white.[1] By the 1970s, however, when the federal government was classifying citizens and then distributing benefits and imposing costs based on those classifications, they were taking a different position. Rather than government responding to social realities, social realities were being shaped by the federal government, which was being lobbied by organizations that were largely unrepresentative of those they claimed to speak for.

While American classification has pushed some groups out of the "white" category, others have been welcomed in. My family immigrated to the United States from the Middle East, and I attended public schools that had a substantial minority of fellow Arab students. Every so often, usually when taking a standardized test, we were asked to identify our race. I remember there once being confusion in junior high over which box Arabs should check. The teacher looked down at a sheet of paper and, with a hint of skepticism in her voice, told us that we were white. Most people do not have deep ideas about race as a biological or anthropological concept and are willing to defer to government categorization. In high school, I was once in a computer lab in which a fellow student came across a demographic survey on a website that asked the respondent for his racial identification. When someone asked where Arabs were among the options, the teacher replied that it would be more accurate to say "Arab-speaking." Steeped in the public school bureaucracy, he had allowed existing categories to shape his scientific and social understandings of the concept of race.

After 9/11, it became clearer than ever that Arabs and Muslims were an "other" in American culture. The Council on American-Islamic Relations (CAIR), formed in 1994 on the model of other civil rights organizations, came to play a more prominent role in American politics. Yet discrimination against Arabs and Muslims has been treated as a relatively minor political issue. One rarely hears about the "underrepresentation" of either group in any particular field, nor does anyone ever discuss their crime rates or standardized test scores. We do not even know for certain whether Muslims, or Arabs for that matter, are underrepresented or overrepresented among prisoners or those of higher or lower socioeconomic status. While some studies on the topic have been done, the Census does not ask about these categories, and neither do those who collect arrest data or administer standardized tests. The data we have is therefore less copious and of lower quality than numbers pertaining to officially designated "races," and as a result, much less relied upon.

In 2020, the "Asian American Pacific Islander" community was said to be targeted as a result of the coronavirus pandemic. On Twitter, #StopAAPIHate became a rallying cry for journalists, activists, and academics. This community was supposedly being represented by an organization of the same name as the hashtag and affiliated with the Asian American Studies Department of San Francisco State University. As of this writing, its website shows a series of faces of people who appear to have no background in common except for the fact that they are neither black nor white. The media in recent years has run countless stories about increasing hate crimes against "AAPIs," along with numbers about "hate incidents" that are based on nothing but unverified and subjective reports collected by activist groups, though relied upon by newspapers like the *New York Times* to build a larger narrative.[2]

A moment's thought reveals how strange this narrative is. The coronavirus, as far as we know, began in China, and it is plausible that Americans of Korean, Japanese, or Vietnamese descent might in the last few years have suffered discrimination at the hands of bigots too ignorant to differentiate between these groups. Yet there is no reason to believe that Americans of Samoan or Indian descent should have seen an uptick in discrimination as a result of the pandemic. Still, any assaults inflicted on people of South Asian or Polynesian descent become part of the narrative about race in America. The Stop AAPI Hate website conveniently lists Punjabi and Marshallese among the languages in which one can report "hate incidents."

Meanwhile, not only is there an official narrative of shared victimhood among Asian Americans and Pacific Islanders, but elite institutions also punish them as a collective for their aggregate success. As of this writing, a lawsuit on behalf of Asian American students accusing Harvard of holding them to higher admissions standards is before the Supreme Court. As noted in chapter 2, Ivy League universities, whether in explicit collaboration or not, by the mid-2010s had an unofficial "soft cap" on Asian enrollment, although in recent years the number of Asians admitted has risen as more public attention has turned to the practice.[3] From the early 1990s to around 2010, the population of Asian Americans of college age more than doubled, while their numbers at the most prestigious universities remained constant, hovering around 16 percent.⁴ While academics in fields such as "Asian American Studies" point out that not all groups that fall into the AAPI category are doing well in socioeconomic terms, their cries are usually ignored. Colleges regularly release numbers on how many Native Americans or blacks are enrolled, but rarely if ever do they talk about the Hmong.

One only has to look at how we think and talk about race in the United States to clear up any doubts as to whether government classification can have a major influence on the larger culture. Activist organizations are formed on the basis of government classification, and individuals who work for these groups are sincere in their attachment to their larger pan-ethnic communities, no matter how imagined. The government itself, and major private institutions living under its system of record keeping, measure progress based on statistics reflecting everything from standardized test scores to the suicide rates of designated categories of individuals. Public policy and mass culture have both been shaped by decisions made decades ago by bureaucrats who in many cases gave little thought to what they were doing.

Although not to the same extent, the government has also helped usher in the idea of gender and sexual orientation as relevant political categories that institutions must take account of. At the time of the Civil Rights Act, there was a consensus in the United States that men and women had different roles to play in society, and the *Diagnostic and Statistical Manual-II* released four years later classified homosexuality as a mental disorder. Relatively few had heard of the concept of "gender identity." Yet over the next few decades, government, mostly through the courts and the federal bureaucracy, would set out to do away with stereotypes in the workplace, micromanage norms regarding dating, and make beliefs based on new academic theories about the subjectivity and malleability of gender mandatory for private institutions.

We see a common pattern in how the government has socially constructed race and how it has helped legitimize a certain conception of womanhood as the kind that deserves to be favored and cultivated by the state. The government decides which categories are relevant to public life, and which are not. It then goes about encouraging a system of data collection and record keeping to justify state intervention and private activism. Law influences culture, as individuals are financially incentivized to lean into accepted identities and play their assigned roles, and may come to genuinely believe that the box they are put in has deep historical, moral, and spiritual importance. All of this happens far from the democratic process; civil rights laws as passed by Congress, incomplete and vague, serve as the justification for bureaucrats and judges to remake society.

Sometimes, government decisions are made with relatively little conscious thought, as was the case with certain forms of racial classification, and the categories decided upon only then take on cultural significance. As will be shown in this chapter, the categories "Hispanic" and "AAPI" existed as bureaucratic concepts before becoming part of the mental model of the world that most Americans hold. In the case of sex, women of course were always seen as a distinct category, but government in the late 1960s began to come down in favor of an extremely specific vision of womanhood, one that prioritized the feelings and ambitions of a certain kind of adult over economic efficiency, freedom of association, or traditional understandings of male-female relations that emphasized the importance of children and family. While civil rights law promises "equality" between the sexes, it prioritizes the interests of some women, those who represent feminist ideals and seek economic self-sufficiency, over women who prefer not to be in the workforce or who would like to use their youth or beauty to their advantage.

Inventing American Races

In 1997, the Office of Management and Budget (OMB) revised Directive No. 15, which required a minimum of five categories for the purposes of government record keeping: "American Indian or Alaska Native, Asian, Black or African American, Native Hawaiian or Other Pacific Islander, and White."[5] There also continued to be two categories for "ethnicity": "Hispanic or Latino" and "Not Hispanic or Latino." This was in contrast to the original 1977 directive, which allowed the Asian American and Pacific Islander categories to be counted together.[6] The federal government uniformly adheres closely to OMB guidance, whether it is the FBI reporting crime statistics by race or the Office of the Director of National Intelligence touting its diversity in hiring.[7] Even more interesting is the fact that practically every major private institution in the United States divides the population into the same five or six categories when talking about race. Harvard currently reports its numbers for Hispanics, blacks, Asians, Native Americans, and Native Hawaiians.[8] Stanford is similar, but instead of "Native Hawaiians," the school lists "Native Hawaiian or other Pacific Islander," copying OMB regulations more faithfully.[9] The National Center for Education Statistics reports test scores similarly, as does Google's 2021 diversity report for its US workforce, although it collapses all Pacific Islanders into something called "Asian+."[10]

Two things are particularly noteworthy about how the United States classifies people according to race. First of all, the racial classifications—the macro-categories and the lines between them—look arbitrary. Groups such as Arabs, Jews, North Africans, and those from the Caucasus are rarely counted either within or outside government. Like the Italians and Irish, they are considered part of the homogeneous white standard against which diversity accomplishments are to be judged. The government cares about your ratio of whites to non-whites; it does not care whether your whites are Jews, Arabs, or Anglo-Saxons. At the same time, those who are non-white need to be aggregated into large enough groups for the purposes of record keeping and reporting; hence the categories "Hispanic" and "Asian." Second, institutions practically never provide religious breakdowns. There is no particular reason to believe that discrimination based on religious status is unworthy of consideration by a society that keeps such detailed records on ethnicity. If the federal government and major corporations were as obsessed with differences in crime rates, test scores, and socioeconomic status between Southern Baptists and Episcopalians as they are with disparities between blacks and whites, we would have a very different society.

This is fundamentally strange, because nearly all the arguments made for government race-consciousness apply to religion. One might say that blacks and Native Americans have historically faced unique circumstances in this country. But society shows a deep interest in the socioeconomic status of other groups, many of which had practically no presence in the US before the 1960s. Haven't Catholics, Mormons, and Jews faced more historical discrimination in the United States than Indonesians, Venezuelans, and Sri Lankans? The differences in income between religious groups are substantial; according to Pew Research, over a third of Hindu, Jewish, and Episcopalian families make $100,000 a year or more, compared to just 4 percent of Jehovah's Witness households.[11]

The story of how the United States got to the point of having, for practically all official purposes, four or five "races" and a binary choice for ethnicity reflects the importance of lobbying, interest group politics, and historical contingency more than it does either anthropology or a good faith effort to address historical discrimination. The modern history of racial classification can be traced back to the 1950s.[12] President Dwight Eisenhower followed Franklin Roosevelt and Harry Truman in signing an executive order outlawing discrimination based on race or national origin in government contracting. In 1956, the executive branch required contractors to count only "Negros" and "other minorities," with the option to engage in more fine-grained analysis. Under pressure from activists and members of Congress, "Spanish Americans" would soon be added. Not until the Kennedy administration did the government start to count Native Americans and "Orientals." Nonetheless, already in 1966 the EEOC required sixty thousand employers, those with one hundred employees or more, to list the gender and racial makeup of their workforce, with the latter based on categories we would recognize today.[13] John Skrentny sees the sending out of form EEO-1 as a watershed that marks the transition from the era of official color-blindness to modern race-conscious governance. He writes that rather than "protecting abstract Americans from the harm of discrimination, the form explicitly created *whites* and *blacks*, who were hired in each firm in varying proportions."[14]

Over the next decades, government would get into the race-counting business in the areas of contracting, education, voting, and employment. Not long after the Civil Rights Act was passed, the state had moved away from focusing on explicit discrimination in favor of looking for disparities between groups, rooting out "stereotypes," and other forms of social engineering. Yet which "groups" were to be counted for purposes of record keeping and analysis was yet to be decided. Blacks and Native Americans were widely acknowledged to have suffered unusually long and brutal forms of discrimination at the hands of the American government. But what about other groups that had come to the United States by choice and, in many cases, already overcome any obstacles holding them back, and even surpassed the white majority in socioeconomic status? As Skrentny notes, in a racially, linguistically, and religiously diverse society, government classification "made some inequalities more real and others invisible."[15] According to Herbert Hammerman, who served for fifteen years on the EEOC until 1981, the racial categories adopted by the government in the aftermath of the Civil Rights Act used to enforce anti-discrimination laws were "the product of sheer historical accident."[16] Yet they remain with us today.

It is important to note that in the mid-1960s, Americans thought about race as a political issue in terms of the status of African Americans living in the South, one that was being solved through the Civil Rights Act and other laws passed under the Johnson administration. Practically nobody saw "minorities" as a government category that should separate certain individuals from the white majority and make them eligible for special government benefits. Yet while whites, blacks, and Native Americans were natural categories with deep roots in American history, even if their borders weren't always clear, who exactly were Spanish Americans and Orientals, the categories invented by the Eisenhower and Kennedy administrations?

Despite what EEOC forms said, the 1970 Census had no category that corresponds to modern Hispanics or Latinos. There was no Asian or AAPI category, either, although there were options for Chinese, Japanese, Hawaiian, Korean, and Filipino, in addition to the standard categories of white, black, and Native American.[17] Only a sample form sent to 5 percent of households that year asked whether the respondent had his origins in Puerto Rico, Mexico, or another Spanish-speaking country. Our modern theories of racial categorization were never natural or inevitable. UC Berkeley sociologist G. Cristina Mora writes that, before the civil rights era, there had been a "consistent empirical finding" that "Mexican

Americans, Puerto Ricans, and Cuban Americans overwhelmingly considered themselves to be separate groups. They 'didn't really identify' with one another, and they 'didn't really know what Hispanic meant!'"[18]

The earliest substantive ethnic activity within the modern Latino category was on behalf of Mexican Americans. In the mid-1960s, representatives of this group were lobbying the EEOC for representation, and in response, President Johnson appointed the first Mexican American EEOC commissioner and established the Inter-Agency Committee on Mexican-American Affairs (IMAA) by executive order.[19] Congress began to consider the organization's fate in 1969, and legislators from the Northeast asked whether the IMAA could also consider the plight of Puerto Ricans. The bill resulting from this debate created the Cabinet Committee on Opportunities for Spanish-Speaking People (CCOSSP). The term "Spanish-speaking" was a compromise, as "Hispanic" was objected to by the head of the IMAA, and Puerto Rican activists sought a term that would include themselves.[20]

The focus on linguistic commonality provides insight into the intentions behind the creation of this new minority. When asked who exactly was "Spanish-speaking," Congressman Edward Roybal (D-CA) replied that the new legislation would not apply to those who had assimilated into the American mainstream.[21] In effect, he was arguing that one day, as soon as barriers to success had been removed, the CCOSSP could be disbanded. Martin Castillo, who had been appointed by Nixon to head the IMAA, agreed that lack of assimilation was the main criterion by which to judge which groups the government should help, therefore rejecting the idea that Cuban Americans shared the same disadvantages as Puerto Ricans and Mexicans on the grounds that they were doing well in the United States.[22] Descent from a Spanish-speaking country or territory was not seen as a source of permanent disadvantage in the US. The focus was on linguistic differences that created difficulties for full participation in American life.

Congress failed to extend the CCOSSP in 1974 after it was accused of having become a partisan tool of the Nixon reelection campaign.[23] In the end, although it had little formal power, the most lasting legacy of the committee may have been its collection of data. Whenever it was necessary, the CCOSSP could provide numbers on Spanish-speaking Americans and what barriers they faced; earlier questions about who qualified and whether government recognition of "Hispanics" as an official minority made sense faded away, given the realities of electoral politics and lobbying from within and outside the government. As it turned out, it was easier to create a race than it was to disestablish one. In 1977, the OMB released the aforementioned Statistical Policy Directive 15, which required all federal data collection to include the Hispanic category.[24] The National Council of La Raza, originally a Chicano organization— that is, focused on Mexican Americans—became a "Hispanic" advocacy group as it found it beneficial to conform to government classifications and inflate the number of those it claimed to represent.[25] By 1982, it was relying on federal grants for 96 percent of its money. The Reagan administration then cut off funding, at which point it began to rely more heavily on private foundations and corporate donors.[26]

While the 1970s saw the solidification of Hispanics as a unified category for purposes of government record keeping, activists still had a lot of work to do in the cultural realm. Lobbying ensured that there would be a question about Spanish speakers on all census forms in 1980.[27] Showing how controversial this was even a few years before that change, the *New York Times* in May 1978 ran a front-page story critical of the new Hispanic category, sympathetically quoting demographers who saw its creation as a response to political pressure rather than as a classification that captured anything worth measuring.[28]

In the end, the Census Bureau went with a Hispanic "ethnicity" question instead of a race question, chiefly because of worries that if it allowed respondents to say that they were part of a Hispanic "race," it could reduce the number of Americans identifying as black or African American.[29] Census officials even met with black organizations to reassure them that the new Hispanic question would not dilute the numbers of their own group. Thus the arrival of an Afro-Cuban would increase both the number of "blacks" and "Hispanics" in the United States. This is why today, when they fill out forms, Americans are usually asked to choose a "race" and an "ethnicity," with Hispanic or Latino being the only kind of "ethnicity" officially recognized.

Even as of 2012, 51 percent of people of "Hispanic" descent preferred to refer to their country of origin to describe their identity.[30] Just under one-quarter (24 percent) chose "Hispanic" or "Latino," and "American" (21 percent) was just behind that. In other words, close to three-quarters of the "Hispanic" category either preferred an assimilationist label that embraced their American identity, or saw themselves as people coming from a certain country, not part of a loosely defined collective created for reasons having to do with political activism and bureaucratic convenience. In the same poll, seven in ten said that American Hispanics did not share a culture. Yet in elite political discourse and institutions, alternative conceptions of identity are all but ruled out. For ethnic activists to have a purpose, they need to claim to represent a group that is distinct from the population, but not so distinct that it can be ignored as irrelevant to national politics.

To most people of Latin American descent, ethnic politics is an abstract issue with little relevance to their social, economic, or political lives. When prompted to name the most important leader of their community, the vast majority of Hispanics say they cannot think of one.[31] The disconnect between elites and the masses was demonstrated in the debate over the term "Latinx" that emerged after the 2020 election, in which an unexpectedly high number of Hispanics voted Republican. Polls showed that few Hispanics had even heard of the word, and an even tinier minority used it, with that minority being vastly outnumbered by those who found it offensive.[32] Nonetheless, the androgynous term continues to be used in the worlds of politics, academia, entertainment, and ethnic activism. The irony of this debate is that even the non-androgynous concept "Latino" itself was a government creation that to this day has limited traction among the wider public.

Creation of the Hispanic category, and its failure to completely prevent assimilation into the American mainstream, can be seen as a reflection of the limits of government social engineering. At the same time, the fact that this category has so much influence on the way powerful institutions operate despite its artificiality raises some disturbing questions. Congress has a Congressional Hispanic Caucus, the government makes institutions keep track of how many members of this "ethnicity" are employed in different kinds of jobs, and grants and status markers are awarded based on the assumption that the category is real. The fact that even a quarter of people of Latin American descent call themselves "Hispanic" is a testament to the power of government classification, given how completely fabricated the label is. It would be as if a substantial number of Americans of Italian and French descent came to call themselves "Romance Americans," based on the languages that their ancestors spoke. Back in the 1950s, such an outcome would probably have looked not much less likely than the emergence of Hispanics.

While there was at least some debate within government and in the broader public surrounding how the government could count the emerging Hispanic group and what it was owed, the Asian category was being formed in an even more haphazard way. The existence of this group as an official minority early in the civil rights era was complicated by the fact that its members were doing quite well. Already in the 1960s, Chinese and Japanese Americans had incomes well above the national average.[33] An "Oriental" category was added to government forms by the Kennedy administration as a result of lobbying from the congressional delegation of Hawaii, just a few years after the state was admitted to the union in 1959.[34] The term was soon changed to "Asian or Pacific Islander" so as not to exclude Native Hawaiians.[35]

While language brought together Spanish speakers into one government category, geographical proximity grouped East Asians with people from the Pacific. In 1960, the population of Hawaii was 16.2 percent Native Hawaiian, in addition to 32.2 percent Japanese, 10.9 percent Filipino, and 6 percent Chinese.[36] This was by far the most racially diverse state in the union, but the overall numbers were small in the context of the nation as a whole. The federal government therefore saw little harm in creating a broad "miscellaneous" category that covered most of the population of one of its states, even if the various groups living there had little in common.

Nonetheless, while Asian Americans could potentially complain that they were underrepresented in certain businesses, the fact that they were doing economically well overall meant that they received little attention from the federal government. In 1978, Congress passed the Small Business Act, which provided set-asides based on "social and economic disadvantage," with businesses owned by blacks, Hispanics, and Native Americans automatically qualifying.[37] Soon, however, the Small Business Administration added "Asian Pacific Americans" after lobbying pressure. Which groups counted in this category was settled within the federal bureaucracy. Between 1982 and 1989, the SBA added individuals with ancestry from India, Tonga, Sri Lanka, Indonesia, the Marshall Islands, Micronesia, Nepal, and Bhutan. In the case of Indonesians, the change came in 1988 when they were included based on the lobbying efforts of one businesswoman after she was originally rejected.

In the next year, the SBA would reject Iranians and Arabs for inclusion, and conclude that the category of "Asian" stopped at the Afghanistan-Pakistan border for the purposes of government classification in this area.[38] Although it doesn't appear to have been given much thought, further up north, Central Asians were and remain considered whites for the purposes of government classification, with the status of Uzbeks being the subject of a 2008 SBA hearing that was settled by the petitioner being declared disadvantaged on nonracial grounds. The Asian standard in practice remains as it was in the 1980s, with those who fall into the category generally being discriminated against by admissions departments in colleges, where they do relatively well, and yet often eligible for minority set-asides at the state and federal levels. As of 2020, the SBA reported more federal contracting dollars going to Asian-owned or Pacific Islander–owned small businesses than those owned by either blacks or Hispanics as individual categories.[39]

When Directive No. 15 was revised in 1997, the resulting document split Asians and Pacific Islanders. Sen. Daniel Akaka (D-HI) had been receiving calls and letters from Native Hawaiians concerned that they were losing out in terms of college admissions and scholarships on the basis of being lumped within the larger and more academically successful Asian category.[40] He asked OMB to put them into the Native American category, a proposal that ended up getting support from the rest of the Hawaiian congressional delegation. OMB was afraid that this would open up the issue of giving sovereignty to Native Hawaiians, a right that is under certain circumstances provided to Native Americans. An official from the OMB recommended giving the group its own category, which it ended up doing in the revision to Directive No. 15 in 1997. Hence Pacific Islanders, a group that represents no more than 0.4 percent of the American population, became one of the five major "races" in the country, separate from Natives of the forty-eight contiguous states and Alaska. Just as lobbying that originated in Hawaii brought the categories of Asian American and Pacific Islander together, it also split them apart.

The exclusion of "white ethnics" from the minority revolution is notable because of the extent to which the idea of including these groups had more grassroots support than did the inclusion of Native Americans, Asians, or Hispanics, who would all be counted as designated minorities.[41] Throughout the 1970s, there was large-scale media coverage of issues related to ethnic Americans, and books written on the obstacles faced by Catholics, Italians, and the Irish. In 1971, the Ford Foundation gave nearly $1 million in a series of grants to address the concerns of the white working class. A 1970 rally in New York City on behalf of Italian Americans reportedly brought to the streets as many as one hundred thousand people. Data was gathered on the underrepresentation of certain categories of white Americans in various kinds of employment and other barriers they faced, much of it summarized in a 1979 report by the USCCR titled "Civil Rights Issues of Euro-ethnic Americans in the United States."

Moreover, there was direct lobbying to the federal government on behalf of white ethnics for inclusion. The EEOC originally denied Poles official minority designation on the grounds that there was no room left on their form, and including them might lead to demands for similar treatment of "Italians, Yugoslavs, Greeks, etc."[42] More extensive efforts were made on behalf of American Jews. Reports from the Truman administration on civil rights gave them substantially more attention than European ethnics, and the Eisenhower administration listed Jews as one group that could be voluntarily reported on by employers in the "other minorities" category. But official efforts to use civil rights law to fight anti-Semitism were eventually dropped; the justifications included high Jewish socioeconomic status and opposition from black activists.

The Nixon administration squashed steps taken by the federal bureaucracy to start relying on religious classifications more generally, on the grounds that doing so would be unworkable and potentially run afoul of the constitutional principle of the separation of church and state.[43]

The inclusion of some groups and not others as official minorities, and how those minorities are divided, has mostly been a story of bureaucratic inertia. Throughout the 1970s, politicians and activists for groups that were excluded from official minority designation asked reasonable questions. Weren't many "Latinos" white? If underrepresentation in important positions was key to determining which groups needed government help, why did the government brush aside data provided by organizations representing Poles and Italians? Speaking before Congress in 1974, Jerome Powell, the head of the EEOC, said that designated minorities were those that the commission had found were discriminated against. Yet the categories it relied on were in many cases created before the EEOC even existed, and were apparently chosen in a haphazard way by bureaucrats looking for practical standards and working off of little to no data.[44]

Whenever a new group has applied for official minority recognition, government agencies have been able to reply that they do not have evidence that they face enough discrimination. Ethnic activists respond that of course there is no evidence, because the government is not collecting the relevant data.[45] These circular arguments have mostly ended, though there was a serious attempt made by Arab and Iranian activists to add a Middle Eastern category to the 2020 Census in an effort that was gaining momentum under Obama but was lost under the Trump administration. Belatedly, it appears that Republicans had learned their lesson about the ultimate effects of creating new government-endorsed minorities.

Eventually, the made-up and largely arbitrary categories decided upon in offices in Washington became "real" in the broader American culture. The racial classification regime has not only had an effect on the self-perceptions of minorities. The last decade has seen the rise of the "great replacement theory," which argues that Democrats and liberals are trying to obtain power by changing the demographic makeup of the United States. While this is often referred to as a conspiracy theory, if we assume that Democrats are self-interested actors, there is no reason to suspect that they do not see demographic change as a benefit for themselves, and it takes only a moment of googling to find countless examples of those on the left celebrating immigration for that very reason. One of my own survey experiments has shown that both conservatives and liberals become more supportive of immigration when told that new arrivals are likely to help their side electorally.[46] This does not mean that anyone designed the immigration system as part of a conscious plan to reduce the influence of whites, but one has to be willfully blind to deny that political considerations play a role in immigration attitudes.

The conspiracy-theory label has allowed liberals to deny the substance of the argument. Nonetheless, what neither side seems to have noticed is that the idea of the great replacement derives from government racial classifications and their downstream effect on culture. Although whites of various ethnic groups support different political parties, there is relatively little interest in how changing demographics within the category of "white" might influence the future of American politics. Arabs and Persians immigrating to America add to the "white" numbers, and in their own small way help make it appear that the relative decline of the majority population is being slowed. But newly arrived Hispanics, even if they look white and will assimilate into the American mainstream, present a "threat" when they are counted in official statistics.

The Rise of Hispanics, Latinos, Asians, and Pacific Islanders

Before the mid-1970s, the word "Hispanic" appeared in fewer than one in every five hundred thousand words in English-language books. By its peak in the early 1990s, the frequency of the word had increased by two orders of magnitude. "Latino" saw a smaller and more delayed rise from a lower base. At the same time, "Mexican American" and "Puerto Rican" reached their peaks in the early 1970s and have appeared at lower rates since. Before this point, Americans were more likely to discuss individuals belonging to either of these groups as notable for their country or territory of origin rather than any wider "ethnicity." Notably, "Hispanic" and "Latino" came to eclipse "Puerto Rican" and "Mexican American" in the years after the CCOSSP replaced the IMAA and when activism centered around racial politics in Washington began to take off. Adding plural forms does not change the results much, but delays the triumph of the Hispanic and Latino categories by a few years, indicating that Figure 4.1 underestimates the recency of the change. The figure shows a logarithmic display, which means that the changes are far more radical than implied below.

It is remarkable that there is less relative discussion of Puerto Ricans and Mexican Americans today than there was in the 1970s, considering demographic trends. The number of Puerto Ricans living on the US mainland increased by two and a half times between 1980 and 2012, and the number of Mexican Americans has risen at an even faster rate.[47] Yet both groups arguably occupy less of a place in the American consciousness as specific national-origins categories than they did in the 1970s, despite our growing overall interest in identity and manufactured panethnicities.

The results for "Asian American" and "AAPI" are somehow more

Figure 4.1

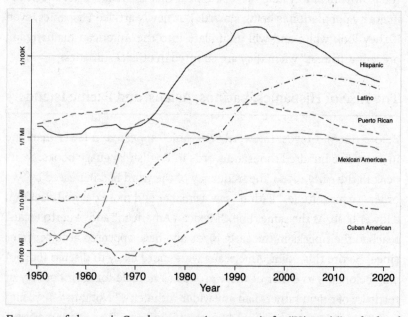

Frequency of phrases in Google n-grams (1950–2019), for "Hispanic" and related terms.

dramatic. For all practical purposes, these concepts did not exist in the English language at the time of the Civil Rights Act. Use of "Asian American" then skyrocketed in the late 1960s, while it took two decades for "AAPI" to catch on. There is no use of "Asian American Pacific Islander" before 1972. The phrase does not even reach one in ten billion n-grams until the 1990s. Before the 1960s, Americans were much more likely to write about "Japanese Americans" or "Chinese Americans" than "Asian Americans." In recent decades, there are more mentions of "Asian Americans" and "AAPI" than of Chinese, Indian, Japanese, and Korean Americans combined.

Thus we can see that while whites, blacks, and American Indians have always been with us, the other major races of contemporary America were largely government inventions. The differences between people from Spanish-speaking countries and territories have been deemphasized as

Figure 4.2

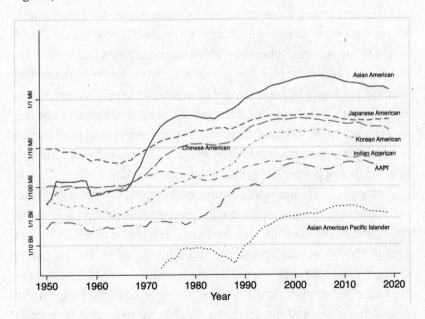

Frequency of phrases in Google n-grams (1950–2019), for "Asian American Pacific Islander" and related terms. There were zero uses of "Asian American Pacific Islander" before 1972.

we have come to see them as one group for the purposes of understanding cultural, socioeconomic, and political trends. The categories that correspond to today's "Asian American" and "AAPI" existed in government forms for decades before they came into common use in the English language. If bureaucratic classification influences how Americans conceive of racial identity, the construction of which is often thought to be an organic process, it is natural to think more carefully about the impact of civil rights law on how people think about concepts like sex, humor, and the nature of the relationship between the individual and the state.

The Two-Front War on Tradition and Sexuality

The idea that the Civil Rights Act would ban employment discrimination based on sex started out as an attempt by a southern segregationist to kill the bill. The proposed amendment to Title VII nonetheless passed, with many voting for it in good faith, although the entire process initially led to confusion among government officials responsible for enforcement. Those who were earnest supporters of the amendment hoped that it would tackle sex segregation—by which was meant men and women being placed in different jobs.[48] In less than a decade, however, the federal bureaucracy would be going beyond even what congressional supporters of civil rights protections for women had intended. Ultimately, the ban on sex discrimination would lead to the government declaring war on gender stereotypes, micromanaging sexual relations, and even inserting new theories of gender and sexuality into public policy.

Although most Americans would be horrified by an explicit acknowledgment that government regulation extends to what are usually thought to be personal matters, "work life" is still part of life, and in the eyes of the law sexual harassment and other forms of discriminatory behavior can occur even when individuals are off the clock. The story of the ban on sex discrimination in employment demonstrates the breadth of civil rights law and the degree to which it has expanded far outside the democratic process.

In the mid-1960s, ideas about the naturalness and inevitability of differential treatment based on sex were so entrenched that even professionals in the EEOC thought that there was no justification for applying the paradigm for fighting discrimination against blacks to women's issues. One staff attorney would recall that because "sex discrimination came in as essentially a ploy by the opponents to try to derail the legislation, it is quite understandable that it was not . . . even on the radar."[49] Public discourse centered around the "bunny problem"; would *Playboy* be forced to hire male models to be compliant with federal law? Journalists used this example as a *reductio ad absurdum* of the idea that government would actually ban discrimination based on sex.

By the end of the decade, however, due to pressure from political activists, some of them working from within government itself, this had changed. The National Organization for Women, which would become the most influential feminist organization in the country, was formed at a luncheon at a 1966 conference for state commissions on the status of women.[50] Over the next few years, the EEOC would stop allowing gender-segregated advertising for jobs and oppose protective legislation at the state level that relied on assumed sex differences to regulate the employment of women differently from that of men.

The first few steps toward combating discrimination were based on explicit differential treatment and clear rules that were easy to follow. As long as an employer did not advertise jobs as only available to one sex, for example, they could go on about their business. Soon, however, the government would move into the area of setting standards for interpersonal behavior and enforcing equal outcomes. Through its war on "stereotypes," it would even move into regulating culture and thought. In *Price Waterhouse v. Hopkins* (1989), a woman accused of aggressive, foul-mouthed behavior sued her accounting firm, claiming that she was denied a partnership because she did not fit its ideas of what a partner should look like. A plurality opinion of the Court held that, once discrimination was proved, to avoid liability it was the defendant's job to show that it would have made the same decision in the absence of discrimination. Importantly, gender stereotypes could be a form of discrimination.

Since the 1980s, courts have enforced a vision of "nondiscrimination" that officially requires that males and females be treated as all but indistinguishable from one another. The war on difference found in liberal jurisprudence is a two-front war, fought against both environments that promote traditionalist ideals that restrict sexual expression and those that would encourage it. To take one illustrative case of the former, the Fourth Circuit ruled in 2022 that a charter school that required skirts for female students was violating the Equal Protection Clause and left open the possibility that the rule also ran afoul of Title IX.[51] The school argued that it taught traditional morality and wanted to encourage chivalrous behavior among its young men. A concurrence brushed aside claims that parents had a right to guide the development of their own children by pointing to the "psychological damage" that young girls faced by being required to dress differently from boys.[52]

While the majority could of course cite "expert testimony" in favor of this view, the idea that differential treatment based on sex is damaging to the development of young girls would imply that institutions controlled by modern liberals are the only ones capable of creating well-adjusted women. The increasing rates of female unhappiness over the last few decades as law and culture have become more egalitarian, along with the close connection between liberal ideology and mental illness among girls, imply that even if it's not clear that liberal ideology makes women unhappy, modern leftists are unlikely to have a monopoly on wisdom in this area of life.[53]

Perhaps nowhere have social engineers been more explicit about their goals to reshape humanity than in the area of Title IX. Courts have held that not only must schools have rough proportionality between males and females in athletic participation, but that female sports must be competitive enough to be included in calculations. Thus, at least in the Second Circuit, a school cannot balance out a male football player with a female cheerleader; maybe the girl doesn't have to play football herself, but hockey or volleyball is generally acceptable, though the state of Florida was at one point sued over its decision to count flag football as a varsity sport.[54]

Moreover, simply offering the right number and mix of female sports is not enough. In 2012, the Seventh Circuit ruled that an Indiana high school could be sued under Title IX for scheduling boys' basketball on Fridays and Saturdays and relegating girls' games to other nights, when fewer members of the community are likely to turn out.[55] While the boys benefited from games with a "packed gymnasium, cheerleaders rallying the fans, the crowd on their feet supporting their team, and the pep band playing the school song," when girls played the "bleachers are nearly deserted; there is a lack of student and community support." Following other court decisions, the Seventh Circuit held that the community being more interested in boys' basketball was no defense; such "stereotypes" could not be the basis of government decision-making, and sports scheduling decisions therefore had to be taken out of the hands of the local community.

The decision reflected the norm of Title IX being used as a method of social engineering, complete with a stand taken in favor of the malleability of gender differences. It cited a previous court case that asserted, practically as a matter of law, that girls' sports can be "just as exciting, competitive, and lucrative as men's sports." The court, of course, never explained why girls' basketball could be as exciting as the boys' version of the sport, given that at any level the best female athletes are inferior to their worst male counterparts. It would be as if the government decided that a basketball league featuring only athletes less than five feet tall could be just as exciting as the NBA, and declared that if any government institution acts based on a different assumption it is potentially in violation of civil rights law. In one Ninth Circuit decision, an unusually explicit court asserted "that women's attitudes toward sports are socially constructed and have been limited by discrimination and gender stereotypes," and that the purpose of Title IX was to change that state of affairs.[56] Title IX is the only reason such insane beliefs can become mandatory throughout the education system, while anyone who sought gender parity in, say, fantasy football interest would be a laughingstock.

Religious conservatives and local governments are not the only ones no longer able to run their affairs as they see fit. Southwest Airlines marketed itself in the 1970s as an airline that appealed to men, employing only young, attractive women as ticket agents and flight attendants in the hopes of creating a fun and informal atmosphere.[57] A group of men sued, arguing that they were being discriminated against under the Civil Rights Act. In its defense, the airline acknowledged that it discriminated against men, but argued that it was legally allowed to do so due to the exception in Title VII that allows for sex discrimination in the case of a "bona fide occupational qualification reasonably necessary to the normal operation of that particular business or enterprise."

In 1981, the Northern District of Texas rejected that argument on the grounds that the primary business of an airline is to transport customers. Since men are capable, the court said, of performing the most necessary tasks of being a flight attendant or ticket agent, such discrimination was illegal in this case. Although Southwest Airlines argued that restricting these positions to females was necessary for its business success, the court was unpersuaded.

In the post–civil rights era, government now decides questions like "Is an airline based on sexy stewardesses a good idea?" A distinguishing marker of a free society, however, is the ability of individuals and institutions to arrange their own affairs as they see fit.

To take another illustrative case, in 2019 five female journalists between the ages of forty and sixty-one sued the TV station they worked for on the grounds of age and sex discrimination, saying that they had been pushed aside for younger women and men.[58] The premise of the lawsuit, as in the case of the Southwest flight attendants, was that it is government, not employers and consumers, that decides the nature or "true essence" of a job. Civil rights law gives artistic freedom to those who cast TV shows and movies, yet it is considered legally questionable whether sex appeal can be used to sell news. One of the allegations of the female journalists was that management was grooming young women to take their jobs.

While this is clearly "age discrimination"—another monstrosity created by civil rights law—the argument raises the question of how a practice that prefers certain women over others can be a form of sex discrimination. A norm that one cannot prefer certain women for jobs because of their youth or beauty does nothing to create equality between the sexes but is consistent with an understanding of civil rights law as a way for academic theories seeking social transformation to be forced onto private institutions.

The worst fears of those who talked about the bunny problem were

never realized. Strip club owners, pornographers, and movie produc-
ers can still discriminate based on sex. Everything else, however, had
to change, even though the notion of the government deciding whether
the news must be read by a young, attractive woman or an older and
unattractive one reflects a fundamental break with pre–civil rights conceptions of the appropriate limits of state power.

Yale Law professor Vicki Schultz argues that the workplace has been
"sanitized" of all sexual content in the name of fighting discrimination,
regardless of the desires and wishes of men and women.[59] Indeed, when
one interrogates the assumptions that are at the center of harassment
law, they are revealed to be those of radical feminists with views that
problematize conduct and ways of living most people find unobjection-
able or even healthy. Election results can ideally represent the preferences of all women equally, regardless of whether they are married or
single, housewives or career-focused. When policy is made by activists
and bureaucrats, however, it naturally becomes tilted toward the interests and aesthetic preferences of a small minority. This is true with regard to men, but even more so in the case of the sex whose members
are less likely to seek full-time employment. Current civil rights law
discounts the views of women with a less hostile attitude toward traditional heterosexual relations, whether they subscribe to a conservative
sexual morality or not.

As with much in civil rights law, universities are on the cutting edge
of the zeal for social engineering. Their ideological leanings and financial reliance on the taxpayer mean that they are usually the institutions
most welcoming to federal regulation in this area. The Dear Colleague
letters of the Obama years reflected a shift away from an understanding of discrimination as an act committed against individuals to one in
which patriarchal oppression is part of American life; hence settlement
agreements with universities that included "systemic" solutions such
as more training for faculty and students and the creation of new bureaucracies.[60] While the American university provides the most extreme
example of what can go wrong when social engineers are given a free
hand, we see similar problems in business and industry, and the triumph
of the radical feminist view that many forms of heterosexual relations

are inherently suspicious, particularly when there is a power differential between a man and a woman. The ideal of womanhood under civil rights law is one in which love, passion, and sex are removed from professional life, but only in the name of equality, not traditional ideas rooted in modesty and restraint.

To say that the state is simply "fighting discrimination" ignores the fact that many women have socially conservative views and, if given a choice between their husbands being able to earn as high a wage as possible or themselves having an equal right to work, would select the former. As of 2017, 57 percent of women were in the labor force. The rest do not directly benefit from anti-discrimination laws. In 2019, 75 percent of men preferred to work outside the home, compared to 56 percent of women.[61] The number of women in the labor force and those who say they want to work is practically identical.

As of the late 2010s, slightly more than one in ten heterosexual couples met at work or through coworkers.[62] According to surveys that asked couples about their current or most recent partner, this was down from about 20 percent at its peak, with the number of work couples having started to decline around the time that the Civil Rights Act of 1991 began to allow punitive damages for sexual harassment claims. While some of this change is surely due to technological developments such as internet dating apps, it is difficult to see how making unwanted sexual advances at work potentially illegal would not have reduced the possibility of new relationships forming. The fact that anyone still dates at work is a testament to human nature; individuals, particularly men, will occasionally take personal and financial risks in order to form relationships with someone they find attractive.

With regard to race, it is clear that government classification came before social change, with Hispanic and Asian identities largely being creations of a bureaucracy. In contrast, of the many developments in gender relations over the last half century, only some of them can be attributed to public policy. Outside of the United States, since the mid-twentieth century we have seen declining birth rates and delayed rates of marriage across rich countries.

Despite a greater focus on achieving equality in the workplace, we see—apart from in Scandinavia, which has unusually high numbers—corresponding trends in female labor force participation rates across developed countries. The numbers increased up till the 1980s or 1990s before plateauing and settling at between 50 percent and 60 percent in recent years, just as in the US.[63]

As discussed in the next chapter, while anti-discrimination laws might have made the workplace a less fun and interesting place, it is unclear to what extent they have remade the culture more generally. Nonetheless, Americans spend a lot of time at school and work, and taking away their ability to build unique subcultures is a major cost to happiness and well-being, even if human nature is resilient enough for things to mostly go back to normal when individuals clock out. It is worth remembering that even a small decline in the birth rate should be taken seriously as a major problem, as stopping families being formed is a much greater sin than allowing certain forms of workplace inequality to continue to exist.

While sexual harassment law is now decades old, a more recent development has been the rise of LGBT rights, which are, at the federal level, mostly creations of the courts. "Gender identity" did not exist as a concept outside of the academy and a few other fringe sectors of American society during the Clinton administration, much less when the Civil Rights Act was passed. Yet in 2020, the Supreme Court ruled that private businesses had to embrace gender theory due to a law signed in 1964. At the time of the decision, more than half of American states had no employment protections based on gender identity, and attempts to create them at the federal level had failed for decades.[64] To be uncomfortable with a man in a dress is now illegal in the American workplace.

Bostock to a large extent codified nationally what had been the legal standard in more liberal states. As the workplace has been cleansed of heterosexual relationships and behaviors that might lead to them, firms have fallen over themselves in their support for nontraditional preferences and lifestyles. In recent years, major corporations have aggressively promoted the LGBT agenda, even threatening capital strikes against states that considered passing religious freedom bills or other legislation understood to be contrary to the LGBT cause. While the development of sexual harassment law has meant that gays are in many ways as restricted as everyone else in how they can behave at work, it is only those on the official list of "sexual minorities" that see their identities legitimized and celebrated by powerful American institutions.

The number of under-thirties who identify as LGBT has, according to surveys, risen from around one in twenty in 2008 to one in five in 2020.[65] Although more reliable government figures from the UK and Canada indicate that the numbers in American surveys might be inflated by a factor of two or three, this would still represent a large increase over the recent past. Moreover, much of the increase in LGBT identity appears to be among those who engage in only heterosexual behavior, indicating that we are arguably witnessing more of a social contagion of identity than a situation where greater tolerance has allowed more individuals to live as their authentic selves. Again, as with changes in gender relations, it is difficult to prove a causal effect of government policy, though it would be surprising if it had none. Nonetheless, with regard to gender and sexual identity issues, we see the same story of social engineering evident in the way we think about and classify individuals according to race.

Official Minorities as a Source of Expanding Government Power

The success of *I Love Lucy* is only one example of what the writer Steve Sailer calls "diversity before diversity" in American society.[66] That is, before it was the norm to celebrate the accomplishments of minorities as minorities and undertake efforts to demographically remake American institutions, people of non-European descent were able to succeed without that fact being considered remarkable. Among his examples are a half-Mexican head of counterintelligence at the CIA who began serving in the 1950s; Charles Curtis, who was three-eighths American Indian and vice president under Herbert Hoover; and a Native Hawaiian who was a famous surfer and won Olympic gold medals in swimming in 1912 and 1920. That the racial backgrounds of some individuals seem more notable in the 2020s than they did a century or even a few decades earlier demonstrates both the influence and the absurdity of government

racial classification. While no one can deny the disadvantages historically suffered by blacks in the South, society did not have to go down the
path of making broad racial categories central to political and social life.

Throughout the civil rights era, we see a feedback loop in which culture affects law and law affects culture. Today, the existence of "Hispanics" and "Asian Pacific Islanders" as natural categories is taken for
granted by many Americans, and entire identities are built around them,
at least among the more educated and politically active portion of the
population. We talk about the impact of the "Hispanic" vote and "AAPI"
representation. Cambodian Americans have a more difficult time getting
into some schools and universities in part because Korean Americans
are academically successful. An attack on a Thai man in San Francisco
is seen as part of a narrative of "AAPI hate" that is rooted in the novel
coronavirus having originated in China.[67] The Biden administration
points to the appointment of an American of Cuban and Jewish descent
to satisfy Mexican American activists clamoring for more Hispanics in
government.[68] Meanwhile, there is little to no pressure to appoint Muslims or Arabs to high positions, and any prominent figure who counts
the number of Jews in government is more likely to be banned from
social media than see his comments perceived as a good faith attempt
to show concern over diversity.

Like broad racial identities, the idea of a sexless workplace—but
one supportive of LGBT and whatever letters might be added in the
future—is now taken for granted in American culture. There is no reason to suspect that this is what the majority of the population wants,
and even if it did, a free country normally allows those with minority
preferences to live as they see fit. The trend in recent decades has been
to get government completely out of the bedroom, as seen in court cases
knocking down restrictions on pornography and homosexual behavior.
Yet sexual harassment law—made by courts and administrators and
justified by appeals to egalitarianism rather than social conservatism—
stands out as a glaring exception. Here, there is no form of intersex
interaction that is too small to escape the potential concern of government. Businesses find themselves having to adopt policies that are less
tolerant of flirtation and other forms of organic, healthy interactions

between men and women, meaning that government has in effect le-galized all sexual behavior that goes on behind closed doors, while also carving out an exception for when two individuals work together—in which case it has problematized every step in the process to get to that point.

When it comes to sexual orientation and gender identity, it appears that activism and culture have moved at least as fast as politics. Support for gay marriage became a fashionable cause among entertainers a few years before it became the norm even for national Democratic politi-cians. Yet there was always a "heads I win, tails you lose" component to the debate. By the mid-2010s, the country was headed toward an equi-librium in which liberal states were expanding anti-discrimination laws to cover LGBT individuals and adopting new ideas about gender iden-tity coming out of social media and the academy. Conservative states, meanwhile, were adopting cultural practices and government policies that reflected their own preferences, and left private parties to decide such matters for themselves.

In his dissent in *Obergefell v. Hodges*, the 2015 case that rendered bans across the country on gay marriage unconstitutional, Justice Sca-lia noted the dictatorial nature of the ruling, which had—with little in terms of sound legal justification—settled a political debate once and for all in favor of one side. The Supreme Court did not recognize same-sex marriage or create anti-discrimination protections for homosexuals and transsexuals as soon as these causes became accepted in liberal circles. Rather, it let the debate occur, and then told those who had achieved victories in the public square that their activism had been in favor of a cause that violated the Constitution the whole time, and therefore a waste of time and money.

One may agree or disagree with decisions to expand the scope and coverage of anti-discrimination laws. But we are a long way from the original intent behind the Civil Rights Act of 1964 or any other piece of major legislation. Sexual harassment law, the war on stereotypes, and new definitions of gender have been forced upon the American people, as we see courts and the federal bureaucracy serve as the pipeline for ideas coming out of universities to make their way into law. None of this was historically or legally inevitable. Nor can it be justified as an organic process responding to larger societal trends. It is the exercise of power by a class that denies it is doing any such thing.

The law creates the concept of "minorities" and draws lines within that category. It assigns each individual either oppressor or victim status, perceiving the latter as belonging to "communities" that stand apart from the larger society. The OFCCP, for example, recommends that contractors encourage the creation of identity groups within their workforce and recruit from race-based organizations.[69] Just as the government constructs and classifies a "minority" for the purposes of data analysis and social engineering, it shapes the kind of woman it wants to be consistent with the preferences of a class that is disproportionately career-focused and single or lesbian.

One cannot fall back on the argument that judges and bureaucrats are channeling "evolving ideas" or "evolving norms," unless we're referring to those of the class that they belong to. Feminists and advocates of LGBT rights had to use the courts and federal bureaucracy because they could not get what they wanted, at least at the federal level and in most states, through the democratic process. With every innovation coming out of academia or the activist community, the left could rely on the legitimacy that originally accompanied the passing of the Civil Rights Act of 1964 and the mechanisms it created to push for legal standards and regulations that would have been considered absurd by those who wrote and voted for the original bill.

Theorists who believe in the complete subjectivity and malleability of gender have never needed to convince a large portion of the population that they are correct. Rather, the prohibition on sex discrimination found in civil rights law—originally introduced as a joke and at most thought to end segregation in the workplace—has acted as a justification for a two-front war against both the expression of human sexuality and the most historically tested methods through which to curb some of its more destructive aspects.

CHAPTER 5

Social Engineering as a Cause of Stagnation, Ennui, and Social Strife

At the time of the collapse of the Soviet Union, never before had an ideological debate been settled with such finality. For half a century, intellectuals debated whether central planning or markets were the better way to organize an economy. Although socialists had lost the debate intellectually by at least the 1970s, few analysts foresaw that the Soviet Union would decide to abolish itself because its leaders no longer believed in the ideology of the empire. Even those who benefited by ruling over a planned economy were now admitting that it could not work. It was almost as if, in the midst of the European wars of religion, the pope announced that he'd had a revelation in which God told him that Martin Luther's critique of the Catholic Church was on point. Today the debate is between those who advocate for a form of free market capitalism with relatively little redistribution, as in the United States, or one with more redistribution, as in Scandinavian countries. China and India, the two largest states in the world, have benefited immensely from the move toward capitalism, despite large differences in their governing systems.

Yet while central planning in the economic realm has been completely discredited, in social matters it has become an accepted part of life in the United States. Most Americans see themselves as part of the "free world." Unlike in authoritarian countries, in the United States, Europe, Japan, and a handful of other places society is run, and distributional

outcomes are determined, according to consistent rules and decentralized processes like markets and elections. This includes the idea of
cultural pluralism; the American system in particular gives people the
power to live their lives and organize themselves however they see fit.
This applies both to politics, in the form of federalism, and to the most
intimate matters of faith through the separation of church and state.

Previous chapters of this book have argued that this view of American
society, while still true in some ways, is also to a large extent outdated.
This chapter makes the case that civil rights law, out of all the problems
one can focus on, should be an area of concern for those interested in
human progress. In broad terms, modern civil rights law has at least
four major effects on American society: the war on merit, restrictions
on the cultural pluralism that is necessary for human happiness, ending
creative destruction in personnel management, and widespread social
strife as reflected in our culture wars.

How could one area of law have such disastrous downstream effects
in so many different areas of life? By way of analogy, this question can be
answered by noting that one might be skeptical of a claim that there is a
medicine that cures a large number of ailments, while being more ready
to believe that there is a poison with a large number of negative health
effects. Like the human body, society is an extremely complex system,
which means that there are many more potentially harmful interventions than there are beneficial ones. Civil rights law has effectively
ended freedom of association as the default assumption in American
private life, and it reaches down to regulate nearly all forms of interpersonal relations. There is no reason to expect the downstream effects of
such a revolutionary change to be constrained to one area of human existence. One cannot make a comprehensive list of all the things that can
go wrong in a centrally planned economy, because the theory the system
being analyzed relies upon fundamentally contradicts sound economic
principles. Likewise, the idea that the federal government can regulate
personal relationships is so contrary to human nature, and reflects such
a misunderstanding of the organic ways in which cultures and norms develop, that it should be unsurprising to learn that the post-1964 regime
has had dire and wide-reaching consequences.

Similarly, the belief that in a world free of discrimination every group would have equal outcomes in every field is—and this is not an exaggeration—contrary to everything one would learn from the most cursory study of human history.[1] As Steven Farron points out, minority groups have often done socioeconomically well in the face of extreme societal discrimination.[2] Some examples include the Chinese in Southeast Asia and the Jews in Eastern Europe. The reason for this is that under most circumstances, people are too selfish for discrimination to play a major role in relative socioeconomic outcomes.

Bigots, like other people, care more about their own personal comfort and financial interests than they do about hurting others. This is true even under the most extreme circumstances.[3] A Nazi Party report from 1937 complained that "large parts of the population, and even of the Party community, do not bother . . . even about the most basic demand, namely not to buy from the Jew."[4] The political leadership in the Third Reich was not immune to this desire for needed goods and services at reasonable prices, as Hitler himself decorated the Berghof with drapery from a Jewish textile-manufacturing firm. The civil rights regime—which holds that government must interfere in free markets to prevent private-sector discrimination and thus create equal opportunity—rests on fundamental misunderstandings of both economics and human nature. There is no way for a government to operate under such an assumption without going to war against important principles such as merit, freedom, and cultural pluralism.

The War on Merit

While large socioeconomic disparities that are not based in underlying differences in productivity cannot exist in a market system, government is of course a different story, and here widespread discrimination can plausibly explain differences in outcomes between groups. Once the need for government is accepted, the question becomes what kind of criteria to use to select state employees. For most of recorded history, nepotism and patronage were the standard methods.[5] Powerful men would distribute state offices to their family members or officials who would then owe them favors. In the American context, patronage took the form of the "spoils system" that emerged in the nineteenth century and became the target of progressive reformers. Government employees were appointed and removed based on loyalty to elected officials, were frequently given paid leave to campaign for them, and might even send a portion of their salaries to politicians.[6] Reflecting the attitudes of many reformers of the time, an 1868 congressional report quoted a Jackson biographer who wrote, "The Government, formerly served by the *élite* of the nation, is now served to a very considerable extent by its refuse . . . a man's holding office under the government is presumptive evidence that he is one of three characters, namely, an adventurer, an incompetent person, or a scoundrel."[7]

In 1881, President James Garfield was assassinated by Charles J. Guiteau, who believed that his support for the Republican Party during the campaign had entitled him to a diplomatic post in Paris. As a result, Congress finally decided that change was needed, and in January 1883, it passed the Pendleton Civil Service Reform Act. The bill authorized the president to appoint a three-member Civil Service Commission (CSC).[8] For the jobs to which it applied, the law, among other provisions, mandated "competitive examinations for testing the fitness of applicants for the public service," banned those "habitually using intoxicating beverages to excess," and disallowed members of Congress from recommending applicants.

The president was given discretion to decide which federal employees were covered under the Pendleton Act. The portion of the federal government covered went from 11 percent shortly after the bill was signed to 46 percent by 1900.[9] Yet the impact of the new merit system was even stronger than those numbers would indicate, since it tended to disproportionately cover the most important government officials.[10] This greatly increased American state capacity. In 1895, Theodore Roosevelt, then serving on the Civil Service Commission, wrote that "every Cabinet officer whom I have seen in Washington has, before the end of his term, come to the conclusion that if there was any bureau in which he needed special efficiency, he had to put it under the civil service law."[11]

Modern science has generally confirmed the belief of nineteenth-century reformers that standardized tests can predict employee performance. The superiority of standardized tests as a method of selection cannot be completely credited to the scientific accomplishments of psychometricians in designing such useful tools; it is less the case that written exams are a perfect measure of performance than that practically everything else is so much worse. Personality tests, for example, rely on self-assessment, and there is no guarantee that a candidate will have a high degree of self-awareness or even answer honestly. Standardized exams that try to measure general intellectual ability, in contrast, do not have this problem, since the whole point of the exercise is to determine if the candidate can figure out what the right answers are. Interviews can be useful in certain circumstances, but the interpersonal nature of the interaction and the human tendency to take into account superficial factors tend to limit their predictive ability.

In the empirical literature, there is no question that intelligence tests are, in general terms, the best predictors of job performance, regardless of the complexity of the job in question.[12] The assumption that one can maintain standards of merit while having selection mechanisms that all racial groups perform equally on simply has no support in the data, despite massive efforts undertaken on the part of psychologists to develop methods that would do precisely that. The difficulty created by civil rights law is so well known that it is referred to as the "validity-diversity trade-off": the better a metric is for predicting job performance, the larger its disparate impact.[13] Nineteenth-century progressives did not have access to modern social science, but they were on the right track when they argued that objective standards provided a better basis for hiring than subjective processes or arbitrary characteristics.

The idea that standardized tests should be used for government hiring—having had the prestige of being a successful Progressive Era reform and been confirmed by psychological research—was therefore uncontroversial by the mid-twentieth century. What had been an issue that was central to American politics just a few generations before was conclusively settled in favor of merit. Yet this consensus would not survive the civil rights era, and the shift from a focus on equal opportunity to one on equality of results. Within one month of the founding of the EEOC in 1965, a White House conference on employment discrimination that included staff members of the new organization foresaw policies based on class action lawsuits, racial balancing, and quotas.[14]

The soft quota approach became all but required in much of the private sector under Title VII and EO 11246, but it was even more successful in government. Private businesses, always worried that incompetence or bad morale can harm the bottom line, have an incentive to hire talented attorneys to fight the more extreme interpretations of civil rights law, while government agencies have a tendency to roll over. Hence while the EEOC failed when it filed early sexual harassment suits against private companies, it had better success when going after the Environmental Protection Agency and the Community Relations Service, in cases where it could establish general precedents.[15]

Despite the move toward race-consciousness in the decade after the passage of the Civil Rights Act, old ideas about merit still had a foothold in the federal government via the Civil Service Commission, with its statutory basis in the Pendleton Act of the previous century. The EEOC and the CSC spent the late 1960s and much of the 1970s in open conflict over the question of merit versus representation. In 1970, the EEOC put out guidelines that explicitly stated that getting employers to switch to tests that rejected whites and non-whites at more equal rates was a goal of public policy.[16] This was opposed by the CSC, and even the precursor to the OFCCP tended to think that the EEOC was going too far in its hostility to merit-based standards.

The USCCR, which advises the rest of the government on civil rights issues, sympathized with the EEOC position. In a 1970 report, it noted that the examination process was the main method for selecting federal employees. Out of 2.5 million applicants a year, 300,000 to 450,000 would be hired after being screened through tests.[17] The USCCR criticized the exams for having an "impersonal, formal, authoritarian" aspect. Reflecting the view of the civil rights establishment of the time, it celebrated the fact that some tests used for federal employment had dropped arithmetic and algebra in the name of achieving equality.

In 1972, Congress created the Equal Employment Opportunity

Coordinating Council, which included among its members the Department of Justice, the CSC, and the EEOC, in the hopes of creating uniform standards for determining employment discrimination under both Title VII and EO 11246.[18] The EEOC and CSC became the main antagonists, and their disagreement centered around the disparate impact standard, as the two sides grappled over highly technical issues like whether it should apply to every step in the hiring process, as the EEOC wanted, or whether to take a "bottom-line" approach that only looked at final results and therefore could preserve a larger role for written tests, as the CSC preferred. The EEOC raised eyebrows when it filed an amicus brief supporting an unsuccessful black applicant to the Department of Housing and Urban Development who sued the CSC over the use of the Federal Service Entrance Examination.[19]

A DOJ official would write in a memo that the effect of the EEOC position would be "to place almost all test users in a position of noncompliance; to give great discretion to enforcement personnel to determine who should be prosecuted; and to set aside objective selection procedures in favor of numerical hiring."[20] The Government Accounting Office released a report noting that EEOC regulations were so confusing that employers were dropping tests altogether and adopting hiring quotas to protect themselves. Showing the attitudes of the civil rights community, the staff director of the USCCR in 1973 told an interviewer, "I don't believe there is such a thing as a merit system," while leaving open the possibility that one could theoretically exist at some point in the future.[21]

In the end, the question of merit versus representation that had been waged within the federal bureaucracy was settled by an election. In 1976, Jimmy Carter won the presidency, and his administration came down on the side of the EEOC and the civil rights lobby.[22] With overwhelming Democratic majorities, Congress passed and President Carter signed the Reorganization Act of 1978, a bill that put an end to the Equal Employment Opportunity Coordinating Council and made the EEOC the preeminent civil rights enforcement agency in the federal government. The Civil Service Commission was abolished as a standalone entity and split up into the Merit Systems Protection Board and the Office of Personnel Management (OPM).

At the risk of oversimplification, we may divide American governance into four eras. From the Founding to the presidency of Andrew Jackson, there was the era of elite rule. Then came the spoils system, which was ended, albeit imperfectly, with the Pendleton Civil Service Reform Act of 1883 and the formation of the Civil Service Commission. The era of meritocratic hiring lasted just under a century. Since 1978, when the Civil Service Commission was abolished, if not earlier, we have been living in the racial spoils era, where government maintains impersonal standards but seeks to distribute jobs across various official categories.

With the CSC on its way out, the EEOC was able to finally get its way on federal hiring. In *Luévano v. Campbell*, a group of civil rights lawyers filed a lawsuit against OPM, the main successor to the CSC, on the grounds that the Professional and Administrative Career Examination (PACE) discriminated against blacks and Hispanics under Title VII.[23] The Carter Justice Department was sympathetic to the plaintiffs. It therefore agreed to settle in January 1981, just as Reagan was coming into office, and PACE was eliminated. This was after the Nixon administration had already thrown out the original civil service test in 1972. After *Luévano*, according to the *Washington Post*, as of 2015, in most kinds of federal hiring, "applicants who make it past the initial screening do so based on résumés, self-assessments and a measure of luck."[24] While reforms have been attempted, the federal government has not been able to solve the validity-diversity trade-off any more than private employers have.

Interestingly, one way to potentially get around the problem is through explicit quotas. In the first decades of the EEOC's war on testing, employers had begun to "race-norm" exams, which simply meant giving extra points to individual blacks and Hispanics by only comparing their scores to those of the same ethnic group. With that method, instead of eliminating standards, one can at least find the most qualified people from each race. The EEOC was in favor of this practice as a means to achieve equal representation, at one point actually prosecuting a Tennessee company for not giving extra points to black applicants.[25] When race-norming became the subject of public controversy, however, it caused an outcry, and the practice ended up being banned in the Civil

Rights Act of 1991.[26] In one of the many ironies of civil rights law, a conservative political victory actually ensured less merit and competence in hiring, since the alternative to explicit quotas has always tended to be a shift toward eliminating objective standards altogether. The EEOC, generally opposed to merit when it makes demographic balance more difficult to achieve, was actually supportive of a "second-best" solution that unfortunately ended up being politically untenable.

Written exams are far from the only standard targeted by civil rights law. Few hiring criteria seem as obvious as the idea that police officers, firefighters, and military personnel need to meet certain physical standards. Unfortunately for the left, almost any non-negligible physical fitness standard that men have to achieve is going to exclude practically all women. Candidates to become police officers, firefighters, and military personnel generally still must meet certain levels of fitness, but here "norming" based on demographic background is not only permitted but practically required. There doesn't appear to be much of a policy justification for this. Rather, it seems that banning race-norming in hiring can obscure favoritism shown toward underperforming minorities, while physical differences between the sexes are so obvious and pronounced that it would do little good to try to hide them. Even height requirements for police officers are a recurring problem under civil rights law.[27] The US Army had for years tried to maintain consistent standards across age and sex for its annual fitness test, but finally gave up in 2022.[28] Only when civil rights law cannot stealthily prefer some groups over others does it do so openly.

While the war on merit has gone furthest in the public sector, it has also had a major impact on private employment. As mentioned before, however, a key difference between the public and private sectors is that government is not incentivized to maximize profit, while businesses are, which means that there are some limits to how much damage civil rights law can do to American industry, as long as it can hire enough lawyers and supposed experts to protect itself. One survey of 2,500 companies conducted a few years after *Griggs* showed that three-quarters of those that used testing planned to cut back, and 14 percent were going to eliminate it completely.[29] Yet paper-and-pencil tests have not completely disappeared. Asked to comment on a venture capital firm that in 2022 asked applicants to include an IQ score, a New York University School of Law professor recommended that "to avoid legal risk, companies shouldn't rely on these tests. They should just be talking to job applicants."[30]

Companies have to worry about legal risks, but they also need to hire competent employees and provide goods and services for prices people are willing to pay. Because government resources are limited and everything has a disparate impact, they are constantly pushing the envelope on what they can get away with. Google, in its early days, famously asked potential employees brainteasers, some of which were collected into a book called *Are You Smart Enough to Work at Google?* Had the federal government checked for disparate impact, they certainly would have found it, although there is no indication that it ever did.

Businesses are often nimble and flexible enough to stay ahead of government. When productivity is measured within a job, white workers are usually found to do better than blacks, indicating that employers are bending over backward to avoid civil rights liability, since a nondiscriminatory process should find little difference between groups selected for the same position.[31] The diversity-validity trade-off exists everywhere, but in the private sector, it actually is a trade-off, while government agencies do not need to be competent to continue to maintain their budgets and influence. What seems to be going on is that the private sector is forced to use tools of questionable legality since the disparate impact standard makes practically everything legally questionable. At the same time, it protects itself from legal liability and maintains access to government contractors through the use of soft quotas. This is similar to the "diversity" justification used to practice affirmative action in college admissions, where schools still use standardized tests but ensure that they have an acceptable racial balance while pretending to do no such thing. Government, in contrast to business, generally puts legal liability rather than performance front and center, and hence settles the trade-off between merit and civil rights decisively in favor of the latter.

Just as employers are forced to pursue diversity indirectly, they are forced to pursue competence indirectly. Generally, more abstract IQ tests are better predictors of job performance than knowledge-specific tests, yet it is precisely the tests with the most validity that are most likely to be targeted by civil rights bureaucrats and lawyers.[32] This does not result simply in a misallocation of resources in the labor market. Recent decades have seen credential inflation, in which more employers require postsecondary degrees than before, despite a lack of any clear link between what students learn in college and the skills needed for the vast majority of jobs.

The quality of the school one attends also matters for job opportunities. It appears that, at least in part because civil rights law dislikes IQ tests but allows degree requirements, employers are glad to outsource some of their screening process to colleges and universities at taxpayer expense. Along with government subsidies for higher education, this leads to too many young people attending college. It has even been argued that the long arm of civil rights law reaches into the nature of childhood. Since universities adopt "holistic admissions standards" to select racially diverse student bodies but are banned from relying on explicit quotas, many American parents have increased time and money spent on ultimately pointless extracurricular activities for their children in order to give them the best possible chance of attending a high-ranked institution.[33]

Cultural Diversity and the Rise of the Miserable Workplace

Just because standardized tests are more useful than other methods for selecting employees does not necessarily mean that they should be universally relied upon. In government, standardized tests have emerged as the best method for selecting personnel because state hiring lacks a price system through which to judge performance. Barring a revolution, a government that performs its tasks poorly does not go out of business, and the same is usually true even when the service an agency provides is no longer needed. Thus the political process is forced to pick methods for choosing, managing, and promoting personnel. There is no need to make such decisions on behalf of the private sector, however. Moreover, it is important to note that increasing economic productivity is not all that matters in the labor market. Even if standardized tests maximize profits and ultimately GDP, people have preferences regarding how they spend their time, and they may well look for various qualities in choosing different aspects of their workplace environment, including the people they spend time with. This applies to both employers deciding whom to hire and employees in determining where they work.

The same government tendency to regulate human thoughts, emotions, and interpersonal behavior found in hiring and consumer preferences can be seen in how government has shaped the workplace environment itself. We usually think of cultural diversity as a concept speaking to differences between countries or religious and ethnic communities. But there is, by some measures, at least as much variation within nations and ethnic groups as there is between them. Think of the "cultural" differences between a law firm, a knitting club, a Pentecostal church in Appalachia, a motorcycle gang, a New York City Orthodox Jewish community center, an Ivy League university, a community college, and a fantasy football league. Each community reflects the aggregate preferences of its members and the ways in which they negotiate the nature and extent of their interactions with one another. One of the main benefits of living in a free society is the ability that individuals have to opt in to or out of various kinds of cultures, and this goes beyond racial and religious communities. People have different preferences regarding whether they seek environments that encourage, for example, extraversion or reservedness, hierarchy or egalitarianism, or a reliance on rationality or instinct.

A workplace is simply another area of life where individuals form a community. The same arguments for letting people choose how to spend their free time—the importance of individual liberty and the belief that individuals know best how to manage their own lives—apply just as strongly to work. In fact, the legal default is to allow workplaces to set their own cultures on most things. Some corporations are conservative, enforcing strict dress codes and traditional work hours. Others, like many Silicon Valley giants, have relatively informal practices and norms. No one suggests that there is a societal interest in turning Google into ExxonMobil, or vice versa. On matters involving relations between the sexes, individuals and communities clearly vary widely in their preferences. Virtually every culture in human history has believed that men and women have different strengths and weaknesses and different roles to play in society. Rarely has anyone explained why it is this particular area of social life that has to be standardized, and few have thought carefully about what kinds of creative energy or sources of human joy might be lost in the process.

The best research on what makes people happy supports the idea that we should allow more freedom in how individuals arrange their work lives.[34] In general, people are happiest when they are outdoors and moving. They are less happy when doing chores, commuting, or working. More passive forms of leisure like watching TV, reading, and sleeping are less conducive to human happiness than one would expect. In a study that relied on real-world data in which people entered their mood and what they were doing into their phones throughout their day, out of forty activities studied, work came in second-to-last place in how happy it made individuals, ahead of only "sick in bed." For most people, work is a source of misery, perhaps by some measures the main source of misery in life, given how much time we spend working and how little we spend lying sick in bed. One exception, however, is when people are working with friends, which can make something that is normally miserable into a source of joy and happiness.

In the name of equality between groups, civil rights law has sought to "depersonalize" the American workplace. Yet research indicates that it is the exact opposite of what we should be doing. Government should not declare a moratorium on the "pursuit of happiness" for forty hours a week. Civil rights law is not like safety, environmental, or health regulations.

Most world religions do not have a straightforward view of the minimum wage or the acceptable levels of particulates of different pollutants in the air. Yet they almost all take a position on recommending different societal roles for men and women. Many also mandate different standards of behavior toward co-ethnics or members of the same faith. Private clubs, even when of a secular nature, often engage in gender segregation. Even without a deep philosophical basis for such views, people understand that the sexes are different, and environments made up of one sex or the other are often natural and healthy. Without any mandates coming from above, humans have naturally invented priesthoods, fraternities, sororities, sports leagues, schools, bands, and countless other organizations, clubs, and institutions that are officially or unofficially for one sex or the other. How the sexes relate to one another when they do interact is also an issue people have deep feelings about.

Economists differentiate between two kinds of discrimination. First is statistical discrimination: someone judges individuals based on group characteristics. For example, if a business is looking to hire someone who must be trusted to count money, it might prefer a candidate from a demographic background that has a lower crime rate, on the grounds that the future employee is less likely to steal. The second form of discrimination is taste-based. An individual may prefer to be surrounded by co-ethnics, or people of one sex, and may even be willing to lose out financially by, for example, hiring less qualified men over talented women because they are considered better company.

Civil rights law, in theory, and usually in practice, makes both kinds of discrimination illegal for protected categories. This leads to some strange moral and legal outcomes. Let's say you believe that people who wear baseball caps are more likely to have criminal records and be prone to theft. It would therefore be legal to simply refuse to hire anyone who shows up to a job interview wearing a baseball cap. However, if it can be shown that a certain race is more likely to wear baseball caps, the same practice becomes arguably illegal. Government efforts to do away with taste-based discrimination lead to similar absurdities. I may dislike people who are too loud or too tall and discriminate against them, but not if my dislike of these traits disproportionately disadvantages members of a protected class. Height-based discrimination might even be legal in a city where the population was made up of blacks and whites, two races that are approximately equal in stature, but violate civil rights law in one where the population is white and Hispanic.

The beauty of markets is that people are free to make such decisions for themselves. As with many other things, some women like to be in an environment that accepts sexually charged jokes, while others find it distasteful, or even frightening and disturbing. Beyond matters of

the heart, some individuals like an environment in which they are surrounded by different kinds of people they can learn from, while others
feel more comfortable with those like themselves. There is no justification for saying that those who have one set of instincts on each of
these questions are good people, while those on the other side are bad
and should have no ability to act on their preferences. The bureaucrats,
lawyers, and judges who brought civil rights law to its current state managed to start from a premise that the vast majority of Americans agreed
with—that instruments of state power should not be used to repress
others—and turned it into an excuse to micromanage people's lives.

Since the 1960s, an elite consensus has developed that government
should not restrict the sex lives of consenting adults. From the middle
of that decade, the Supreme Court began to override the democratic
process on issues related to sex and reproduction in a libertarian direction, striking down restrictions on birth control (*Griswold v. Connecticut*, 1965, and *Eisenstadt v. Baird*, 1972), interracial marriage (*Loving v.
Virginia*, 1967), and abortion (*Roe v. Wade*, 1973). These cases formed
the legal basis for eventually invalidating bans on homosexual relations
(*Lawrence v. Texas*, 2003) and gay marriage (*Obergefell v. Hodges*, 2015). In
Planned Parenthood of Southeastern Pennsylvania v. Casey, a 1992 decision
reaffirming a woman's right to choose, the Court famously wrote that
"at the heart of liberty is the right to define one's own concept of existence, of meaning, of the universe, and of the mystery of human life."
While this principle was arguably brought under attack by *Dobbs v. Jackson Women's Health Organization* (2022), which overruled *Casey* along
with *Roe*, the majority opinion vehemently denied that it was calling
into question earlier cases based on its reasoning.[35]

At the same time, liberals aren't the only ones who have had reason
to celebrate the increasing emphasis the Supreme Court has placed on
individual rights over ideas about the collective good. In *Wisconsin v.
Yoder* (1972), it ruled in favor of Amish parents who resisted compul-
sory education laws and did not want their children to attend school
past the eighth grade. The religious freedom of parents outweighed
the interests of the state in educating the child. This decision paved
the way for granting more rights to families that wanted to homeschool

their children, a practice that used to be much more restricted and only became legal in all fifty states in the early 1990s. As the legal scholar and philosopher Brian Leiter argues, religion is given special status in American law, allowing people not to comply with mandates they would otherwise be required to follow.[36] While this trend has unquestionably privileged religious belief over secular philosophies and political convictions, it allows for more pluralism and communities to live their lives free from government interference. Given this context, civil rights law does something very strange. On most questions, the American system takes a relatively laissez-faire attitude toward the economy and the culture. Yet it also engages in social engineering when it comes to the private sector. This is no small matter in a society where people spend large portions of their lives at work, and often have more contact with their coworkers than members of their own families.

It is important to stress that, because of how broad and vague most of its proscriptions are, civil rights law does not simply make views or attitudes that are clearly bigoted illegal. Even conservative political views, or views held by a majority of the population, can be problematic. For decades, polls have shown that Americans oppose race- and sex-conscious programs in college admissions and in the workplace.[37] While one can sometimes get a contradictory result by framing the question differently in a way that obscures what affirmative action actually looks like, when voters have gone to the polls to decide on such programs, they generally vote against them. This was true even in California, a state where the voters in 2020 rejected affirmative action in the public sector and in university admissions by a vote of 57 percent to 43 percent.

Opposition to affirmative action is therefore about as mainstream a position as one can find. Yet color-blindness or gender-blindness, whether in terms of speech or practice, is illegal for major employers. Americans who talk about politics are used to being able to debate questions such as the causes of group differences and how much public policy should seek to equalize outcomes between different races. In the workplace, however, the practical impact of civil rights law can be to create an environment in which only the left-wing position is permitted, and any employer who thinks otherwise is opening himself up to legal liability.

Occasionally, those making and interpreting civil rights law have made their intentions explicit. As the Sixth Circuit Court of Appeals wrote in 1988,

> In essence, while Title VII does not require an employer to fire all "Archie Bunkers" in its employ, the law does require that an employer take prompt action to prevent such bigots from expressing their opinions in a way that abuses or offends their co-workers. By informing people that the expression of racist or sexist attitudes in public is unacceptable, people may eventually learn that such views are undesirable in private, as well. Thus, Title VII may advance the goal of eliminating prejudices and biases in our society.[38]

In other words, speech and conduct deemed "offensive," defined by courts and bureaucrats of course, is to be purged not only from the workplace but from private life. One can debate whether this kind of social engineering is a legitimate function of government, but what cannot be denied is that practically no Americans thought this was what they were signing up for in 1964.

Civil rights law legitimizes some identities while delegitimizing others. It therefore pretends to speak for the powerless and marginalized, even when it is clear that its protection of groups and its division and classification of individuals are products of political processes. For example, characteristics of Asperger's syndrome include a naive concern with truth and a poor ability to read social cues. Of course, people with this disorder should have no more right to make others uncomfortable than should homosexuals, and in the labor market, we might expect Asperger's to be selected against. Yet one could imagine the traits associated with the disorder being a net positive under some circumstances, as it may immunize an individual against groupthink and allow him to see certain truths that others are better at avoiding. In 2021, Elon Musk told the world that he was "on the spectrum," which appears to have contributed to his success. It is not the place of the government to either favor or place obstacles in the way of people with Asperger's syndrome. No state is wise enough to understand in what contexts the traits associated with that condition are beneficial for society, and when they cause too much distress or disruption to be tolerated. Markets and private institutions making the best decisions for themselves and those they interact with, free from government interference, should be the mechanisms for figuring such things out.

A thought experiment can show the absurdity of government attempts at social engineering. Courts have ruled that sex stereotypes can be a form of discrimination on the job. A woman who acts too "masculine" by arguing with her colleagues and interrupting them during meetings cannot be "discriminated" against based on these behaviors, at least if they would be more acceptable in a man. But if a woman acts too "feminine" for a workplace—say, if she is considered too nice and passive to manage employees—and is not promoted for that reason, she has no legal recourse. In other words, the government maintains that defending masculine behavior in women is something worth restricting freedom for; it does not adopt a similar paternalistic role for women more generally. A woman who has too feminine a demeanor for her employer's liking might have a disparate impact claim, if anything, though here a business necessity defense would be available. It would not be available if an employer fired the masculine woman.

Practically, of course, trusting courts and bureaucrats to make such determinations requires them to have unrealistically high levels of information and discernment. In the real world, if a woman says that she was fired for behaving in a traditionally masculine manner, few employers are likely to respond that they would have tolerated her behavior up to a certain level, but that she was acting so obnoxiously that they would have also fired her had she been a man. One would have to prove to social engineers the level of masculine behavior that a workplace finds acceptable in men, and show that this woman crossed that threshold. How does one prove such things? In effect, firms in many cases must end up placing limits on traits associated with extreme masculinity among men, while encouraging them among women.

Are the above ruminations absurd? If so, it is only because civil rights law itself is absurd—extreme in the extent to which it limits freedom; the power it puts into the hands of judges and unelected bureaucrats; and the trust it puts in their judgments. Human relations are complex, so much so that, according to the social brain hypothesis, the reason we have such high levels of cognitive ability in the first place is because intelligence is necessary to navigate and manage our social relations.[39] Within any relationship between two individuals, there are subtleties and subtexts that will escape even the closest observer, and often the participants themselves. Critics of television shows, movies, and literature can have a panoramic view of what happens in a scene and what came before it and nonetheless spend hours debating the motivations that led to a particular action. As the number of relevant actors in an institution grows, the number of dyads, and therefore the complexity of the system, increases exponentially. Our large brains have evolved to navigate the social world, mostly without explicit rules about appropriate standards or behavior. Religious traditions and bottom-up social institutions provide order amid chaos. They work because guidelines emerge organically and have withstood the test of time.

Civil rights law has the ambition of religion, without benefit of the right to exit, and without having competed with other systems of societal organization and having proved more functional than them. It constructs and shapes racial identities, has ideal types of each gender it tries to mold into being, and claims jurisdiction over a potentially unlimited range of speech, thought, and behavior. All the while, it is of a fundamentally dishonest character. It speaks of equal treatment but requires different treatment of various groups; justifies itself as temporary and limited even as it has become permanent and expansive; and claims to be based in the rule of law while creating subjective and ever-changing standards.

The End of Creative Destruction in Personnel Management and Institution-Building

The problem with social engineering goes even deeper than the fact that there is nothing inherently illegitimate about allowing individuals to indulge in certain forms of taste-based discrimination. For on what basis can we be sure that the most productive economy is not one where people can seek their happiness to the greatest possible extent in how they organize their private relations? Industrial-organizational psychologists may measure what predicts the productivity of worker A versus worker B, but they have no tools with which to foresee the kinds of environments and institutions that would emerge under a system that allowed complete freedom of association.

Humanity generally does not advance through central planning, or because some wise individuals foresaw the best ways to organize our affairs and then put their plan into action. Most exceptions to this rule that have ended relatively well, like the American Revolution, involved individuals creating a system that refrained from central planning and instead allowed scientific, technical, and economic progress to result from decentralized processes of information and preference aggregation. By setting the rules and largely leaving individuals and institutions to make their own decisions about the best ways in which to cooperate with others, well-functioning governments help facilitate growth. This requires what the economist Joseph Schumpeter called "creative destruction," which he defined as the "process of industrial mutation . . . that incessantly revolutionizes the economic structure *from within*, incessantly destroying the old one, incessantly creating a new one."[40]

It is easy enough to understand the concept of creative destruction in a narrow sense. One business sells widget A, another sells widget B, and the firm with the better or more affordable product outcompetes its rival. In practical terms, the benefits of the free markets are much more extensive. Each individual who is taking an active role in commerce has an endless number of decisions to make. At what scale should a firm exist? If one does have employees, how does one motivate them to put forth their best efforts? What image should the individual or company providing a good or service present to the world? Reasonable minds can differ on all of these questions, and many others, and the answer to each of them will depend on factors such as the technical requirements necessary to provide the good or service and the local market in which the firm is operating.

Capitalism does not guarantee optimal societal outcomes—such a thing is too much to hope for. But it aggregates information in a way like no other process on earth, and produces a result that, if not perfect, continuously builds on previous improvements and makes people's lives better.

This is why the standardization of the American workplace that resulted from civil rights law has likely had such disastrous effects on productivity. A series of practices, such as structured interviews, the deemphasizing of tests, and HR departments managing social relations did not emerge necessarily because they reflected the best ways to run a business. Rather, they emerged as a compromise between market pressures that reward productivity and aggregate human preferences, on the one hand, and arbitrary government fiats aimed at achieving demographic parity while hiding what they are doing, on the other.

In addition to issues related to economic efficiency, the practice of social engineering, as alluded to above, also prevents the culture from developing in organic ways that reflect the underlying preferences of individuals. The discussion thus far has drawn a line between economic productivity and taste-based discrimination. In reality, however, the two must be balanced, and we have no way to do so other than through markets. If women and non-whites have something to contribute in a market economy—and they of course do—then it is overly simplistic to believe that they have no bargaining power in their interactions with white men. At some point, discrimination against a particular group presents an incentive to hire them, and the market will be constantly selecting against taste-based prejudice.[41]

Private-sector discrimination may unfairly harm some groups, but there is a limit to the extent to which that can happen in a free market.

Through civil rights law, government still allows individuals to live how they want in the private sphere, but the space of the private sphere has been shrinking. One can choose one's spouse, friends, and fellow church members based on any criteria one wants, but not one's coworkers, employees, neighbors, or even, in some cases, roommates. Yet work is not simply a place to make money, and it should not be turned into a sanitized environment in which the only possible values are efficiency and treating people fairly based on a few arbitrarily chosen dimensions. Government is not wise enough to know the best ways to produce manufactured goods and get them to the consumer. Why do we believe that it has the wisdom to regulate no less complicated issues related to friendship, humor, and romance?

Many religious believers consider how they behave in their work lives to be part of their faith, not separate from it. In *Burwell v. Hobby Lobby Stores* (2014), the Supreme Court held that a private corporation could refuse to provide contraception for employees on religious grounds. While this was the right decision, the fact that the case was decided by a 5–4 vote, the narrowest of margins, shows the extent to which those with minority religious views face an uphill struggle in living their faith in their day-to-day lives. *Our Lady of Guadalupe School v. Morrissey-Berru* (2020) was another victory for religious freedom, as the Court found that the protections that religious institutions have against anti-discrimination laws go beyond a narrowly defined "ministerial exception," and also apply to other employees, in this case those given the job of teaching the faith to children. Yet if there are some relatively robust defenses against the application of anti-discrimination laws for the religious, those with secular political views have practically no right to freedom of association at the workplace when the principle collides with the supposed rights of protected groups.

Civil rights law is killing experimentation at work, with implications for the rest of life. As a matter of simple logic, more diversity within institutions will lead to less diversity between them.

Younger generations are less likely to marry or have children, and there is a gap between how many kids people want and how many they end up having. Americans have fewer close friends than they have had in the past, and many journalists and scholars have talked of an "epidemic of loneliness."[42] There are good reasons to doubt that governments can provide meaning to most people, and when they have tried, the results have often proved disastrous. Political power and the search for spiritual meaning are a dangerous combination, and one of the recurring ideas of the Enlightenment is that they should be kept apart.

Yet while the state shouldn't, and likely can't, cure what appear to be many of the pathologies of modern life, it can at least get out of the way. Under a legal system that allowed more institutional diversity, it is not difficult to imagine firms taking a more laid-back approach to how employees interact with one another, or even deciding to take steps to actively facilitate the forming of personal relationships. If individuals forming communities with others like themselves is legally suspect, civil rights law can be seen as taking away what for many people might be a deep source of meaning.

Even larger and more diverse firms have lost the ability to experiment and innovate in the area of interpersonal relations. In late 2021, the *New York Times* ran a piece about "ice-breaking activities" at the Chinese tech giant Alibaba, which included uncomfortable questions about one's sexual history.[43] Such practices would be all but unthinkable in the American context given the state of civil rights law, and the reporters writing about Alibaba appeared to judge the company by those standards. Still, one of the strengths of American society has traditionally been its willingness to allow experimentation in the ways in which people live. While Americans still have more freedom than the Chinese in their personal lives, as soon as they participate in commerce, we see social engineering that, in many ways, goes further than almost anything employed by most authoritarian regimes.

Civil rights law may explain why American culture portrays corporate life as dreary, lonely, and often leading to existential crisis. TV series like *The Office* and *Severance,* along with films like *Office Space,* have been enjoyed by millions because they speak to the experiences of many Americans. The white-collar workplace is portrayed as an environment where employees are hired as replaceable widgets, with interpersonal chemistry nonexistent. It may be of little surprise, then, that in one study published in the *Harvard Business Review* of readers surveyed in eight regions of the world, those responding in North America were least likely to say that their organization emphasized "enjoyment" as one of its top two most important cultural traits.[44]

A more sanitized corporate environment would still be possible even in the absence of civil rights law. Yet what current law does is take late-twentieth-century elite cultural attitudes and assumptions about the nature of work and make them permanent, though with occasional updates based on new theories put forth by the academy. Among these assumptions that are frozen in place are the ideas that work should be completely separate from all other areas of life; that it should have nothing to do with building relationships with others; that one must surrender free speech and freedom of association to participate in commerce; and that different kinds of businesses should be siloed, without new kinds of institutions and arrangements being allowed to develop. In a society that allowed institutional pluralism, one could imagine organizations that combined aspects of a church, a social club, a matchmaking service, and a traditional business. That is all but impossible now.

If individuals desire a sexless, androgynous, and sanitized workplace free of anything that might cause offense, the market will create such spaces. But as things stand, if such institutions are contrary to human nature and as miserable as happiness surveys suggest and how they are portrayed in pop culture, we have no corrective mechanisms. Civil rights law, with its expansive definition of "discrimination" and social engineering with regard to personal relationships, does not allow institutions to opt out, except in the case of religious exemptions. We are therefore stuck with stagnant institutions that micromanage the thoughts, relationships, and personal conduct of hundreds of millions of Americans.

Civil Rights Law Is Why We Hate Each Other

The United States is experiencing historically high levels of "affective polarization," the term political scientists use to describe the phenomenon of different political factions disliking one another. A 2020 study found that out of twelve developed countries, the US had both the highest level of affective polarization and the greatest increase over the past thirty years.[45] Various theories have emerged about why we hate each other so much, with the most convincing having their roots in a more fragmented media landscape and the growing trend of individuals becoming more likely to collapse various forms of identity along a single dimension.[46]

Political analysts on the left often blame polarization on "white resentment," arguing that whites, and particularly white men, feel threatened by their loss of status and are irrationally angry at justifiable calls for equality.[47] This is often combined with a psychosocial theory wherein rich people create false consciousness among the masses in order to distract them from their true economic interests and thereby cause them, for instance, to vote for policies that benefit the wealthy. One problem with this theory is that during the period in recent history when racial issues were most salient in our politics, the country was overwhelmingly united. Just a few months after the passage of the Civil Rights Act, Americans approved of the bill by an overwhelming margin and in November 1964 gave Lyndon Johnson the largest share of the popular vote received by any candidate since 1820, as the Democrats gained thirty-seven seats in the House and two in the Senate. Clearly, white Americans were not opposed to any attempts to improve the situation of blacks. The Civil Rights Act was framed as a bill that would primarily end Jim Crow and ensure nondiscrimination in employment without creating quotas or forcing the hiring of less qualified individuals based on their background. This was seen by most Americans as eminently sensible.

Yet the election of 1964 was the last we would have without the cultural cleavages that are recognizable to us today.[48] Very quickly, it became clear that there was a large gap between what the Civil Rights Act of 1964 promised and how it would be interpreted. In less than a decade, the federal government would be forcing school busing, looking for discrimination through the lens of disparate impact, and mandating "goals" and "timetables," while still claiming to forbid quotas. The broad reinterpretation of the CRA was not the only thing that shifted the country to the right. Political elites claimed to have new solutions to old problems surrounding issues like discrimination and crime, yet when they took federal action consistent with their theories, social indicators appeared to get worse. The mid-1960s saw the start of explosions in crime, drug use, and illegitimacy, with numbers today having come down from their peak in some of these areas but still looking unfavorable relative to America before the Johnson administration. The American people responded to increasing crime and disorder, along with the bait and switch of civil rights law, by giving Republicans the presidency in five out of the next six presidential elections beginning in 1968, with the only Democratic interruption being one term in the aftermath of Watergate.

If we are going to look for polarization as caused by one or a small number of factors, civil rights law is a good place to start. Political scientists have reached something of a consensus: American politics are driven by racial and cultural attitudes, which are, as a general matter, better predictors of political and partisan affiliation than economic circumstances or views on other topics.[49] Due to the political biases of most academics, these findings are interpreted to mean that, for example, conservatives are simply more racist than liberals, with scholars often providing a definition of "racism" that corresponds to conservative positions and arguments.[50] Nonetheless, even if the interpretation of the data by academics has, ironically enough, shown a political bias, the results themselves are indisputable, and they tell us that racial attitudes—and cultural attitudes more generally—are of fundamental importance in determining how Americans divide themselves politically, and shifts in party affiliation over time.[51]

Given US history, and the largely united front in favor of civil rights law among major institutions, white Americans have been more likely to favor discrimination against their own group than perhaps any other people in the world. That doesn't mean that they like it. From the earliest days of affirmative action, during the first term of the Nixon administration, supporters of such policies in Congress and the executive branch have worked carefully to avoid direct votes on the topic.[52] More recently, the website Ballotpedia lists nine instances of affirmative action being put to a state referendum between 1996 and 2020, and it has been rejected eight of those times, including twice each in the liberal states of California and Washington.[53]

Dishonesty is poison to political discourse. Those on the left are able to understand this when they see lies on the other side. The rise of Trump and his style of politics in the Republican Party has been accompanied by liberal denunciations of the "post-truth" atmosphere that has taken over the political right. When a president falsely says, for example, that he had a larger inauguration crowd than his predecessor, or that he actually won an election that he lost, there is a widespread understanding that blatant lies make honest discourse impossible, and ultimately harm the kinds of deliberation and debate on which democracy ultimately depends.

Yet the left has failed to grapple with the harmful effects of the lies of their own side, in part because the dishonesty is wrapped in packaging that is more presentable and also superficially resembles dispassionate academic or legal analysis. It is one thing to discriminate against a group; it is another to do so while professing the exact opposite principle. The "EEO Is the Law" poster that a firm is required to place in a conspicuous place informs its workers, among other things, that "Executive Order 11246, as amended, prohibits job discrimination on the basis of race, color, religion, sex or national origin, and requires affirmative action to ensure equality of opportunity in all aspects of employment."[54]

In other words, major American institutions are required to declare *within the same sentence* both that they do not discriminate and that they practice affirmative action. Americans know that almost every time they apply to a school or for a job, they have to check a box to indicate their sex and race, and that checking white or male is almost always a hindrance in the process. One may doubt the wisdom of the average voter, but she is not so blind as to be unable to see that she lives under a regime that doles out rewards and punishment based on sex and ancestry, while disclaiming any such role for itself and always being hypersensitive to the point of absurdity in trying to ferret out "racism" and "sexism" against different targets.

On this point, the liberal columnist Jonathan Chait has written about how "the left is gaslighting Asian Americans about college admissions."[55] He notes that elite universities use soft quotas because they do not want their schools to become too Asian, but have built an elaborate system of admissions on the false premise that they do no such thing. Chait is right, but he does not go far enough, as the entire affirmative action system is built on lies, including when it discriminates against white people. Institutions that talk about the need for diversity in practice define the concept as balancing according to US Census categories that have only a tenuous relationship to social reality, while not showing any concern about increasing the number of individuals with underrepresented viewpoints held by conservatives.

Racial preferences were originally presented as temporary expedients, yet their supporters do not seem to want to phase them out. Nor do they seem even to wish to provide a road map for doing so. Meanwhile, the category of preferred groups has come to include those with no substantial history of being discriminated against in the United States. And while the system claims to do all of this in the name of merit, objective standards like cognitive tests are not allowed, to be replaced by subjective criteria designed to achieve the goal of racial balancing.

It is worth thinking about how Trumpian lies and those of the civil rights regime are different, and how they interact with one another. For half a century, Americans have seen a clear disconnect between what elites and the institutions they control *say* about divisive issues relating to race and sex and what they actually *do*. The entire system is propped up by networks of politicians, activists, academics, and journalists who can always be counted on to either ignore inconvenient facts or justify the current system in ways that cannot possibly fool even the least sophisticated among us, no matter how impressive the credentials of those making the arguments are. Can anyone say with certainty that lies like this are less harmful to social trust and democratic deliberation than misrepresenting the crowd size at an inauguration?

The shift to a "post-truth world" long predated Trump. He was the product of a system in which many Americans had come to see elites as dishonest pseudo-experts who hide behind credentials and scientism to push a political agenda hostile to people like themselves. Some have argued that Trumpian lies play a social role in binding the right—that by expressing belief in falsehoods that are clearly absurd, followers of the former president show their loyalty to him.[56] They have failed to notice that the same can be said regarding lies couched in legalese or academic jargon. Trumpian lies at least make clear the rules of the game and delineate the sides. They at the very least do not insult anyone's intelligence through obfuscation.

One might hold that racial set-asides and preferences are a way to achieve social peace, even if they cannot be justified constitutionally or through an honest argument that would be found convincing by the broad public. There are a few problems with this view. First, there is little evidence that we gain social peace from the lies that surround civil rights law. In fact, American inner cities started erupting in riots in the mid-1960s after the greatest burst of civil rights legislation in the history of the nation. This famously puzzled President Johnson, although it did not cause him to rethink his premise that racial preferences help maintain public order. By the end of his presidency, he had gone from advocating nondiscrimination to brow-beating business executives into giving advantages to blacks in hiring on the grounds that doing so would prevent riots in the future.[57] Nixon accepted similar logic when he launched his "black capitalism" program in response to the urban race riots of the late 1960s.[58] Urban violence did not decrease with the rise of racial preferences and reverse discrimination but actually increased. While one cannot say for certain that things would not have been worse under a color-blind regime, this is at least some evidence against the theory that poverty and discrimination are the "root causes" of violence. Thomas Sowell's study of affirmative action across the world shows racial preferences to consistently be a source of intergroup tensions.[59]

Second, if "white lies" are necessary, it defeats the purpose if those lies are not believable. Despite the fact that voters are often ignorant of policy specifics, the lies told to justify affirmative action and civil rights law more generally are so blatant that even the least-informed citizen can see that there is a gulf between the words used by elites and the practices that they mandate. Finally, the social peace theory does not even try to explain why preferences have been expanded to women and other groups without histories of engaging in large-scale violence.

White lies might be desirable or necessary in some circumstances, but we should never begin with the assumption that they are in any particular case, particularly when they are used to justify a policy that has much to answer for. While slavery and Jim Crow were evils that government needed to take strong action to stamp out, there is little reason to believe that government can eliminate disparate outcomes. That entirely predictable failure then angers both those who were promised results and those who never bought into the social engineering project.

The Right That Ate All Others

Strenuous social engineering and a complex web of lies have fundamentally transformed American society. Critics of civil rights law have wisely pointed out that a system of preferences and quotas hurts all of us because it puts less competent people in positions of power and influence. Yet they generally underestimate the damage, since the science on the predictive validity of tests that measure general intelligence is not very well known. It is the strengths of such tests—the fact that they provide clear, consistent, and unambiguous rankings of ability—that make them suspect under civil rights law.

We've all had the experience of seeing a couple that fights over seeming trivialities, and realizing that they have much more serious problems that they have decided to suppress rather than deal with honestly. A marriage that decides to live with a big lie that both parties know is false is fundamentally unhealthy. The same is true of societies. American conservatives and liberals are like a couple that is always fighting about surface-level issues while burying the true sources of their disagreements, which leads to growing contempt for each another.

Civil rights law declares some practices related to sex and race unacceptable and others mandatory, restricting personal freedom and harming economic efficiency. It prevents creative destruction in the economic and social realms and taste-based discrimination, while making life more difficult for certain "unofficial minorities," including the neuro-atypical, the socially inept, the highly religious, and the hypermasculine. By championing certain ideals of womanhood, controversial academic concepts surrounding gender identity, and a bureaucratic and arbitrary system of racial coexistence, the state moves away from being a neutral arbiter in disputes between citizens or even a vehicle for seeking the common good and toward social engineering. Civil rights law can be blamed for hyperpoliticization, as issues that should be negotiated and settled locally and through the democratic process are decided far from public view, creating a sense of hopelessness and anger among those on the losing side.

It is difficult to think of a bedrock principle of liberal democracy that is not at odds with civil rights law as practiced since the late 1960s. A partial list would include freedom of speech; freedom of association; the right to private property; and the belief that government gains its legitimacy from the consent of the people. Similarly, capitalism is justified based on the principles that people have heterogeneous preferences; creative destruction is necessary for social progress and technological advancement; and government has neither enough information nor the right incentives to engage in central planning. When it comes to civil rights law, all of this is thrown out the window. Individuals are assumed to be homogeneous, or they need to be made homogeneous, when it comes to everything from how they choose their associates to what kinds of jokes they tell. Systems of personnel management and human relations are standardized across industries and nearly all of economic life. Civil rights law gives all of this power to a government that practically every knowledgeable observer agrees should not be setting prices or guiding industry as a general matter.

The system is not only based on lies. It is also based on meta-lies: that is, lies about lies. Proponents of civil rights law are not only being dishonest when they, for example, say that they support affirmative action but not quotas, or that they are seeking a critical mass of a minority group for diversity purposes instead of racial balance based on census categories. The system also lies when it claims its original lies are necessary for social peace, or even that certain policies actually have a purpose instead of being the result of bureaucratic inertia and the efforts of a small and unrepresentative number of activists within and outside government. For the sake of progress and overall societal health, the premises that underlie this entire regime must be brought out of the shadows and rejected in the political and legal arenas.

CHAPTER 6

Republicans and Civil Rights Law

Up until now, this book has skated over a puzzle that has been mostly only hinted at. Current interpretations of civil rights law are massively unpopular. Moreover, most of the post-1964 innovations are based on actions taken by the executive branch and the judiciary, but Republicans have held the presidency for most of that period. Since 2000 alone, the Republicans have had unified control of government in three Congresses (108th, 109th, and 115th), and parts of a fourth (107th). Yet mandatory racial classification and ethnic and gender bean counting are still standard parts of American life, as is overbroad harassment law that micromanages social relations. Republicans in power have only made at best marginal changes to the status quo. At worst, as during the administrations of Nixon and the elder Bush, they have pushed the civil rights regime further than their Democratic predecessors had.

Given that championing an anti-woke policy agenda should unite Republicans and also put them on the right side of public opinion, why have they done so little?

There have been three eras that reflect different Republican approaches to civil rights. First was 1964–1980, when conservative politicians spoke to the fears and concerns of the majority of Americans on civil rights excesses but allowed government bureaucracy to move forward on issues such as disparate impact and consent decrees that mandated racial balancing. This is because Republican elites, while willing to appeal to cultural grievances to win elections, were far from antagonistic to the civil rights establishment and often intimidated by a hostile media landscape. This changed with the election of Ronald Reagan in 1980. From 1981 to 2008, we saw the second era, one in which Democrats continued to be completely united on civil rights law while the other side was split. Reagan and those around him did more to push back on civil rights law than any other president since the 1960s, but disagreements within his cabinet and resistance in Congress prevented him from taking decisive action. The administration of George H. W. Bush spoke out against "quotas" but capitulated to a Democratic Congress and signed the Civil Rights Acts of 1991 while actively supporting the Americans with Disabilities Act (ADA). His son would sign a bill in 2008 expanding the definition of "disability" under the ADA.

After the 2008 election, we started to see the culmination of decades of political sorting and elite polarization as conservatives took charge of the Republican Party. On a wide range of issues—including guns, abortion rights, and environmental regulations—Republican officials moved to the right. Yet civil rights law simply fell off the radar. Conservatives grew increasingly concerned with wokeness as a cultural phenomenon while ignoring its origins in policy. This coincided with a rise in education polarization, wherein a disproportionate share of college graduates, particularly elites, identify as Democrats. Fewer conservatives were interested in the mechanics of government, or well-versed in the topic. Had the right had a debate on civil rights law during this era, surely the more conservative wing of the party would have won, as it has on nearly all social issues, but the topic was simply neglected. Republicans in the 2016 election fell in love with Trump in part because he made liberals angry, but he was the only major GOP candidate to express support for affirmative action. Once Trump was in office, however, we saw the effects of the conservative takeover of the American right. The administration did push back in areas like Title IX sexual assault tribunals, overturning the previous administration's push to mandate gender theory in the nation's schools, investigating colleges for anti-white discrimination, scaling back EEOC enforcement, and, near the end, clamping down on critical race theory trainings in the federal government. Yet the lack of focus on civil rights issues ensured that there would be no major legislation in the area passed when Republicans had unified control of government, nor even many fundamental shifts in the regulations made by the executive branch that would not end up being undone by the next administration.

I call these three eras of Republican civil rights policy Bipartisan Cartel, Republicans Divided, and Conservative Neglect. With liberal elites having been sorted out of the party, an assault on civil rights excesses can be the issue that unites Republicans into a fourth era, leading to electoral success and shifting the culture in a more conservative direction. Numerous factors that have stopped this from happening before are no longer in play.

The economist Robin Hanson asks us to imagine political debate as a tug-of-war, with each side pulling on one side of the rope. If one wants to have an unusually high level of influence, the best strategy is to pull the rope sideways—that is, take a position not clearly aligned with either side of the political spectrum.[1] The argument for the effectiveness of this approach seems to be consistent with the idea of the "Secret Congress" theory.[2] While Republicans and Democrats strenuously debate high-profile issues and find it difficult to compromise on them when voters and activists are actually paying attention, below the surface much in Washington keeps getting done. Understanding this should encourage activists to seek to depoliticize their issue of concern in most cases. One is in a better position to successfully advocate for a position if one arranges to have it seen as an issue of "good governance," "health," or "safety" rather than as a litmus test of the right or left. Often it is better to not have one's pet cause be given much attention at all, because the second a policy program is exposed to the light of our contentious politics, polarization begins to play a major role in shaping the debate surrounding it, which can be fatal in a system like ours with a large number of veto points.

While "pull sideways" is in most cases good advice when one is introducing a relatively new issue, it provides less guidance when a policy area has already been polarized or is at the heart of the differences between the two major American coalitions. There is no hope of depoliticizing abortion or gun rights, for example, at least at the national level. Woke-ness is an animating concern on both sides of the political aisle. There are liberals who have come to see propositions such as "men can be-come pregnant" and "the US is a white supremacist nation" as scientific truths that can only be denied due to irrational prejudice or a hostility to democracy itself.

Conservatives perceive the growing acceptance of these ideas in elite institutions as the clearest sign we have of a world gone mad. For this reason, I don't believe I would have been able to write a book like this directed to policymakers on both sides of the political aisle. It would have been naive to try, and ultimately would have made the work less effective in accomplishing its goals. While intellectuals on both the right and left can benefit from the historical, legal, and bureaucratic analyses provided in these chapters, the current state of our politics and an un-derstanding of the issues around which our two great political coalitions have formed indicate that, to the extent to which it is read as a practical guide, this work will be useful mostly to conservatives and Republicans.

The New Right and the Establishment Can Unite on Civil Rights Law

In a two-party system, if one party wants to enact a policy program, it must be internally united. Today the main intellectual fracture within the Republican Party is generally seen as one splitting the new right, animated by populism and concern with controlling institutions, and the establishment, with its commitment to the more libertarian-leaning philosophy of Ronald Reagan and his successors. This divide can be seen in the debate over "David French-ism" that broke out in May 2019, when the conservative writer Sohrab Ahmari attacked his fellow pundit for placing individual liberty and respect for gradual change within institu-tions above all else, and not taking seriously enough the cultural threats that conservatives face from a variety of private and public institutions.[3]

To members of the new right, represented most clearly at the institu-tional level by the Claremont Institute, the Reaganite consensus is what led us here. Republicans have done little more than mouth outdated platitudes about "freedom" and "small government" as the culture shifts under their feet and everything they believe in is destroyed. They point out that government is not the only possible threat to the common good or things conservatives care about: social media companies censor their views; they are cut off from supposedly neutral payment-processing platforms; and large corporations force individuals to go through humiliating training programs that attack individuals based on their race and sex. All of this has supposedly shown that mainstream conservativism, its adherents brainwashed by decades-old dogma, is insufficient to deal with modern problems.

To libertarians and many members of the Republican establishment—even those who share many of the cultural concerns of the populists—this kind of talk is dangerous. They wisely point out that government cannot solve every problem. The Constitution and American federalism do not allow rapid and wholesale social transformation from the top; if they did, that might well be to the benefit of the left, whose ideas dominate among the federal bureaucracy, the activist class, and the legal profession.[4] Critics of the new right are further able to point out that many of the ideas that populists put forth do not seem to have anything to do with their underlying concerns. For example, many conservatives are angry at social media censorship and have therefore embraced breaking up big tech companies on antitrust grounds. Yet a more decentralized internet is not guaranteed to be any freer than what we have now; after all, universities are decentralized, and conservatives never stop talking about their high levels of repression and left-wing bias.[5]

Despite the seeming intractability of these debates, if the arguments put forth in this book are correct, then conservatives do not have to choose between adhering to principles of small government and pushing back on destructive forces that are harming society, at least when it comes to fighting back against wokeness. Wokeness is government policy. The state orders private corporations to classify their employees by race and sex, tells them how much and what kinds of aesthetic pleasure customers are allowed to derive from their goods and services, and regulates humor and dating. Not only does it mandate nondiscrimination against protected classes, but it defines this as requiring discrimination against the non-protected. For a Reaganite or libertarian, using government power to roll back the excesses of civil rights law is no more philosophically problematic than reducing environmental regulations or lowering taxes. Doing so is not only something libertarians shouldn't feel uncomfortable about, it is something they should actively support.

For this reason, libertarian-leaning Republicans have for decades warned about the excesses of civil rights law. Barry Goldwater's nomination was seen as the first triumph for movement conservatism in presidential politics. In his Senate speech on why he was opposing the Civil Rights Act, he affirmed that, while he had been willing to support a bill that ended government-sponsored discrimination in the form of Jim Crow, bans on private discrimination would create "an 'informer' psychology in great areas of our national life—neighbors spying on neighbors, worker spying on workers, businessmen spying on businessmen, where those who would harass their fellow citizens for selfish and narrow purposes will have ample inducement to do so." The powers that government was claiming and the psychological features that it relied on were "landmarks in the destruction of a free society."[6] The provisions of the CRA relating to employment and public accommodations in particular would "require for their effective execution the creation of a police state." Goldwater was correct on that point, even if the creation of the bureaucratic army he foresaw developing was largely outsourced to the private sector in the form of human resource managers and trial lawyers. There, the enforcers of the law could earn much more money than it was possible to earn in government service.

As discussed below, Ronald Reagan himself, the bogeyman of much of the new right, did much more than any other Republican president in recent history to push back against civil rights law. Nationalists, libertarians, and members of the traditional Republican establishment may debate free trade, immigration, or foreign policy, but on opposition to wokeness they should be united in a common goal. The next time Republicans have unified control of government, rolling back the excesses of civil rights law should be near the top of their agenda, before leaders move on to issues that are potentially more divisive within the party.

Not only does the war on wokeness unite the conservative movement internally, but it is good for winning over larger swaths of the public. As mentioned in the previous chapter, almost every time affirmative action has been on the ballot it has lost. What makes these results all the more impressive is that the pro–affirmative action side is often much better funded and has the support of prestigious and powerful institutions. In 2020, when affirmative action was on the ballot in California, the state was 37 percent white, and Biden got 63.5 percent of the vote, giving him a margin of 29.2 percent over Trump. The side in favor of racial preferences outspent the opposition by 19 to 1 and could count among its ranks, according to the Associated Press, the "chambers of commerce, tech companies, sports teams and Democratic leaders."[7] The other side was "fueled by smaller donations from a grassroots network that included Chinese immigrants." In 2021, Blue Rose Research surveyed 113 Democratic policy positions and found affirmative action to be the second most unpopular.[8] More recently, a different firm conducted a survey of Democratic voters in which they were asked to choose their three most important issues for Biden and Congress to pass legislation on. Structural inequality, in the form of aid targeted at minority communities, came in last place.[9]

Framing the topic in other ways can lead to different results. If respondents are asked about "affirmative action programs" or how they feel about "ensuring nondiscrimination," polls often indicate majority support.[10] This is an old trick in polling: a question is presented as a binary choice with no downside, and one gets a predetermined result. For example, a pollster may ask whether people want to protect the environment, without mentioning that this may require higher gasoline costs. A better question would indicate the trade-offs involved. When Americans are given information about what modern civil rights law actually looks like, they recoil. For example, between 1977 and 1989 Gallup asked Americans whether "women and minorities should be given preferential treatment in getting jobs and places in college" or if "ability, as determined by test scores, should be the main consideration." In each of four polls, Americans favored ability as determined by test scores by over an 8-to-1 margin.[11] Ballot initiatives require clarity about what is or isn't allowed, which is why affirmative action performs poorly when put to a direct vote.

Polls and ballots may still underestimate just how unpopular civil rights law would be if people had a better understanding of how it works. It is not simply that blacks and women are given "preferences" in jobs; rather, nearly every aspect of hiring, promotion, and behavior in the workplace is regulated in the name of anti-discrimination. How would Americans vote in a referendum on whether the government should be able to regulate jokes or the expression of political and religious views in the private sector? A more honest conversation about topics like disparate impact, sexual harassment law, and affirmative action would mostly benefit conservatives.

Three Eras

On many issues, conservative principles lead Republicans to champion positions that are unpopular, like entitlement reform. In contrast, when conservatives have principles that put them on the right side of public opinion on a particular cause, they should be expected to raise the salience of the issue. In the 2004 election, when most Americans still opposed gay marriage, Republicans worked to put the issue on the ballot in multiple states, with pundits later speculating that it helped George W. Bush's reelection effort by turning out more conservative voters.[12] Quotas in one form or another have been central to liberal governance since soon after the passage of the Civil Rights Act, yet Republicans have talked less about the topic than one might expect throughout the decades, and have completely ignored the issue since the early 2000s. As little as they have talked about civil rights excesses, they have done even less. To understand the conservative movement and its relationship with civil rights law, it is worth looking at developments in each of the three eras outlined above. The dynamics of each have been determined by the state of communications technology at the time, and by the level of policy maturity within the movement.

Bipartisan Cartel, 1964–1980

After the Great Society, conservatives spent a decade and a half going along with, and in some cases actually being the force behind, innovations in civil rights law. The Nixon administration, along with Republicans in Congress, helped institutionalize racial preferences, lower standards for proving discrimination, and make women and designated categories of non-whites more analogous to blacks, in what John Skrentny calls the "minority rights revolution." This was far from inevitable. Although Goldwater electorally went down in flames, something close to his vision of conservatism ultimately triumphed. Given the backlash to the excesses of civil rights law among the general public that emerged in the mid-1960s, one might have expected Republicans to have put an end to policies like affirmative action and disparate impact, rather than accepting or even helping facilitate their expansion. The two main reasons they didn't were the centralized nature of the media at the time, and the fact that the conservative movement had not yet reached maturity as an ideologically coherent force with control over the Republican Party.

Sometimes when different factions of the elite agree on a policy approach, they can exclude alternative viewpoints that might resonate with the masses. This was easier to do before the fragmentation of the media landscape. In the 1960s, national politics was covered on television by three major news stations. While most journalists saw themselves as arbiters of truth delivering a valuable public service, the nightly news broadcast represented a left-wing point of view on most things, particularly on the issue of civil rights, support for which during the 1960s became a class marker in the United States. Before the rise of talk radio, conservative news channels, and the internet, those who wanted an alternative viewpoint could subscribe to newsletters or magazines like *National Review*, the conservative publication founded in 1955 and still influential today. But for anyone other than political junkies, most information about national politics came filtered through a center-left lens.

This does not mean that the bias was so pervasive and effective that liberals could make reality bend to their will. The Great Society legislation passed by Congress in 1964 and 1965 was widely popular. But Americans very quickly saw that not only did liberal reforms fail to treat social pathologies, but they were soon followed by levels of urban crime and disorder that had no precedent in American history. The murder rate approximately doubled over the course of the 1960s, and violent crime more generally increased fivefold between 1960 and 1992.[13] The fact that the increase in crime was overwhelmingly concentrated precisely where Great Society legislation aimed to help—that is, in the inner cities— helped further discredit the liberal project, as did the rise of race riots in those same communities. The country that in 1964 gave Lyndon Johnson 61 percent of the popular vote would four years later give only a slightly lower percentage to Richard Nixon and George Wallace, and go on to elect Republican presidents in most elections over the next four decades.

Yet the conservative political backlash did not mean that the Great Society would be rolled back. This is because while voters were paying enough attention to see with their own eyes the failures of the 1960s and vote accordingly, policymaking shifted from Congress to the federal bureaucracy and the courts. Moreover, while the media, which was highly centralized and liberal, could only change public opinion on issues to a limited degree, it had overwhelming control over how proposed policies under consideration were framed. It determined which policy proposals were uppermost in the minds of the masses, along with the facts presented about those issues.

Liberal media bias could not get Americans to like racial quotas, or even make them fail to understand that they exist in the first place. What it could do, however, was obscure the legal and institutional sources of power of the civil rights regime, how it could be rolled back, and the nature of any particular policy under discussion. While Americans would cast votes in opposition to crime or affirmative action in the abstract, Congress could pass the Civil Rights Attorney's Fees Award Act of 1976 secure in the belief that the public would remain unaware of the connections between increased funding for the civil rights lobby and growing race- and sex-consciousness in American life.

Moreover, prominent conservatives who went along with innovations in civil rights law would be portrayed as acting as tolerant statesmen, while those who resisted would be painted as bigots. It did not matter if most Americans agreed with positions that liberals and the civil rights establishment considered "racist," like opposition to school busing. The public has never been composed of policy wonks, and a media with centralized control of information had a wide degree of freedom in how it presented policy debates. None of this implies a conspiracy or a conscious campaign to deceive on the part of most journalists; rather, like politicians, reporters are generalists, and in the 1960s and 1970s they deferred to the issue frames provided by a civil rights establishment that still had a great deal of prestige after its victory over Jim Crow.

In addition to the effect of the media environment, it took conservatives decades to complete their takeover of the Republican Party. Congress therefore went along with executive and judicial decisions moving policy to the left and occasionally passed legislation pushing in the same direction, even while prominent Republicans spoke out against the excesses of civil rights law.[14] Nixon in particular adopted the language of conservatives, but he was a centrist on domestic policy whose primary interest was in foreign affairs.[15] As he focused most intently on geopolitical issues surrounding Vietnam, China, and the Cold War, at home Nixon gave moderate staffers a dominant policy role while letting conservatives handle speechwriting and PR.

The president was smart enough to realize that, in his words, "those who write about politics really care more about style than substance."[16] While voters and political pundits were relatively unsophisticated with regard to developments in federal law, the legal and public interest communities that did understand what was at stake in various policy battles were overwhelmingly liberal, and it would be decades before a conservative counter-establishment would form.[17] Conservatives had used the backlash to the Great Society and its effects to win votes—with Nixon himself being the greatest beneficiary. Nonetheless, the political right had yet to form an activist class that could keep politicians accountable to its ideals, nor had it developed a media ecosystem that could pressure politicians to adopt the conservative perspective on issues.

The failure of conservatives to arrest the progress of civil rights law was not completely Nixon's fault. He made the judiciary a central issue in the 1968 campaign, but once he got into office he had trouble

finding qualified Republican judges. There were simply few conservatives within the federal judiciary who could be realistic candidates for
the Supreme Court. As of 1969, there were only four Republicans under sixty serving on any US court of appeals.[18] Similarly, conservatives
were so underrepresented in elite circles that the Nixon administration
in many cases didn't even understand the implications of what it was
doing. Title IX would become one of the most potent weapons in the
hands of government social engineers. But in 1972, supporters of the
provision consciously adopted a strategy of trying to publicize it as little
as possible so as to not stir up opposition. It was added to the Education
Amendments Act of 1972 by voice vote, and when Nixon signed the bill
he released a statement that made no mention of what would become
one of his most lasting domestic policy changes.[19]

Thus while Nixon the man was the personification of the backlash to
the 1960s, Nixon in power represented the continuation of the revolution that had been started under Johnson. On many issues, his administration went further than the executive branch had ever gone before.
Nixon signed Executive Order 11478, which established affirmative action in the federal government; before, similar regulations were forced
only on the private sector. In the Philadelphia Plan, government construction contractors were first held to a "goals-and-timetables requirement" to hire more minorities, with Nixon having personally lobbied
members of Congress on behalf of the policy in December 1969 as a way
to pit civil rights organizations and labor unions against one another
and split the Democratic coalition.[20]

A few months later, the OFCC expanded affirmative action in contracting beyond construction to all industries, a development of which
the president may have been unaware. The Nixon administration also
pioneered the practice of the federal government giving contracting
preferences to female- and minority-owned businesses, as well as using
Title VI to pressure universities to consider race and sex in hiring.[21] Finally, the president signed the Equal Employment Opportunity Act of
1972, which increased the enforcement power of the EEOC.

It was not only on civil rights that Nixon championed or helped facilitate a liberal shift in policy. He also presided over the creation of

the Environmental Protection Agency and a major expansion of government. Nixon was not alone in supporting policies that were, to conservative intellectuals and ideologues like Goldwater, examples of government overreach or even steps toward tyranny, as bills that represented the expansion of the Great Society received bipartisan support in Congress. Between 1940 and 1976, every Republican platform except those of 1964 and 1968 endorsed the Equal Rights Amendment, which would have enshrined in the Constitution what would surely have been a feminist ideal of gender equality.[22]

Even Nixon's judicial appointments did not overwhelmingly reflect a conservative philosophical orientation, or at least not to the same extent as would those selected by later Republican presidents, although, as mentioned above, this was not entirely his fault. The conservative legal movement, which for all practical purposes did not exist during the Nixon administration, would pressure future Republican presidents to appoint judges that would reflect its worldview and understanding of the law.[23]

Republicans Divided, 1981–2009

On the issue of civil rights, Ronald Reagan was philosophically closer to Goldwater than Nixon. Because he was more strongly grounded in conservative ideology than his Republican predecessors, his administration made some efforts to push back on the civil rights establishment. Yet they failed due to bipartisan opposition not only in Congress but among cabinet officials. On voting rights, the president and his Justice Department opposed policies and practices that would have—by mandating the drawing of electoral boundaries and instituting voting procedures meant to maximize the number of black public officials—created racial quotas for political representation. Yet Reagan decided to sign an extension of the Voting Rights Act of 1982 after it received veto-proof majorities in both houses of Congress.[24] The bill increased the stringency of federal supervision of the electoral systems and of the practices of states and localities, judging their acceptability based on whether they elected enough black candidates, not simply whether they protected the right of individuals to vote.

Reagan had a bit more success in pulling back the scope of affirmative action, albeit temporarily. His appointees and staff worked on several initiatives that eventually failed, due to resistance from within and outside the administration. These included proposals to reduce the number of contractors that had to produce affirmative action plans by three-quarters; reduce the frequency of affirmative action compliance reports from annual to once every five years; close the OFCCP; and end goals and timetables for private firms.[25]

In general, it was the Department of Justice that was most consistently conservative on these issues, and when it tried to act in ways consistent with the policy wishes of the president, it faced pushback from Labor and other agencies. At the EEOC, Clarence Thomas, then chairman, stopped approving agreements with employers accused of discrimination that included goals and timetables. Fewer contractors were disbarred for noncompliance with government affirmative action policies, and the EEOC and OFCCP both saw staffing cuts, with the latter shrinking by over half between 1979 and 1985 to fewer than one thousand employees as its budget was reduced.[26]

The Reagan administration was fairly cautious in its approach to affirmative action in its first term. This began to change after the appointment of Ed Meese as attorney general in early 1984 and the president's landslide reelection victory that same year. In 1985, Meese drafted an executive order that would have prohibited the OFCCP from using statistical evidence to charge contractors with discrimination.[27] In the words of Raymond Wolters, conservatives saw an opportunity: "With the stroke of a pen, they believed, President Reagan could deliver a crushing blow against quotas and put an end to the government's policy of forcing firms with federal contracts to practice racial discrimination."

Secretary of Labor Bill Brock argued for a small revision to EO 11246 that emphasized the color-blind language of the Civil Rights Act. The right-leaning press, in contrast, held that now was the time to act, given the president's recent electoral mandate. Reagan unquestionably sympathized with the more strenuous critics of affirmative action. Yet in early 1986, as a result of media coverage of the debate going on within the administration, 69 senators—including Majority Leader Bob Dole and 24 other Republicans—and 180 members of the House sent a letter urging the president not to sign Meese's executive order.[28] While Republicans had the Senate, Democrats had come out of the 1984 election with a 72-seat majority in the House, despite having lost 16 seats. Faced with such overwhelming political pressure, Reagan punted and never signed the proposed executive order. Despite the fact that most Americans opposed racial quotas, civil rights activists and journalists sympathetic to them were able to make life difficult for conservatives in the Reagan administration.

Also during Reagan's second term, in 1987 Congress passed the Civil Rights Restoration Act, which said that institutions that received federal funds had to comply with Title VI and Title IX in all areas of operation. This was in response to the Supreme Court decision *Grove City College v. Bell* (1984), which held that under Title IX the government could only threaten to cut funding off from the program or activity of a school or university that was found to be engaging in discrimination. Reagan vetoed the bill, but the veto was overridden via nearly unanimous support among Democrats in the House (242–4), with only a slight majority of Republicans voting against it (73–94). Just under two-thirds of Senate Republicans voted for the override.

These votes accurately represent the positions of the two parties on civil rights issues during the 1980s: Democrats united in more strenuous enforcement, Republicans about evenly split. Congress was therefore able to pass the bill, and even override the president's veto the next year. One can hardly exaggerate the importance of the Civil Rights Restoration Act; *Grove City* had effectively ended OCR jurisdiction over athletics for a few years.[29] Under the Supreme Court's interpretation of Title IX, the Department of Education no longer had jurisdiction over college sports, because the federal government did not provide money to athletic programs. After Congress overruled *Grove City*, Title IX enforcement would not only go back to what it was but ramp up and become ever more intrusive, as the mainstream left became more radical in its ideas about gender and forced its views onto higher education. Had Republicans united in upholding Reagan's veto, as they would be united on major civil rights legislation in later decades, OCR would likely never have had the opportunity to begin its project of micromanaging athletics programs and the sex lives of college students.

Reagan and many of those around him clearly wished they could go further on rolling back the excesses of civil rights law. Democrats were only able to stop the president because they had help from Republican politicians. The *Grove City* controversy roiled official Washington but was mostly ignored throughout the rest of the country, meaning that it was not public opinion but elite attitudes that determined the outcome.[30]

After the 1984 election, Republicans were still a minority in the House but controlled the Senate. Democrats alone could not negate the effects of a new executive order repealing or significantly modifying EO 11246 and ending mandatory affirmative action among government contractors. Yet Reagan faced pushback from Republicans in Congress, whether acting from genuine conviction or political pressure. Mainstream media reports on the debate over government contracting within the Reagan administration would often include accusations of racism from civil rights activists and do little to inform readers about the substantive issues involved, when not actively misleading them.[31]

As the *Grove City* decision and its aftermath reveal, during the Republicans Divided era the judiciary was moving to the right faster than other parts of government, as Republican appointees were grounded in conservative philosophy and relatively immune to the kinds of media pressures faced by politicians. Yet Democratic unity on civil rights issues and Republican internal strife ensured that any judicial victories would go to waste. By 1989, Republicans had controlled the White House for all but four of the last twenty years, and in that period appointed six of the nine justices then sitting on the Supreme Court. This included John Paul Stevens, who came to vote with liberals on hot-button issues, but enough of the Republican appointees had a conservative judicial philosophy to significantly change the nature of the Court.

This was reflected in two major cases in 1989. In *Wards Cove Packing Co. v. Antonio*, a 5–4 decision, the Supreme Court ruled that having a different percentage of whites and minorities in different jobs did not create a prima facie case for discrimination. Disparate impact was not thrown out, but to establish their case complainants had to at least show which practices resulted in the relevant disparity, not simply point to the fact that a disparity existed. The Court held that if a statistical disparity was all that was required to create a prima facie case for discrimination, then the "only practicable option for many employers would be to adopt racial quotas . . . this is a result that Congress expressly rejected in drafting Title VII." This commonsense argument, which conservatives had been making for two decades, was only accepted by the Supreme Court after Republican presidents had appointed enough judges. In the same year, the Court also ruled, in *Lorance v. AT&T Technologies, Inc.*, that a system that protected employees from firing based on seniority was not against the law just because it had a disparate impact that disfavored women.

As Yale Law professor William Eskridge Jr. noted, Reagan differed from previous presidents in undertaking "a virtually unprecedented confrontational strategy *against* civil rights legislation."[32] George H. W. Bush's election would ensure that not only would Reagan's changes to civil rights enforcement practice not continue, but that the most important Supreme Court rulings in this area would be overturned. The Americans with Disabilities Act of 1990 prohibited discrimination against the disabled, and went beyond the Civil Rights Act in requiring employers to provide "reasonable accommodations" and imposing accessibility mandates in public accommodations. More controversy accompanied the debate that would ultimately culminate in the Civil Rights Act of 1991. In October 1990, Bush vetoed its predecessor bill on the grounds that, in his words, it "employs a maze of highly legalistic language to introduce the destructive force of quotas into our national employment system."[33]

He was in a politically precarious position, as the bill had enough bipartisan support that it was shy of a veto-proof majority by only two votes in the Senate and twelve in the House. After the midterm elections, Democrats would be in an even stronger position, and the administration and Congress came to an agreement on the Civil Rights Act of 1991, which passed with overwhelming bipartisan support and was signed by the president. For the first time, the bill allowed for punitive damages under Title VII, capped at $300,000 for the largest corporations and at lower amounts for smaller firms.[34] It also shifted the burden of proof onto the employer for showing that a practice that had a disparate impact was "job related for the position in question and consistent with business necessity" in order to avoid a violation of Title VII.

Bush justified signing the Civil Rights Act of 1991 after vetoing its predecessor by declaring, "this is not a quota bill."[35] It is interesting to note the parallels with what happened in Nixon's first term, when the new president saw his party do poorly in the midterms and then acquiesced in liberal efforts to expand civil rights law, all the while obscuring the nature of the reforms he enacted, even down to disingenuously denying that new laws and regulations had anything to do with imposing a quota system.

As discussed above, the Civil Rights Act of 1991, overshadowed by its predecessor and all but forgotten today, had a major effect on employment law, and when combined with vague standards inherent in concepts like "discrimination" and "harassment" led to an explosion in EEOC complaints and Title VII lawsuits. The election of 1994 again followed the norm of recent American history in which a president's party lost seats in the midterm elections, although in this case the gains the Republicans made were massive: they picked up eight seats in the Senate and fifty-four in the House, winning the latter body for the first time since 1952.

Newt Gingrich, upon becoming Speaker of the House, lent his support to the ultimately successful effort to end racial preferences in California and in early 1996 promised a conservative audience that he would "pursue an all-out effort to end affirmative racism in America."[36] Yet congressional Republicans came to defer to the only two black members of their caucus on the issue. Gary Franks of Connecticut wanted to move ahead with taking apart affirmative action, while J. C. Watts of Oklahoma tried to put the brakes on any such efforts.[37] In July 1995, the Senate defeated a measure to end federal contract set-asides for women and minorities by 61–36. The *Washington Post* reported at the time that Republican congressional leaders "found that the issue is more divisive within their party than some had initially believed" and "have demonstrated little enthusiasm for an emotionally wrenching debate."[38] Soon after, Bob Dole introduced the Equal Opportunity Act of 1995, which would have prohibited or limited affirmative action in government contracting and employment, effectively undoing the legacy of EO 11246 and decades of EEOC regulations and court decisions. The bill never went to a vote.[39]

Sometime in 1995, Republican leaders apparently concluded that winning the public relations battle over affirmative action was hopeless, and they stopped talking about the issue. In 1996, Dole selected as his running mate Jack Kemp, an outspoken supporter of racial preferences who promised that he would use his influence in the party to make sure it focused on taxes and economic issues "rather than on reducing immigration by one-third or stopping affirmative action," which according to him would involve dividing people by race and sex.[40]

The issue after that point was mostly forgotten. Continuing a long-term trend of ideological sorting between the parties, meaning that more specific positions come to be clearly associated with one side of the aisle or another, the administration of Bush the younger was more conservative on civil rights issues than that of his father. Yet this was not saying much, and the administration was still to the left of the average American voter, being unwilling to even go as far as supporting policies that had been enacted through ballot initiatives in states like California.

When the Supreme Court was considering *Gratz* and *Grutter* in 2003, Bush gave a statement opposing the affirmative action programs at the University of Michigan then under consideration while stopping short of saying that all racial preferences were unconstitutional.[41] And unlike under Reagan, there was no real attempt to roll back civil rights excesses through the executive branch, although decades of conservative appointments to the judiciary did continue to have an impact on the law under the younger Bush.[42]

As it had with the doctrine of disparate impact in the 1980s, the Supreme Court in 1999 started pushing back on the expansive interpretations of the Americans with Disabilities Act. In *Sutton v. United Air Lines, Inc.* (1999), the Supreme Court allowed courts and employers to consider mitigating measures to determine whether an individual is disabled, and *Toyota Motor Manufacturing, Kentucky, Inc. v. Williams*

(2002) narrowed the concept of "disability" to mean something that hinders the ability of an individual to carry out daily tasks, not something that simply prevented one from doing a specific job. In response, Congress passed and President Bush signed the ADA Amendments Act of 2008, which set a broad standard for what counts as a disability and prohibits considering mitigating measures. Hence alcoholism is now clearly a disability under the ADA, even if an individual could at any moment decide to stop drinking.

The ADA Amendments Act passed through a voice vote in the Senate and an initial vote of 402–17 in the House.[43] Incredibly, one of the changes of the law was to strike from the record a congressional finding used to justify the ADA saying that 43 million Americans had some form of disability. This was used by the Supreme Court in *Sutton* to find some limit to the number of Americans who could be covered. In that particular case, it meant excluding those with poor vision, of which there were nearly four times that number.

Having the ADA cover only one-sixth of the American population was apparently too restrictive for President Bush, Congress, and disability activists. The divergence here between the Court and politicians, including Republican politicians, can likely be explained by the fact that while civil rights law as applied to race and gender had become polarizing by the late Bush administration, disability law was still approached in the same way civil rights more generally were under Nixon. The Supreme Court actually listened to the arguments of disability activists and rejected them once it understood how radical they were, while politicians outsourced their thinking to those claiming to speak for what was perceived to be a sympathetic minority, even if the law Congress passed made them into an official majority. The ADA Amendments Act would be the last major civil rights law that was debated and ultimately enacted by a near consensus in Washington without major opposition from any sector of the American political elite.

Conservative Neglect, 2010 to the Present

While the Reagan administration represents a clear break from the bipartisan consensus that came before it, it's less clear where to draw the line between the second and third eras of conservatism and civil rights law. I choose 2010 because it was the year that the Tea Party movement achieved electoral victories, with ideologically committed conservatives knocking off a series of establishment figures in primary elections and Republicans performing well in the midterms. Mitt Romney had been a moderate for most of his career, but would have to grovel before conservatives in order to secure the Republican nomination for president in 2012. The conservative takeover of the Republican Party had been ongoing since Goldwater's nomination, but by 2010, with the end of the Bush presidency and the electoral loss of John McCain, we can say that the process had become mostly complete.

This means more polarization on civil rights law, which has simply been a part of greater polarization more generally and a likely contributor to it. An analysis of congressional voting patterns shows steady polarization in both houses of Congress from the 1960s to the late 1970s, before it took off and increased at a more or less consistent rate up to the present day.[44] While in the past there was some overlap in voting behavior between the most liberal Republicans and the most conservative Democrats, since around 2010 there has been practically none.[45] Increasing polarization does not necessarily mean that Republicans are getting more conservative and Democrats more liberal, only that the two parties vote more differently on the laws that Congress actually considers. Thus while both parties are more in favor of gay marriage than they were in the late 1990s, such a fact would be unlikely to be reflected in the data. Nonetheless, the most casual review of the programs and initiatives supported by Nixon and Ford, when compared to most of the policies favored by Republicans since 2010, confirms that the data gathered by political scientists on congressional voting reflects trends that are consistent with what is happening on the right and left more generally.

One explanation of conservative neglect of civil rights issues in this era is the fact that the US has been experiencing increasing education polarization over the last few decades.[46] Republicans are the less educated party, particularly underrepresented in policymaking circles and among elite college graduates. While there is a conservative intellectual elite, the movement as a general matter finds it less natural to connect its concerns to public policy. There are simply fewer activists, journalists, and legal scholars on the right than on the left, with the views and attitudes of American conservatism being in large part driven by the news cycle, purely partisan concerns, and the idiosyncrasies of political leaders and entertainers.[47] The conservative legal movement, well represented in the judiciary and the executive branch, has often seen the problems with civil rights law, but it has gotten little help in this area from state legislators and members of Congress, who are more reflective of the Republican base.

From the 1960s on, conservative intellectuals and pundits were always vociferous critics of affirmative action, race-conscious electoral laws that tried to maximize minority voting power, sexual harassment law, and disparate impact. Judges appointed by Republicans, many of them coming out of the conservative intellectual tradition, were willing to push back on the excesses of civil rights law as early as the 1980s. Yet until the last decade and a half, principled conservatives were only one faction within the Republican Party. Bipartisan majorities were responsible for the major post-1964 legislative expansions of civil rights law: the Equal Employment Opportunity Act of 1972, the Civil Rights Attorney's Fees Award Act of 1976, the Civil Rights Restoration Act of 1987, the Americans with Disabilities Act of 1990, and the Civil Rights Act of 1991. Aside from the ADA Amendments Act of 2008, however, there has been no new important civil rights legislation passed since 1991, not because the left is satisfied with how far we've progressed as a country but because Republicans will no longer cooperate on these issues.

Writing in 2018, R. Shep Melnick lists twenty-eight times Congress has expanded civil rights law since 1964, and six cases in which Congress overturned a conservative Supreme Court decision in this area.[48] The last of the latter category was the Lilly Ledbetter Fair Pay Act of 2009, which extended the statute of limitations under Title VII. It was an almost completely party-line vote, with all fifty-eight Democratic senators (with one not voting) and all but eight Democratic House members (three not voting) supporting the bill.

Republicans opposed it by margins of 3–172 (three not voting) in the

House and 3–36 in the Senate. Thus by 2009 liberals were able to get only a very small expansion of civil rights law, and even that needed to be in the aftermath of a large election victory and without being able to count on Republican support. Figure 6.1 shows how Republicans in each body of Congress have voted on eight major pieces of civil rights legislation since 1972 that involved modifications to the Civil Rights Act of 1964 in a liberal direction by expanding its reach, changing the definition of "discrimination," lowering the burden of proof for showing discrimination, extending a statute of limitations, or awarding attorney's fees to successful litigants.

Figure 6.1

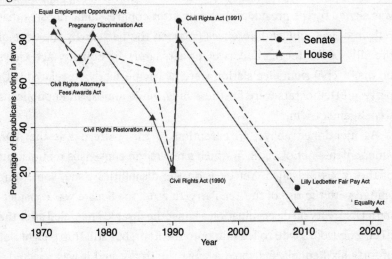

Percentage of Republicans in each house of Congress voting for eight civil rights bills considered since 1972. Excludes those who did not vote in calculating percentages. The Civil Rights Restoration Act votes refer to the votes to override Reagan's veto, not those taken on the original bill. All bills in the chart passed, except for the Civil Rights Act of 1990, which was vetoed by President George H. W. Bush, and the Equality Act, which was never brought to a vote in the Senate. Each proposed bill included provisions making civil rights laws stronger or more expansive. In general, major civil rights bills have become less ambitious and less common as Republicans have turned against them.

We see the three eras discussed in this chapter reflected in the graph above. During the Bipartisan Cartel era, that is, before Reagan came into office, congressional Republicans overwhelmingly supported the Equal Employment Opportunity Act of 1972, the Civil Rights Attorney's Fees Awards Act of 1976, and the Pregnancy Discrimination Act of 1978. Vote tallics on the next three bills reflect the fact that Republicans were divided on civil rights legislation over the next few decades. The Civil Rights Restoration Act was supported by a majority of Republican senators and a minority of House members, which was enough to overcome President Reagan's veto. By 1990, there was a major split between the parties, as most Republicans voted against the Civil Rights Act of that year, which President Bush vetoed. The version of the bill voted on in 1991 passed with overwhelming support and was signed by the president, but only after congressional debates that reflected deep policy differences between the parties. By the time of the Lilly Ledbetter Act and, twelve years later, the Equality Act, views on major civil rights legislation were nearly perfectly correlated with party: all Democrats were for these bills, while almost all Republicans were against them.

As mentioned above, an exception to this pattern was the ADA Amendments Act of 2008, in which a bipartisan consensus reminiscent of the 1970s prevailed. Yet even on the disabilities issue, something shifted with the rise of the Tea Party. In 2012, the Senate was considering a UN treaty on discrimination against the disabled modeled after the ADA. Bob Dole's wife rolled him onto the floor, but still thirty-eight out of forty-six Republicans voted against the treaty, and it was rejected.[49] Given Sen. Dole's role in passing the ADA, the Republican rejection of this UN treaty in his presence was highly symbolic of how much had changed.

In 2017, Republicans in the House, with support from a handful of Democrats, voted to pass the ADA Education and Reform Act, aimed at stopping frivolous lawsuits and reducing business costs. In retrospect, it looks as if the ADA Amendments Act of 2008 was the end of the bipartisan consensus in favor of stronger federal laws to protect the disabled, meaning that the issue today is almost as politically divisive as new proposed laws relating to race and sex. The rise of polarization in the area of disability law came decades after polarization on other civil rights issues, but the direction of the move in each case has been similar.

The failure of congressional Democrats to make discrimination against LGBT Americans illegal under federal law also reflects the new reality, and although the 2020 ruling in *Bostock* gave them much of what they wanted, they have been unable to go any further. In February 2021, the Democratic-controlled House passed the Equality Act, which would have explicitly made gender identity and sexual orientation protected classes, but it did so with a small majority that included only three Republican votes, and the bill has gone nowhere in the Senate.[50] With high levels of polarization, getting major legislation on social issues through has become extremely difficult. The continuing existence of the filibuster in the Senate, even though it is not a constitutional requirement, makes passing two houses of Congress and obtaining a presidential signature that much more daunting.

Looking only at the percentage who vote for the conservative position on various bills underestimates the shift away from the bipartisan consensus model of civil rights lawmaking, as it fails to show all the laws that never come to a vote. And there is yet another sign of how much things have changed. The Trump administration's Title IX policies undid regulations of a previous president, breaking the cycle of the last several decades in which Democratic administrations expanded social engineering through OCR and Republicans maintained the novel policy. This holds only until the next time a Democrat comes into office and starts the process all over again.[51]

How Republican attitudes have changed on voting rights roughly tracks their evolution on civil rights more generally. The original Voting Rights Act was passed in 1965, and subsequent amendments were adopted in 1970, 1975, 1982, 1992, and 2006. All became law with overwhelming majorities. As with the Civil Rights Act of 1964, the first Voting Rights Act was intended to respond to the racial caste system in the South; but the legislation quickly became an open-ended license for government social engineering. Republican acquiescence on the issue was not simply a matter of the party having moderate and liberal members—many conservatives have believed, with apparent good reason, that packing blacks into their own districts maximizes not only minority representation in Congress but also Republican representation.[52] In *Shelby County v. Holder* (2013), the Supreme Court did away with the requirement that certain states and localities gain permission from the federal government before implementing any changes to their voting laws or practices. This decision was met with outrage by the civil rights establishment, and in a previous era, it might have inspired new legislation, just as *Wards Cove* and other rulings led to the Civil Rights Act of 1991. After *Shelby County*, Democrats began to push for new voting rights legislation, but their efforts have gone nowhere, as there is no longer a Republican constituency in Congress for overturning conservative Supreme Court decisions.

Trump's victory in the 2016 Republican primaries and his subsequent election to the White House were seen by many as a refutation of a previous generation of conservatives and their ideas. Yet while Trump the candidate talked like a moderate by, for example, expressing openness to taxing the rich, he for the most part outsourced his legislative agenda to Republicans in Congress, and chose his judges and cabinet officials based on who was acceptable to the conservative establishment. When Republicans had unified control of government in Trump's first two years, their major legislative accomplishment was a tax cut that disproportionately benefited the wealthy, and they also sought significant cuts to Medicare and Medicaid in the process of trying to repeal Obamacare.

Trump, like other Republicans since the 1960s, was elected largely because people vote on cultural issues, not economics.[53] Nonetheless, at the national level Republicans have proved better at accomplishing foreign policy and economic policy goals than they have at doing anything regarding civil rights law. Perhaps the main reason is that courts have assumed an unusually large role on social issues, as has the federal bureaucracy. Still, decades of Republican power, and the conservative influence within the GOP, have meant that the judiciary in particular has moved to the right. This gives conservatives more of a chance to have an influence on cultural and social issues.

Despite only serving one term, President Trump was able to put three new justices on the Supreme Court. Senate Republicans serving during his administration, though lacking much of a legislative agenda, worked hard on pushing judges through the Senate. Trump appointed fifty-four appellate court judges in four years, just one shy of how many Obama was able to appoint through his eight.

The history discussed above shows that on civil rights issues both sides have gone to their respective corners. Republicans have not gone back to supporting the Equal Rights Amendment, and Democrats at the national level show practically unanimous support for even the kinds of racial preferences that were once controversial on the left. Moreover, the days when Republicans would join with Democrats in Congress to overrule a Supreme Court decision that upset the civil rights establishment are long gone.

Yet although the Republican Party has been taken over by conservatives, civil rights law has not been rolled back, in part because the issues involved have lacked salience. And while partisan polarization now prevents Republicans from working with Democrats to expand civil rights law, education polarization ensures that they find it difficult to move policy in their preferred direction. This is why the era is called Conservative Neglect; because moderates and liberals have left the Republican Party, it now generally ignores civil rights law except to fight a rearguard action against its expansion. Measures, laws, and court decisions that were controversial when new have become part of the legal, cultural, and social fabric. When an issue related to civil rights becomes politically relevant, Republicans can be expected to rally behind the conservative position, with recent controversies over the UN disability treaty, the Voting Rights Act, and the Equality Act being examples of this. When the Supreme Court or Democrats in Congress confront Republicans with a new issue, they resist going along due to the conservative view that government should not be doing all that much to fight racism, sexism, or homophobia. This is justified by the beliefs, generally sensible, that these things aren't major problems in American society; that government would not be well equipped to fix them if they were anyway; and that protecting individual rights and encouraging economic efficiency are more important than attempting to achieve equality between groups.

Acting on his own instincts and encouraged by conservatives within his administration and right-wing media, Trump took the conservative position on major civil rights issues that came to his attention. The administration rolled back anti-discrimination protections for gay and transgender individuals in the army, health care, and education when they conflicted with principles like religious freedom and federalism.[54] It also eliminated Obama-era Title IX regulations, including the requirement that universities lower the burden of proof for disciplining men accused of sexual assault.[55]

In the summer of 2020, President Trump happened to be watching Fox News when Tucker Carlson was interviewing Chris Rufo, who had done some reporting on critical race theory trainings within the federal government. The guest called on President Trump to issue an executive order to "stamp out this destructive, divisive, pseudoscientific ideology at its root."[56] A few weeks later, he did just that. On January 5, 2021, The *Washington Post* reported that the Justice Department was thinking about no longer considering disparate impact as a form of discrimination under Title VI of the Civil Rights Act. The paper noted that the administration had been considering the move for two years, and described the initiative as "a last-ditch effort to accomplish a longtime goal of conservative legal activists."[57]

The change would have been limited to the Justice Department but could have had ripple effects throughout the government. Already in 2018, the administration had revoked Obama-era guidance under which the Department of Education would investigate schools that disciplined minorities at higher rates than whites, even without discriminatory intent. The events of January 6 put an end to the possibility of anything being done on disparate impact—even if that policy shift in such a short period of time had been plausible in the first place—but the fact that the effort was even made shows how far Republicans had come since Nixon was pioneering new forms of affirmative action.

The Time for Action

The history sketched above helps show why the time is right for conservatives to act on rolling back the excesses of civil rights law. The political and policy benefits of doing so that existed in the past are still there, while modern developments only add to the case for action. Mass opinion is overwhelmingly against racial quotas, disparate impact, and the results-oriented approach to seeking group equality that has been the hallmark of civil rights law for half a century now. While the public has moved left on other issues, here the conservative position remains the majority one, as can be seen in recent polling and ballot initiatives.

Now, in addition to having public opinion on their side, conservatives have three new reasons to act that are the result of relatively recent changes in the political environment. The first involves already mentioned shifts within the Republican Party. The moderates who thwarted Ronald Reagan's effort to repeal affirmative action and who made sure that the Civil Rights Act of 1991 passed with large bipartisan majorities are no longer there. The rise of populism means that, at least on the issues involved here, there is a growing faction within the Republican Party that is aligned with libertarianism rather than hostile to it. When a party is internally divided on an issue, decisive action can be impossible. Republicans after taking the House in 1994 found that abolishing affirmative action split their own caucus while uniting Democrats, tilting the playing field in favor of the latter despite there being majority support for the conservative position in the country as a whole. A unified right is very important here because of the tendency of the left to misrepresent their own positions in order to make them more palatable to the public. When they get help in such efforts from prominent Republicans, what starts as a political advantage for the right can quickly become a liability. Fortunately, there are few Republicans left willing to side with Democrats on these issues.

Second, Republicans have not only become more conservative and less subject to left-wing pressure campaigns, but they and their base are more obsessed with wokeness than at any point in the past. The idea that conservatives prioritize "owning the libs" over all else has become a running joke among liberals and other critics of the right, including those within the movement. "Cancel culture" was a theme of the 2020 Republican National Convention and has been at the center of more than one annual CPAC. Trump's appeal can be explained in this way—he was far from the most conservative presidential candidate in the 2016 primaries, but he inspired the most hatred from the other side. To many Americans motivated by anger and bitterness toward an elite culture that they believe has gone insane, that was enough.

Yet while conservatives know that they hate wokeness, they have had a difficult time knowing what to do about it. Trying to fight the phenomenon can feel like flailing at the wind, as it seems to be a force that is both omnipresent and unstoppable. Especially since 2016, it would be easier to make a list of prominent institutions that have not gone woke than it would be to count all those that have. Conservatives have united around the idea that something has gone terribly wrong, and the emotional reaction that is the backlash to wokeness has helped solidify a sense of tribalism and an accompanying hatred of an enemy that are conducive to taking real political action.

Finally, not only are Republican officeholders more likely to be committed conservatives than they were in decades past, but the political pressures operating on them are different. In a 2001 essay, John Skrentny found that, when he asked Republican congressional staff and think tank operatives why the party did not end affirmative action, the first thing they usually mentioned was fear that they would be called racist as their views were criticized and misrepresented in the media.[58] In the last two decades, however, conservatives have grown increasingly immune to such concerns, as can be seen perhaps most notably in the rise of Trump and in the kinds of culture war legislation being adopted at the state level. Fox News, along with the growing importance of the internet and social networking sites, has helped create a conservative media ecosystem that has gained influence over Republican policymakers, drowning out traditional media and left-leaning civil rights organizations.

Looking back at the 1970s and 1980s, it is striking the degree to which these activists were able to frame the issues under debate. The Reagan administration took positions on civil rights law that would have sounded reasonable to most Americans if they could have gotten an accurate picture of what those positions were. Color-blindness, and requiring direct evidence of intent to infer discrimination rather than simply relying on statistical differences in outcomes between groups, in and of themselves made sense. Yet in an era before cable news, talk radio, and the internet, debates about civil rights law were filtered down to the public in the form of "liberals are more anti-racist than conservatives." Today, hyperpolarization, and the existence of media outlets that reflect different prejudices and worldviews, can sometimes lead to socially undesirable outcomes, as in recent years when large numbers of Americans who got their news from right-wing sources came to doubt the effectiveness of Covid-19 vaccines.

Yet the hyperpolarization of media and society can also allow for a fairer debate than in the past, particularly on issues where left-wing biases are particularly extreme. In few areas is the mainstream press less trustworthy than on issues of identity, as can be seen in recent years in various supposed hate crimes that journalists have championed being exposed as hoaxes, and the narratives about police shootings that they credulously reported on that turned out to unravel over the course of time.[59] On the question of civil rights law, if there is anything resembling a fair debate, conservatives can win. The way that the left understands identity issues—namely their acceptance of a results-based approach to justice and theories such as institutional racism—is simply unpalatable to most Americans. It may be unacceptable to any people anywhere, as it is so illogical and full of contradictions that the whole system may require constant lying in order to survive. Hence the battle over teaching critical race theory, in which conservatives have been winning a series of political and legal victories ever since Chris Rufo brought the issue to the attention of the public.

Our current high level of polarization means that it is easier than it used to be for parties to get things done even when those things are unpopular. It is interesting that the last three presidents have all seen less variation in their approval ratings than any other president since the beginning of modern polling.[60] Despite all the ups and downs of the Trump presidency, the public did not shift much in its appraisal of the job he was doing, with his approval rating staying in the low to mid-40 percent range across his entire time in office, except for a dip to 34 percent after the events of January 6, averaging 41 percent.

Contrast this with the record of George H. W. Bush, whose approval rating ranged from 29 percent to 82 percent, averaging 61 percent. Trump's signing of an unpopular tax bill as his major legislative achievement, the perceived failures of the coronavirus pandemic, and two impeachment proceedings, one while he was in office and the other on the horizon as he was leaving, did little to change his approval rating over time.

While with all else being equal it is still better for politicians to do things that are popular, less variability in how the public sees its leaders means that unpopular policies won't necessarily sink their political fortunes and popular ones are no guarantee of victory. This gives more room for ideology to play a role in governance—something that is particularly true at local levels. In many states, one party is all but guaranteed to rule indefinitely into the future, which means that Republican leaders in Alabama and Democratic leaders in California can both be more extreme than their constituents. Although rolling back civil rights law would likely be popular, even if it wasn't it would still be easier to do today than it was in the past.

CHAPTER 7

What Is to Be Done?

The idea that society needs to be permanently managed for the sake of making the sexes interchangeable and doing away with unintentional biases—even when they are based on statistical truths—appeals to very few people. Moreover, despite the fact that the civil rights regime has developed to encompass practically all of work life, the First Amendment still protects the speech rights of individuals when they are not on the job, and there are only a limited number of trial lawyers and civil rights bureaucrats in the country. This is why wokeness and the assumptions that underlie it can still be criticized, at least by those of us not under the jurisdiction of an HR office, and businesses and other private institutions can for the most part still function without becoming completely absorbed by issues of race and gender in the way universities have.

For these reasons, wokeness is likely easier undone than would appear at first glance, despite its having seemingly influenced almost every prominent institution in the country. We live under a political duopoly, with one of the two major parties strongly united in opposition to wokeness as both a cultural and political phenomenon. Once individuals are convinced that things can change, and that change can come through the political process, the question becomes, what exactly is to be done? That is the focus of this chapter.

Thankfully, there is low-hanging fruit in the policy space—actions that can be taken through the executive branch or judiciary that are likely to be either actively supported by or ignored by the public, meaning they present few political risks. Amending Executive Order 11246 can be done on the first day of a Republican administration. Abolishing disparate impact as a standard for determining whether an action is discriminatory under Title VI can similarly be done through the executive branch, and the same is likely true to a limited extent for Title VII.

The Supreme Court can throw out disparate impact as a violation of the Equal Protection Clause the moment it gets the right case. Even when it was more liberal, the Court had already shown skepticism toward the doctrine, and now it is simply a matter of litigants being strategic in getting the matter before the judiciary. Harassment law likewise rests on shaky constitutional grounds. The regulation of sex and sports under Title IX resembles disparate impact in that it is the result of bureaucratic and judicial innovations that have little resemblance to the original intent of the statute it relies on. Once again, the legal arguments here are straightforward enough, and do not require new legislation.

These should be the most immediate priorities of an anti-woke political movement. Beyond that, one can discuss more ambitious proposals to take on wokeness that involve passing legislation, or more than simply getting the government off the backs of individuals and private institutions. It is worth considering such proposals, their potential unintended consequences, and what they can and cannot do. Before thinking about any actions one can take to combat wokeness, however, it is worth thinking more about the issue of political salience as a determining factor in what kinds of policies are enacted and the kinds of court cases that are decided.

Political Salience

In mid-2020, a tweet went viral claiming that in most states police could legally have sex with or rape someone in their custody if the officer claimed the act was consensual.[1] This was a highly misleading claim, in that rape is illegal under all circumstances, and the words of a police officer are not required to be taken as gospel in any legal system. The part of the statement that was true, however, was also a sort of half-truth. It was correct that in many states there was no law specifically prohibiting sex between a police officer and an individual in their custody. But the tweet gave the impression that legislators had considered the question and in a majority of states decided that they saw nothing wrong with the practice. In fact, federal law as of mid-2020 did ban sex between officials and inmates in prisons and immigration detention facilities. However, Congress had neglected to also criminalize sex between officers and arrestees who have not been convicted of a crime, a loophole that most states had not bothered to close.

There are likely few or no legislators in the country who believe that such conduct should be legal. Yet because the issue had never been salient, government had not acted. This story teaches us something important about policymaking. There can be a practice that 100 percent of people think should be banned, but it can remain legal if no one thinks about the issue or brings it to the attention of the public.

In a typical year, Congress enacts hundreds of pieces of legislation, and the president signs dozens of executive orders.[2] In the judicial branch, the Supreme Court uses its discretion to hear fewer than 150 cases of the over 7,000 petitions for a writ of certiorari.[3] State governments, regulatory agencies, and lower federal courts likewise selectively use their authority to change policy in areas where they believe it is appropriate to do so. Government officials have a great deal of discretion over what to focus on, and they direct their attention to causes when they believe doing so can make the world better, or when they feel political pressure to act. The job of a political entrepreneur is to raise the profile of his own issue and convince government officials that his particular concern is worthy of consideration on at least one of those grounds.

As mentioned in the previous chapter, highlighting a cause can backfire if it leads to the issue becoming partisan. Yet drawing attention to a cause may be the only way of provoking action in the judicial and executive branches. Ideally, a political entrepreneur wants his issue to be high in salience but low in polarization. High in salience and high in polarization is a second-best option, while if no one cares about an issue at all, nothing will happen. Table 2 summarizes the idea.

Table 2. Political change as a product of salience and polarization

	Polarization Low	Polarization High
Salience Low	Nothing happens, maintenance of status quo (2)	Nothing happens, maintenance of status quo (currently wokeness as law) (1)
Salience High	Legislation, executive branch actions, and judicial decisions all possible (3)	Executive branch actions and judicial decisions possible, legislation very difficult, great deal of public rancor about an issue (currently wokeness as culture) (4)

Right now, wokeness as a cultural phenomenon is in the bottom-right quadrant (4). It dominates our political discourse, but government officials do not spend their time changing the culture, or at least not directly. Wokeness as law—for example, affirmative action in government contracting and the disparate impact doctrine—is in quadrant (1). Government officials do not act, often because they never feel the pressure to do so. A goal of this book is to move "wokeness as law" from (1) to (4), therefore at least making executive branch actions and judicial decisions possible.

Ideally, wokeness as law would be in (3), though this may not be achievable. Even if mass opinion opposes affirmative action and color-conscious policy, what matters most is elite opinion, and the nature of political polarization is such that public opinion among liberals could move to the left once conservatives make wokeness as law more salient in public life, as happened when Trump ran for president and made opposition to immigration a centerpiece of his campaign.

One argument of this book is that wokeness as law can relatively easily be moved from (1) to (4), which might be enough to bring about significant change, since major innovations in civil rights law have mostly come from the executive and judicial branches, where they can also be undone. Nonetheless, the idea of passing federal legislation should not be completely dismissed, although the path to doing so is more difficult and uncertain.

Chris Caldwell writes that over the last several decades, "Republicans, loyal to the pre-1964 constitution, could not acknowledge (or even see) that the only way back to the free country of their ideals was through the repeal of the civil rights laws."[4] Yet this is not exactly right, at least if by "laws" he means "legislation." It is true that criticizing the Civil Rights Act, as it was passed in 1964, remains unthinkable for nearly all Republicans. Yet every extension of the nondiscrimination principle beyond color-blindness—affirmative action, the threat to free speech that comes from regulations against sexual harassment, the soft quotas that are the natural consequences of the disparate impact doctrine, and so on—has been fiercely criticized by at least some conservative thinkers and Republican politicians for over half a century now. While there once were Republican politicians who refused to oppose, or who even supported, these doctrines, ideological sorting across parties has meant that there are now fewer of them.

Civil rights law has not been rolled back by Republicans in power mainly because the issues involved have stayed below the radar. The doctrine of disparate impact, which fundamentally changed the country, was created by the EEOC and accepted by the Supreme Court. The process that produced it was even more obscure than normal agency action, which is subject to the Administrative Procedure Act. That law requires that regulations be subject to a public comment period and makes them appealable to a court.[5] Under federal law, the EEOC does not make rules, it provides "guidance," which in theory gives it less power but in reality provides more ability to innovate without any oversight.

OCR in the Department of Education has the ability to make rules under Title IX but generally does not do so, and has pushed forward new innovations through Dear Colleague letters that make major policy changes under the guise of issuing clarifications of long-accepted standards. Affirmative action for federal contractors has its roots in an executive order that is nearly half a century old, and the text of the document gives no hint as to what it requires. As with the Civil Rights Act and Title IX, the details were to be worked out in federal agencies and the courts.

If affirmative action for government contractors and the doctrine of disparate impact were invented today, Republicans would be united in opposition, and while public opinion would be polarized, it would likely tilt to the conservative side, leading Democrats to be tepid in their support for these policies and others like them. But because the main developments in civil rights law preceded our current era of extreme ideological sorting by party, they today are mainly ignored. New liberal initiatives that extend the logic of civil rights law are strongly opposed by conservatives, who are able to put the brakes on such policies, either through legislators or the courts. Two recent examples are the teaching of critical race theory, which has been banned in several states, and a policy of earmarking grants for black farmers under the Biden administration, which has been criticized by Republicans in Congress and as of this writing remains in a "legal quagmire" as it faces difficulties in court.[6]

A referendum is the ultimate act of making a political issue salient. When affirmative action is put on the ballot, it almost always loses, regardless of the political leanings of a state. Legislative votes are less salient than referendums but more so than agency actions, and here the civil rights lobby has had much less success, with few major victories at the federal level in over thirty years. Yet within the DOJ, the EEOC, and the OFCCP, professional activists and those with the most expansive definition of discrimination have largely been able to do as they please. Ultimately, federal bureaucracies get their funding from Congress and derive their authority from legislation. When they surpass that authority, Congress must be willing to use the power of the purse and presidents to undertake executive action to rein them in.

The focus on "woke capital" as a cause rather than the symptom of what has gone wrong in our culture reveals a lack of knowledge about the extent to which government has been an active player in shaping informal rules and norms. There is widespread understanding on the political right that old approaches to fighting the left have failed. The crucial step for taking political action involves presenting specifics about exactly what the reaction to wokeness should look like.

The concept of political salience has a different meaning for judges than it does for elected officials. As Steven Teles writes in his history of the conservative legal movement, for a judge to reach a decision re quires an intellectual foundation grounded in previous decisions, ideas being debated and shared within elite law schools, and lawyers and advocates strategically bringing sympathetic cases and framing them in ways in which they can make the most impact.[7] Liberals had these necessary prerequisites for impactful litigation decades before conservatives did. While the left still outnumbers the right in number of committed lawyers, nonprofits, and activists on its side, conservatives have built enough of a critical mass to be effective and are now well represented in the judiciary, with Republican presidents having appointed most federal judges as of 2022. Where the conservative legal movement focuses its energy helps determine which cases conservative judges will ultimately rule on. Thus affirmative action in college admissions has been a target of conservative activists for generations, and the Supreme Court now hears a case on the topic a few times a decade.

Yet disparate impact under Title VII and affirmative action in government contracting rarely make it to the Supreme Court, as the higher education sector is more likely than private business to inspire activism on behalf of individuals of all political backgrounds. Highlighting wokeness as law in different areas of public life—from university classrooms and academic journals to social media and talk radio—creates a self-reinforcing cycle through which conservatives can take advantage of public opinion being on their side to effect political change, whether through the presidency, regulatory agencies, legislation, or the courts. This chapter presents what should be the main aspects of an antiwokeness political program, as summarized in Table 3.

Start with the Low-Hanging Fruit

Legally and institutionally, the most important low-hanging fruit available for pushing back against wokeness as law would include repealing or amending Executive Order 11246, abolishing the disparate impact doctrine in Title VI and Title VII, and reworking the rules on Title IX through OCR in the Department of Education. There's a clear path to doing each of these things through either the executive branch or the judiciary, where conservatives have some representation and control.

Table 3. An anti-wokeness agenda

Low-Hanging Fruit		
(Little liberal buy-in required)	Executive Branch	Amend EO 11246 and 11478, ban affirmative action instead of requiring it in government hiring and contracting; change regulations requiring goals, timetables, and race- and sex-consciousness and preferences
		Define discrimination as intentional discrimination, not disparate impact, whenever possible
		Change rules for OCR: permanently establish intentional standard of discrimination; remove all statistical standards under Title IX; make discrimination a matter of treatment of individuals, not of systemic issues that require institutional solutions
	Judiciary	Overrule *Griggs v. Duke Power Company* (1971), on statutory or constitutional grounds
		Restrict reach of harassment law based on the First Amendment
		Declare affirmative action and set-asides illegal under Title VI and Equal Protection Clause (*Students for Fair Admissions v. Harvard* likely to be decided by the time this book is released)
		Declare OCR social engineering in schools and universities contrary to Title IX
		Revisit *Christiansburg Garment Co. v. EEOC* (1978), to allow defendants, not just plaintiffs, to more easily collect attorney's fees in civil rights suits
	Red states	Use power of contracting and control over pensions to ban affirmative action and race- and sex-consciousness in firms
		Call for an inventory of race- and sex-conscious programs with an eye to elimination
		Defund diversity bureaucracy within state employment, schools, and the university system; create legal causes of action to deter undesirable behavior
More difficult projects		
(Require liberal buy-in or defeat, or rely on more difficult legal arguments or executive actions)	Congressional action	Defund or take away power from OCR, OFCCP, and EEOC
		Repeal Civil Rights Act of 1991, Civil Rights Restoration Act of 1987
		Federal ban on programs that are race- and sex-conscious
		Remove punitive damages for civil rights lawsuits

Aggressive executive action	Use OCR to go after schools that engage in reverse discrimination or suppress speech	
	Use OCR, EEOC, and OFCCP to attack corporations and local governments that engage in reverse discrimination	
	Find ways to go after accreditation bodies pushing identity politics	

Sweeping judicial decisions are generally preferable as they cannot be easily rolled back by Democratic administrations, though even executive actions at the very least grant reprieves from the extremes of wokeness as law and create costs for future presidents wanting to adjust the status quo back toward unpopular policies. Regardless, executive and judicial actions are complementary, not substitutes for one another. The executive branch taking a new position on Title IX, for example, might lead to lawsuits and bring the issues involved to the attention of the judiciary.

Executive orders are the easiest form of action a president, or perhaps any official, can take in the American system. This is why presidential and gubernatorial candidates specify which ones they will sign upon coming into office. Affirmative action is mandatory across major institutions because of Executive Order 11246 and how that document has subsequently been interpreted. It now mandates detailed record keeping on the part of employers and all but requires quotas throughout major corporations. Only a few years later, in 1969, President Nixon signed EO 11478, which required affirmative action in the federal government. A Republican president should amend both these documents to specify that nondiscrimination cannot be established based on disparate impact, and that the law does not require either identity-based record keeping or affirmative action.

Going further and instituting a ban on racial record keeping and goals and timetables would potentially be even better, as it would make life much more difficult for any institution that simply wanted to either get around presidential directives or openly bring back old policies. Ending affirmative action mandates under a revised EO 11246 would likely lead to corporations keeping their current policies so that they can be ready for the next time a Democrat comes into office and regulations inevitably go back to what they were. While freedom of association would be ideal, pressure needs to come from both sides to counter the left's deep commitment to race and sex preferences. A Supreme Court decision finding that there is no legal basis under which EO 11246 can require affirmative action from contractors would solve this "ping-pong problem" across administrations. In the meantime, conservatives need to be able to use their own leverage in response to liberal demands for race- and sex-conscious corporate governance.

The disparate impact doctrine has been applied to the federal government and institutions it funds through Title VI, and through Title VII to hiring in the private sector and state and local governments. Eliminating this standard can be done exclusively through the executive branch, with executive orders or within individual agencies. This is the step that the Trump DOJ tried to take in its last days in office. There was also consideration of getting rid of disparate impact in the Department of Education and in Housing and Urban Development.[8] While the standard was never officially revoked, the Trump administration did step back from applications it deemed dubious, ending, for example, the Obama-era policy of investigating schools with differential rates of discipline between white and black students.

Some of the excesses of Title VII can also most likely be taken care of through executive action via appointing sympathetic EEOC commissioners and executive orders. The only complication in this case is the Civil Rights Act of 1991, which specifies details regarding the burden of proof in a disparate impact claim. However, it does not explicitly mandate that standard in the first place, and the reason that the statute is vague is because its authors themselves were divided and decided to cede the issue to the courts.[9] In contrast, the framers of the Civil Rights Act of 1964 were unanimous in rejecting disparate impact and wrote their objections into the bill. Thus it is reasonable to believe that the explicit rejection of disparate impact in 1964, reflected both in the legislative history and in provisions that have never been repealed, trumps the indirect approval of the standard in 1991. The executive branch should, in interpreting Title VII, rely on the intent of the Congress that passed the Civil Rights Act.

Either way, relatively new developments in Supreme Court jurisprudence point to the conclusion that disparate impact violates the Constitution. It has become well-established law that all racial classifications used by the government to treat citizens differently can only be constitutional if they pass a test of strict scrutiny, which means that they must be narrowly tailored to achieve a compelling government interest.[10] Importantly, this includes racial classifications meant to help non-whites, which is why affirmative action cases involving public universities are judged under that same standard. Yet this leads to some ludicrous conclusions under disparate impact doctrine. Let us say that an employer wants to use a test of cognitive ability to hire employees, and that the employer assumes that, as with all cognitive tests, it should be expected to reveal a performance gap between whites and blacks. Using that test is, since *Griggs*, the textbook case of the kind of action that can lead to a disparate impact lawsuit. But not using the test, because whites will do too well on it, should in theory run into its own problem under Title VII. In fact, here the discrimination is not even unintentional, as in a disparate impact case, but intentionally meant to exclude a certain group.

As made clear in Scalia's concurrence in *Ricci v. DeStefano* (2009), disparate impact under Title VII is naturally in tension not only with the prohibition on intentional discrimination under Title VII but more fundamentally with the Equal Protection Clause. If the EEOC or some other government agency will enforce only certain kinds of disparate impact claims, that is, those targeting practices that disproportionately harm the hiring prospects of non-whites or women, and will not enforce even intentional discrimination cases when whites or men are harmed, this also violates the Fourteenth Amendment.[11] Similarly, when the OFCCP requires goals and timetables, it is forcing private firms to engage in racial discrimination, which is constitutionally prohibited. The legal arguments here are straightforward once one accepts that disparate impact and mandatory affirmative action in government contracting are policies that discriminate against whites.

The constitutional problems with disparate impact applied to Title VII do not end there. Let us say that, completely contrary to the historical record, Congress had intended for disparate impact to be the relevant standard for all laws and regulations aimed at combating discrimination—and, moreover, that this was somehow allowed under the Equal Protection Clause. Disparate impact would still be unconstitutional, because it delegates unlimited power to government agencies to regulate the behavior of employers. The Due Process Clause of the Fifth and Fourteenth Amendments has been used to invalidate statutes in both criminal and civil cases. The doctrine of disparate impact, which says that basically everything is illegal and the government will decide which violations it goes after, is unconstitutionally vague regardless of whether it has statutory authority or not. The argument that it would be a stretch to say that Congress did in fact delegate this authority to the executive branch and courts is interesting to note, but a moot point under this analysis.

Finally, it has been federal bureaucrats and the courts that have used Title IX to engage in social engineering across schools and universities. As Melnick points out, this has been through a highly unusual sequence of events, in which OCR avoids the APA rule-making process by issuing "guidance" documents, those documents are cited by the courts, and the agency in turn cites the courts for justification for what it is doing. The Trump administration withdrew the Obama-era regulations in this area, but in summer 2022 the Biden administration began the process of reinstating similar policies through notice and comment procedure.[12] This will make them more difficult to withdraw by a Republican administration, and also more difficult for courts to overturn than they otherwise would be. Nonetheless, even if an administration goes through notice and comment procedure, it cannot go beyond the plain text of a statute. Title IX says no student can be "excluded from participation in, be denied the benefits of, or be subjected to discrimination under any education program" on account of sex.

The idea that sexual harassment committed not by employees of an institution but through actions taken by other students could be a form of sex-based discrimination would have appeared odd to the Congress that passed Title IX, and would have been a radical interpretation of the statute until the 1990s. Courts are to give more deference to regulations that undergo notice and comment procedures than they are to those released through Dear Colleague letters, but that deference is far from absolute. Even as the new Biden regulations make their way through courts, the next Republican administration should similarly undo them through APA processes, at the very least giving institutions a temporary reprieve and making life more difficult for the next Democratic administration. As with the move away from affirmative action in government contracting and disparate impact, the goal should be to define discrimination in a way that limits it to direct evidence of unfair treatment of a specific individual, rather than basing the concept on statistical outcomes such as differences in test scores or sports participation.

The four fundamental pillars of wokeness as law—affirmative action, disparate impact, harassment law, and Title IX—can to a large extent be handled through the executive branch and the courts alone. A president who wanted to do so could end mandatory affirmative action in government employment and among government contractors practically overnight. This would be of no small impact; OFCCP regulations cover 25 percent of the American workforce, and another 6 percent works for the federal government.[13] Two strokes of the pen could therefore change the major regulations under which a third of American workers live. This is a great deal of power to put in the hands of one individual, and may be seen as inconsistent with the principle of separation of powers. But it is important to note that this is the way affirmative action among government contractors and in the federal bureaucracy became mandatory. Clarifications on Executive Order 11246 and Executive Order 11478 that got rid of affirmative action policies would relinquish government power that had been illegitimately taken in the first place.

The path forward on disparate impact is no less clear. There are signs that the Supreme Court is poised to act in this area. In *Alexander v. Sandoval* (2001), it punted on the question of whether Title VI allowed discrimination based on disparate impact, but sounded a skeptical note. Eight years later, *Ricci* arguably clarified that the Civil Rights Act of 1991 had written disparate impact into Title VII, while the decision only made it slightly more difficult for plaintiffs to win such cases. Justice Scalia wrote, in his concurrence, that the decision "merely postpones the evil day on which the Court will have to confront the question: Whether, or to what extent, are the disparate-impact provisions of Title VII of the Civil Rights Act of 1964 consistent with the Constitution's guarantee of equal protection?" In *Texas Department of Housing and Community Affairs v. Inclusive Communities Project, Inc.* (2015), the Supreme Court upheld disparate impact as applied to the Fair Housing Act of 1968, but only by a vote of 5–4, the slimmest of margins.[14] Justice Clarence Thomas dissented in order to "point out that the foundation on which the Court builds its latest disparate-impact regime—*Griggs v. Duke Power Co.*—is made of sand."

The swing votes over the last few decades were until recently wielded by Justices Anthony Kennedy and Sandra Day O'Connor, which helps to explain why a supposedly conservative Supreme Court did not move more aggressively on disparate impact or other areas of civil rights law. Kennedy was the author of both *Ricci* and *Texas Department of Housing*. Like O'Connor, he had a habit of denouncing the more extreme interpretations of civil rights law, clarifying, for example, that whites are just as protected as blacks, and mandating a "strict scrutiny" standard for government racial classifications. At the same time, both justices usually shied away from articulating sweeping principles that would fundamentally remake civil rights law, giving bureaucrats, trial lawyers, and other judges enough wiggle room to continue on as before. The *Ricci* decision ruled in favor of white and Hispanic firefighters who were denied promotions but left the disparate impact regime largely untouched.

O'Connor was the author of *Grutter*, which banned a strict quota or point system in college admissions but allowed the use of race as a plus factor, a distinction that, as the Rehnquist dissent pointed out, could only be maintained by burying one's head in the sand regarding how affirmative action is actually practiced. *City of Richmond v. J. A. Croson Co.* (1989) was another O'Connor decision, this one throwing out a minority set-aside program by ruling that government can only distribute resources according to race as a way to redress discrimination against a specific group that has occurred in a narrow context. The decision was practically ignored by the Bush and Clinton administrations at the federal level, but at least caused 230 state and local authorities to suspend racial set-aside programs, with only 100 of them remaining by 1995.[15]

Six years after *Croson*, O'Connor wrote the opinion in *Adarand Constructors, Inc. v. Peña* (1995), which again raised the standard for justifying minority set-asides, this time tossing out a federal program. In response, the Clinton administration announced that minority set-asides would only be allowed after a study could show credible evidence of discrimination.[16] Unsurprisingly, federal, state, and municipal authorities would go on to commission studies and reviews that told them what they wanted to hear, and contracting preferences based on race and sex continue to be a normal part of the machinery of government.

One can summarize Kennedy-O'Connor jurisprudence on civil rights issues in the following way: courts should denounce racial preferences in strong terms, and throw them out in certain cases, while clarifying that they will be allowed as long as government can do enough paperwork justifying them, in which case things can continue as before. This worldview faces the fatal flaw of placing confidence in the ability of politicians to fund and reasonably evaluate unbiased social science research on our most divisive hot-button issues. Given how poorly we've seen social science hold up even when it has been conducted far away from political pressures, this faith is completely unreasonable, and the results of cases like *Grutter* and *Adarand* were easily foreseeable.[17]

Whether by conscious intent or not—and the clarity of evidence presented in the Rehnquist dissent in *Grutter* along with other judicial opinions argue for a less charitable interpretation of motives—the Kennedy-O'Connor regime we have been living under was a political compromise that gave government officials and universities that wanted to discriminate the best of all worlds as long as they were willing to spend enough money. It let them do what they wanted, while giving the false impression that their favored programs had been scientifically established as well-tailored efforts to meet a societal need. In reality, they were a means for achieving redistribution and balancing according to racial criteria.

In 2006, O'Connor was replaced by Samuel Alito, and a little over a decade later President Trump would appoint Brett Kavanaugh to fill the seat vacated by Kennedy. Trump further moved the Court to the right by appointing Amy Coney Barrett after the death of Justice Ginsburg. The doctrine of disparate impact was hanging on by a thread before; now is the time to strike a blow against the tool that, with very little basis in democratic legitimacy and even less in the Constitution, has managed to remake American governance, politics, and culture. The political right now has a sympathetic court, and it is simply a matter of conservative lawyers and nonprofits recognizing the importance of the issue and being strategic in finding the right cases to bring before it.

The same logic holds for minority set-asides and other forms of government race-consciousness. In contrast to disparate impact, affirmative action in college admissions has been in conservatives' crosshairs for decades, and by the time this book is released, *Students for Fair Admissions v. Harvard* may have already been decided. Given how often affirmative action cases are litigated, it was always certain that the Supreme Court would have an opportunity to hear one soon after the rightward shift of the Trump years was completed. Meanwhile, disparate impact was accepted as the correct interpretation of Title VII in 1971, and in the years since, the Court has rarely revisited the fundamental constitutional and statutory soundness of that ruling. While conservatives wait for the judicial branch to act, they should use the power of the executive branch to roll back the disparate impact doctrine, although it will take the Supreme Court finally addressing it head-on to make any changes permanent.

On Title IX, the courts have done an excellent job in striking down sexual assault tribunals. They should also revisit long-held precedents about the regulation of sports, which rest not on statutory language, or even rules made by a federal agency, but unilateral statements that lack both democratic legitimacy and the legal deference accorded regulations enacted in compliance with the APA. Until we get more reasonable regulations on the Title IX issue within the executive branch, courts should revisit the First Circuit decision in *Cohen v. Brown University*, which ratified an OCR policy encouraging balance in the number of male and female students participating in sports. There was nothing in the plain language of Title IX, and no official rule adopted by OCR, that required such a result. Courts are in a position to put an end to the regulation of sports and sexuality in college life.

Limiting the power of OCR through the courts may prove difficult, as it has evolved a strategy of enforcement that relies on reaching settlements with universities and avoiding the judiciary; it should be a priority of conservatives to find creative ways to get its Title IX regulations in front of federal judges. Ironically, it may have been Trump's victory that prevented judicial review of the regulatory regime OCR has established. In 2016, the Supreme Court agreed to hear the case of *G. G. v. Gloucester County School Board,* which challenged Title IX guidance on transgender issues. Upon Trump's victory and the revocation of the policy under question, the Supreme Court remanded the case back to the Fourth Circuit.[18]

Pushing back against Title IX regulation is low-hanging fruit in the sense that the legal arguments one would rely on are within the mainstream of established jurisprudence. At the same time, finding the right case that can establish a broad principle is more difficult, though all it ultimately requires is financial and legal support for one university or school system willing to take a stand.

Harassment law is an area in which the legal arguments for pushing back against wokeness are straightforward, but an actual decision would require a somewhat radical break with precedent. Recent decades have seen the Court move toward a more absolutist interpretation of the First Amendment on issues as diverse as hate speech, campaign finance laws, and pornography. Yet anti-harassment law remains siloed from this legal development. It is far from obvious why this should be the case. Courts should rely on the arguments put forward by Eugene Volokh and others to at the very least acknowledge the trade-off between the First Amendment and the current state of civil rights law. The ultimate aim should of course be to make regulating speech in the workplace just as difficult and constitutionally problematic as doing so anywhere else.

Finally, Section 1981 could potentially be a problem and pick up the slack in any rollback of Title VII. Right now, the effect of the law is limited. As recently as 2020, in *Comcast Corp. v. National Association of*

African American–Owned Media, the Supreme Court unanimously affirmed that the Reconstruction-era statute requires but-for causation to make a claim, unlike Title VII, which only requires the plaintiff to show that discrimination is a "motivating factor" in any prohibited behavior. The relevant difference between "but-for causation" and "motivating factor" analysis is one of those distinctions that is good enough for lawyers but could easily be picked apart by an amateur logician. The important thing to understand is that but-for causation is treated as a higher standard. In addition, Section 1981 requires intentional discrimination and only applies to race, thus making it less relevant than Title VII to the way most institutions operate.

Still, one wonders whether liberals in the judiciary have allowed Section 1981 to remain relatively weak simply because they already have an expansive Title VII; if the latter had never been passed, one can imagine them having been much more creative in interpreting its predecessor from nearly a century before. Once Title VII is limited to its proper role, it will be important to remain vigilant against judges inclined to find new meanings and applications in Section 1981 cases. To further constrain the reach of the law would be an even better option. The Supreme Court did not even recognize a private right to action under Section 1981 until 1975, a fact that the *Comcast* opinion seemed to attribute to the overzealousness of a previous era.[19]

During my first summer in law school, I worked as an intern for the Center for Individual Rights, a conservative nonprofit that had been involved in *Gratz* and *Grutter*.[20] This gave me a background in civil rights law and affirmative action issues. As part of my job, I would sometimes search for initiatives and programs at universities that likely violated the law. Even when it has upheld affirmative action, one thing that the Supreme Court has made clear is that quotas are an unacceptable form of racial discrimination outlawed by the Equal Protection Clause. I remember once finding a scholarship that a university made available to non-white students only, which struck me as more extreme than a quota and the kind of thing that would get thrown out in court. An attorney was supervising my work, and when I went to him with what I thought was new and interesting information, he made clear that such programs were normal. We were a small office with fewer than ten employees, even if one counted the second intern and me. I left the meeting with the impression that universities and businesses were doing things all the time that would be ruled illegal if they came to the attention of the Supreme Court. But lawsuits are long and expensive, and conservatives doing nonprofit work are heavily outnumbered by liberals. Lawyers are more likely to be liberal than conservative, and the ratio is particularly lopsided at the top firms and in the nonprofit world.[21]

It is not enough to bring the effects of civil rights law to the attention of the president and members of his cabinet and encourage them to make changing them a priority. One also has to let idealistic individuals in favor of progress and liberty and opposed to wokeness know that there is a practical way to fight back. Civil rights law, like other legal areas, is something of a battle of attrition between bureaucrats and lawyers. Progress depends not only on getting judges and bureaucrats to see things in the way one prefers, but also on galvanizing enough members of what is sometimes called "the managerial class" within and outside of government to build upon legal victories and blunt the impact of defeats. Wokeness has no problem attracting opposition among the young and idealistic. This can be seen in the proliferation of authors at Substack who have been hounded out of major publications due to violations of PC orthodoxy, and in the success of outlets like *Quillette*. If popular energy surrounding the anti-wokeness cause can combine with the legal knowledge, infrastructure, and mass appeal of the conservative movement, it may be a formidable enough alliance to break the excesses of civil rights law.

Going on the Offensive

Once we get past the low-hanging fruit—that is, important policy changes that can be taken care of through the courts or the executive branch without liberal buy-in or support—other questions regarding what to do about wokeness present themselves. This section considers four issues: what to do about reverse discrimination, the prospects for federal legislation, what can be done at the state level, and the need to draw lines in the sand regarding further expansions of civil rights law.

Reverse Discrimination

Even if civil rights law helped create wokeness, that does not mean that removing its legal underpinnings would immediately change the culture. Many major corporations seem committed to the principles of "diversity" and "inclusion," euphemisms for affirmative action, even beyond what the law would require, and the universities are even more extreme in this regard. What attitude should opponents of wokeness have toward such programs? It can be argued that any anti-discrimination law in the private sector interferes with freedom of association and hinders social evolution and market efficiency. Thus anti-white and anti-male discrimination should be tolerated in the name of these values and goals, for the same reasons other forms of discrimination should be.

Indeed, as argued in previous chapters, markets can solve the most egregious forms of discrimination. Even if they do not, a free country as a general principle believes in freedom of association even if people make unfair or bad decisions in their personal lives, as long as they are willing to suffer the consequences of their actions—in this case, lost profits and financial opportunities that result from discrimination. As the legal scholar Richard Epstein has pointed out, the classic justification for government abridging freedom of association or freedom of contract is to account for negative externalities—that is, costs imposed on third parties. But when someone engages in an act of private discrimination, they suffer the costs of doing so themselves.[22] While third parties might suffer due to their distaste for discrimination, if we are going to take taste-based preferences into account, there is no principled way for society to decide to prefer some people's desire for integration or a society that doesn't discriminate over those with the opposite preferences making decisions about their own private lives.

There is thus a philosophically elegant, perhaps irrefutable, libertarian case for getting rid of all anti-discrimination laws. Perhaps its logic might break down in a society with strong social taboos against mixing between groups, as in the Jim Crow South and caste-based India. Yet in modern America, discrimination is culturally taboo, and those who want to favor whites or men while doing business are likely to face huge costs in terms of public relations and consumer sentiment, plus the aforementioned costs resulting from the discrimination itself.

That being said, no matter how strong the philosophical or practical case is for doing away with anti-discrimination laws in the private sector, political reality means that they are here to stay. Legislation requires broader consensus than judicial decisions or executive actions, and liberals are unlikely to agree to get rid of anti-discrimination laws anytime soon. Even most Republicans would likely be uncomfortable taking such a step. Because of the status quo bias inherent in a system that makes it difficult to pass legislation and the popularity of anti-discrimination laws—that is, as written and debated in 1964, not what came later—any realistic proposal for action has to begin with accepting that they are not going anywhere. The rise of environmental, social, and governance (ESG) investing, in which Wall Street firms acting as corporate shareholders push for diversity in hiring and promotions as well as other left-wing causes, represents an acute threat to American ideals based in the private sector, and may make a purely libertarian approach to fighting wokeness unrealistic.

What, then, should the conservative or libertarian position be with regard to anti-white and anti-male discrimination? As mentioned above, civil rights laws as written are generally blind to race and sex. This is something that tended to be ignored by the judiciary in earlier decades, but by the 1980s, there were Supreme Court decisions emphasizing the fact. Nevertheless, in most institutions today even unintentional discrimination against protected groups, defined and interpreted by judges, bureaucrats, and lawyers as disparate impact, is forbidden, while intentional discrimination against whites and men is accepted, if not mandatory.

This is the result of what I earlier called Kennedy-O'Connor jurisprudence, which involved a series of decisions that appeared to mark a right-wing shift in civil rights law but if anything may have made the left-wing position stronger. Given this reality, it would be a mistake to ignore anti-white and anti-male discrimination in the private sector; as long as anti-discrimination laws exist at all, institutions need to feel pressure from both sides in order to achieve some kind of balance. Taking a different approach would cause employers and institutions to continue to bend over backward to favor protected groups, even if one could argue that reducing enforcement across the board could at least lower the overall burden of civil rights law in terms of hindering economic efficiency and restricting freedom.

Given this reality, the best option is to call for a return to the original meaning of the Civil Rights Act of 1964, which would involve government simultaneously taking a harder line against anti-white (and in some cases anti-Asian) and anti-male discrimination, while narrowing the definition of discrimination as applied to women and minorities. Current practice is so far removed from the law as written and originally interpreted that such a suggestion may seem like a radical innovation. But this is clearly the direction to move in, as it is consistent both with sound legal reasoning and public opinion.

There does not need to be a trade-off here. In April 2021, the Project on Fair Representation wrote a letter to Coca-Cola warning that quotas it had set for outside counsel were illegal.[23] Corporations have felt free to undertake such initiatives. Moreover, they have likely thought that, even if they invite anti-white or anti-male discrimination lawsuits, the risk is worth taking. This may result from ideological preference, or because such programs provide a defense to any charge that could be made alleging discriminating against groups that civil rights activists and lawyers care more about defending. It is important to change that calculation. While conservatives and libertarians can debate the wisdom of anti-discrimination laws, as long as they are on the books, they have to be applied equally across different demographics.

One likely cannot expect the EEOC or state civil rights offices to be willing to treat all kinds of discrimination equally. The Supreme Court has made it clear that whites and men are protected by the Civil Rights Act and the Equal Protection Clause. But, as Gail Heriot writes, "to my knowledge, the EEOC has never brought a disparate impact investigation or lawsuit on behalf of white males. Nor has the Supreme Court entertained a disparate impact case on behalf of anyone other than women and racial and national origin minorities."[24] This is unsurprising, given that the EEOC was the organization that pioneered disparate impact and made it part of American law, with the explicit goal of being able to do more to root out discrimination against non-whites and women. Yet different standards of justice were not what the framers of the Civil Rights Act intended, and the Supreme Court has made clear that if they had, such a system would be unacceptable.

This means that it is likely impossible to turn the EEOC into a force that fairly and prudently applies the law as written. The fact that it focuses so much on disparate impact indicates how little evidence there is for blatant discrimination within American society. If racism—as the concept was understood in the 1960s—was a major force in the US today, then an agency with around two thousand employees would have its hands full stamping out intentional discrimination and not have the time or energy to create and enforce new standards that contradict statutory language. Each bureaucracy attracts certain kinds of employees based on the issues it champions and its reputation. Given the central role that the EEOC has played in creating the system we live under, it is no surprise that it is staffed mainly by ideologues committed to a far-left-wing understanding of race and gender issues. Those who disagree with them should seek to restrict the power and funding of that organization to the greatest extent possible, with complete abolition being the ultimate goal.

The same goes for the Office of Federal Contract Compliance Programs, which should have much less to do once the executive order mandating affirmative action for government contractors is repealed or modified. The organization can either continue to exist as a body that simply receives complaints alleging intentional discrimination, or it can be abolished and replaced with a new organization that takes a similarly passive role. The Reagan administration cut staff at both the EEOC and the OFCCP and in practical terms gave them less to do.[25] This is the correct model for future Republican administrations to follow, although they should also seek more lasting changes that will reduce the power of these agencies in the long run.

The EEOC and the OFCCP are the most important institutions in the executive branch to reform or abolish, but they are far from the only ones that should be forced to move away from quotas, affirmative action, and race- and gender-consciousness. Top officials at the White House and the Department of Justice should promulgate guidance and directives that make sure that all government activity is consistent with the original intent of the Civil Rights Act as clarified by new executive orders. In 2021 the SEC approved new diversity requirements for corporate boards listed on Nasdaq's US exchange. This attracted relatively little attention, despite the fact that all federal agencies are officially required to practice nondiscrimination. This decision and others like it should be undone.

The federal government can also go after state and local governments that engage in anti-white and anti-male discrimination. The tool to leverage in this case is Title VI, which bans discrimination among state and local entities that receive federal funding. The website of the California secretary of state, for example, informs the public that all corporations with executive offices located in the state must meet certain board quotas for women and minorities.[26] Title VI was originally written to help undo state-sponsored discrimination in the South. Unfortunately, it has itself morphed into a tool of social engineering. That being said, Title VI does provide the methods through which to undo some of the harm it has previously caused.

The Role of Congress

Legislation is generally more transformative and long-lasting than actions taken by the executive branch. It is also much harder to enact, especially with regard to hot-button issues and in an era of mass polarization. While the Civil Rights Act of 1964 and other pieces of legislation set most of the groundwork for wokeness as law, it has been the executive and judiciary from which the most damaging innovations in this area have sprung, and one of the main arguments in this chapter is that they can be undone through the same channels. Nonetheless, if wokeness is as harmful as this book argues, it is at least worth considering whether and to what extent there can be congressional fixes. Legislative initiatives, even ones that do not ultimately pass, are another useful tool.

Congress could, in theory, abolish disparate impact and EEOC, set reasonable standards for Title IX, and limit the breadth and reach of harassment law. As it is unlikely to do any of these things, individual members can at the very least raise awareness of the issues involved and demand information that can expose and make clear the extent of civil rights abuses. Sen. Bob Dole was able to commission a report from the Congressional Research Service in 1995 on federal programs that used racial or ethnic standards, of which it turned out there were 160 at the time.[27] Nearly three decades later, it would be interesting to find out what that number is now. Gail Heriot likewise calls for a "disparate impact inventory" that would uncover all places in the federal government where that standard is used to infer discrimination.[28] Finding and publicizing such information can have two effects. It both provides a list of programs that can be discontinued—either through legislation or executive order, the latter perhaps coming in the aftermath of a favorable Supreme Court decision—and helps create the political conditions under which such action can be taken.

Ambitious federal legislation such as eliminating all racial and gender preferences would have no hope of passing, given the continuing existence of the filibuster and the current state of the Democratic Party, and trends in polarization indicate that this will be the case for the foreseeable future. Moreover, the president signing such a bill would simply accomplish much of what can be done through what this chapter earlier referred to as low-hanging fruit actions, those taken through the judicial and executive branches. Yet while a legislative effort to ban race and gender preferences would be close to impossible and perhaps unnecessary, Republicans may decide that conducting regular votes on the topic would be to their political advantage. Whether it is at any particular point in time will likely depend on the political context. Republicans may want to direct the attention of the public to issues on which they have an advantage during the administration of an unpopular Republican president, but not when the flailing incumbent is a Democrat. At the very least, drawing attention to wokeness as law would send a message that would reach conservative judges, bureaucrats, state legislators, lawyers, and funders of political causes, even if it is ignored by or even inspires a bit of a backlash among others.

Instead of more sweeping bills, a Republican-controlled Congress could nibble around the edges of civil rights law, passing legislation that attracts little public attention but may have major effects on the incentive structures faced by bureaucrats, lawyers, and potential plaintiffs and defendants in court cases. Topics like federal jurisdiction, whether a plaintiff can get attorney's fees and how much, and the burden of proof in different kinds of actions arouse little in the way of mass sentiment; nevertheless, as seen in the rise of certain kinds of lawsuits in the aftermath of the CRA of 1991, they can have a profound impact on how the law is practiced and its societal effects. Sean Farhang has written about how liberals in Congress have managed to outsource much of the enforcement of civil rights law to the courts, which was a deliberate strategy to create a perpetual administrative regime immune to challenges from future Republican presidential administrations that might seek to scale it back.[29] The two lessons from his work are that executive actions to roll back civil rights law are not enough, and that conservative lawmakers and judges should follow liberals in always being on the lookout for ways to weaken this system. Moreover, if there are measures to enforce an anti-wokeness policy agenda through the courts, they should be pursued. The 2021 Florida bill creating a cause of action against schools that teach critical race theory is a good example of this.[30] It even includes attorney's fees for parents who successfully file suits, mimicking federal civil rights law.

State Governments

This book has for the most part ignored state law, which in any case tends to be less important than federal regulations. But to the extent that an argument can be made for effective policy change by state governments, it would look very similar to federal efforts. As implied above, creating legal causes of action to go after wokeness as law, as Governor Ron DeSantis did in Florida, can be done at either the state or the federal level. The fact that some states tend to be under unified Republican control most of the time creates more room for action, and it is worth exploring how far things can be pushed.

When possible, states should enact the kind of sweeping legislation that would be nice to have but is likely impossible at the federal level. To repeat, this means banning racial and gender criteria in government hiring and programs and, when that is not feasible, making data available that can shine a light on unpopular practices. Unlike the federal government, a state exercises direct control over its higher education system, and there is little reason not to go to war with the diversity bureaucracy, with the ultimate aim of getting universities out of the business of social engineering or taking a side in the culture war.

State control over contracting and pensions is another form of leverage. Republicans in recent years have with some success used this leverage to go after ESG investment firms that have expressed an intent to divest from fossil fuels or gun manufacturing.[31] In the field of contracting, states can use legislation or executive orders to require color- and gender-blindness among those receiving government funds, in effect doing the opposite of what the federal government has done through the OFCCP.[32] Businesses may have to decide whether they want to comply with federal or state programs, which can lead to lawsuits that challenge the regulations promulgated under EO 11246. Government contracting is unique in the extent to which it gives the state leverage over corporate actors. The OFCCP and its regulations have become so influential not because EO 11246 had a strong constitutional or statutory basis—in fact, the opposite is true—but because it was in this area that liberals working in Washington could most easily assert their power. The same may be true for those who exercise power in state capitals.

Lines in the Sand

Those opposed to wokeness should also take a close look at age and disability discrimination. Both have led to absurdities, though perhaps not yet at the level of policy related to race and gender. The ban on age discrimination in particular is a major hindrance to reasonable initiatives related to everything from public safety to scientific innovation. Fitness standards for police officers and firefighters are normed based on age just as they are based on sex. More importantly, the threat of lawsuits for mistreating older employees is likely a major barrier to progress in industries that require a great deal of physical energy or high levels of cognitive capability. This can be seen in the fact that tech companies have been targeted in age discrimination lawsuits, sometimes explicitly for acting on the belief that younger workers might be more innovative and productive.[33] Meanwhile, the Americans with Disabilities Act has made everyone a potential victim, and has imposed massive burdens on businesses, communities, and individuals without any consideration of costs and benefits. Civil rights law as applied to disability does not particularly rely on bureaucratic and judicial innovation. As such, what can be done here might be limited. Still, the generalized case against anti-discrimination laws—that they infringe on liberty and are bad for technological and social progress—should be kept in mind when deciding how to define disability and what counts as discrimination in this area.

With the exception of demanding consistency in the government opposing discrimination against all citizens on account of race and sex, conservatives must draw a line in the sand on any and all further expansions of civil rights law, including expanding the definition of discrimination and creating new protected categories. Twenty-one House Republicans were co-sponsors of a bill that would write gender identity into civil rights law. Under pressure from journalist Nate Hochman, writing for *National Review*, several dropped their names from it in late 2021.[34] Given the way that many of the key clauses of the Civil Rights Act have been twisted to mean the exact opposite of what they originally meant, and the creativity with which the trans movement has sought to manipulate language and thought, it does not take much imagination to see the threat to liberty that such a bill becoming law would present.

In March 2022, the House of Representatives passed, with bipartisan support, the Creating a Respectful and Open World for Natural Hair (CROWN) Act, which, bans "discrimination based on natural and protective hairstyles that people of African descent are commonly adorned with" under civil rights law.[35] While I certainly have no desire to see individuals discriminated against for their natural hairstyle, it is not the place of the federal government to dictate standards of grooming, aesthetics, and style in private institutions, even if one may reasonably take a different position when it comes to government institutions themselves.

In addition to preventing liberals from allowing the anti-discrimination principle to begin covering hair or any aspect of grooming, conservatives should fight any attempt to expand the old category of "official minorities." The Obama administration was considering adding Middle Easterners as a racial classification, an effort that was quashed under Trump but has been revived under Biden. Under the current system, every creation of a new "minority"—whether through further splicing the races or a conceptional innovation like "hair discrimination"—is a threat to the principles of merit, freedom, and limited government. In the area of civil rights law, this is one of the clearest lessons we have from the last six decades.

Getting Water from the Ocean

Asking what should be done to fight wokeness while in power is somewhat like asking where to get water from the ocean. Opportunities abound. The only question is the best ways to move forward. The two concepts of affirmative action and disparate impact are the key innovations that have helped deform government policy and ultimately American culture. A line can be drawn from the simple directive that employers can't discriminate, to the EEOC coming up with disparate impact, to ultimately the elimination of merit-based hiring and the regulation of humor and romance in the workplace. Every link in the causal chain can be conclusively established. Ideology and the official justifications for current practices eventually caught up with law in the forms of cancel culture and claims of systemic racism infecting all American institutions. Seeking to modify affirmative action executive orders and adopting the plain meaning of discrimination that Congress voted for in 1964 are clear first steps that any administration or legal movement opposed to wokeness should take.

This should not be the end of the battle but the beginning. Conser-

vatives in government must be constantly on the lookout for wokeness in government policy. Republicans have made it unthinkable for
the United States to have a federal government that promotes abortion
rights or gun control. This is because members of the party have certain
convictions on these issues, as do many of their voters, who will hold
them accountable if they simply go along to get along whenever liberals
want to use the federal government to push their own values. In 1976,
Congress passed the Hyde Amendment, which banned federal funding
for abortion. It has with certain modifications been renewed every year
since.[36]

If such an act were proposed for the first time today, there is no way
it would become law as long as Republicans did not have unified government control, and perhaps not even then. Yet not only do Republicans
help ensure that the Hyde Amendment keeps getting renewed, but they
also bring their pro-life convictions with them to the negotiating table
when they debate Democrats on bills related to economic stimulus and
health care.[37] Conservative politicians similarly don't just support gun
rights; they remain ever vigilant, perhaps even paranoid, regarding potential threats to the Second Amendment. There needs to be a similar
attitude toward civil rights law, with all attempts at dividing citizens
based on race, sex, or other identity-based criteria seen as contrary to
American values. Just as in other areas, it is worth purging from the
party Republicans who deviate from this consensus.

The right hates wokeness, but its failures have resulted from seeing
the phenomenon as simply a cultural trend or class marker rather than
as a left-wing mode of bureaucratic governance. Changing this perspective requires leadership from intellectual entrepreneurs, which in many
cases involves recovering the memories of past battles that were hard-
fought at the time but are practically forgotten today. We are now at
a point where wokeness, aided and supported by judicial and bureaucratic interpretations of the law and the industries that they have created, has become increasingly radicalized and inspired a backlash. Over
the last decade, this backlash has lacked a coherent theory about how
we got here. The legal developments that undergird the whole system
are in many cases nearly half a century old, and so interwoven within the

fabric of government and corporate life that even many critics of wokeness have at most only a faint understanding of their existence.

When the resistance to wokeness has stepped into the policy arena, it has focused on a few narrow topics, such as the doctrine of critical race theory, which had become the basis of education curricula and corporate and government training programs. Such efforts are to be applauded, but they do not yet get at the root of the problem. Many of the things conservatives and moderates fight are just surface-level phenomena—manifestations of what are deeper assumptions and requirements that are not only built into institutions but required to be there by law. Much like critical race theory, civil rights doctrines that were developed in the late 1960s and early 1970s serve to divide Americans into oppressor and oppressed classes, apply different standards to each, and infer discrimination from statistical patterns. The main difference is that critical race theory self-consciously does away with much of the hypocrisy that was inherent in pushing both color-blindness and a disparate impact definition of discrimination while paying lip service to the ideals that motivated the passage of the Civil Rights Act in the first place.

The fight against wokeness will require a pragmatic acknowledgment that it is going to have to be Republicans who, in the short run at least, fight the battle. Understanding and being explicit about this fact may mean alienating some natural allies, but it is a necessary concession to reality. Public opinion surveys show that woke ideas now have widespread support on the political left, particularly among whites, women, and the highly educated, demographics that have disproportionate influence within the Democratic Party. Liberal elites and the institutions they run have developed a strong attachment to the equity agenda, which is why Democratic politicians tend to overreach in this area. All of this may change over time, as Republicans create political costs for the left by highlighting, and bringing to the attention of the public, race- and gender-related issues on which conservatives have an advantage. Moderates and open-minded liberals, too, continue to make the case for individual liberty to their own side. For now, however, it will have to be conservatives who take the political initiative.

It is important to realize that there is no free marketplace of ideas as long as civil rights law remains what it is. Institutions are only allowed to have certain official positions about the causes of group disparities and are forced to be race- and sex-conscious as they suppress speech and micromanage social relations. I have argued that an anti-wokeness agenda would be politically popular. Even if it wasn't, however, the battle would still be worth fighting, as freedom of speech and freedom of conscience are necessary to protect other values. And as long as we have "civil rights" as currently defined, all other rights are either in abeyance or at the very least in a much weaker state than they should be.

Unleashing American Freedom and Creativity

Societies differ greatly in their attitudes toward issues surrounding work, sex, religion, and interpersonal norms. As a general matter, such differences do not create major problems for those in other communities. Individuals have major differences in taste, and such preferences, like all cognitive and personality traits, are shaped by genetic differences within the population. We would all be better off accepting these differences at the individual, local, and institutional levels. While this might mean that certain individuals, localities, and institutions make decisions that others find unappealing, the only alternative is an endless culture war that neither side can ever win. Unless there is some way to truly accept pluralism and cultural diversity, the nature of the disagreements that have caused educated Americans to split up into two great mutually hostile tribes will permanently consume our politics.

Civil rights law is an extreme form of central planning in an area of life where centralization of power can do some of the least good and some of its worst damage. What was originally sold as a law needed to reform the social system of one part of the country to deal with one major issue—that is, the status of black people in the South—became an open-ended commitment to ending "discrimination" in all its forms, with no natural limits placed on what kind of behavior is covered or even which dimensions of equality we should care about and which groups are protected. The civil rights revolution is now deeply embedded in American law. Because of its vagueness and the soft nature of its standards and requirements, it has created its own internal bureaucracies within major institutions. Enforcement depends only partly on government, being otherwise outsourced to the court system and private parties, who have access to grievance mechanisms both within and outside their own institutions. This makes it reasonable to wonder whether a book like this one, focusing mostly on legal doctrine and developments, provides a plan that is adequate to address the challenge, or whether there is too much inertia in the system.

This conclusion has two purposes. First, it is to show that wokeness is not as strong as it looks. Analogies to religious faith—which carry with them the implicit argument that the phenomenon may last for thousands of years—rest on a weak foundation. Previous chapters have made this argument partly by showing the intellectual shoddiness of woke doctrine and the historically contingent nature of its triumphs. Nonetheless, even religions that owe their start to state power and without much internal logic to them can last a very long time, which is why we may wonder whether wokeness is here to stay. I argue that it is not.

The second purpose is to provide a vision of what a post-wokeness world might look like. This book has by necessity been a work of description and negation, focusing on where wokeness comes from, why it is so harmful, and how to dismantle it. I trust the reader brings his own philosophical inclinations to a work like this, and may see wokeness as a hindrance to other societal goals, whether freedom, economic growth, progress, or social stability. Therefore, this chapter tries to paint a picture of what victory over wokeness would look like and how it would foster them. That picture is by necessity speculative as is any work of fiction, but it can at least give a hint as to what is worth fighting for.

Is Wokeness Inevitable, or a Paper Tiger?

Some have argued that to see wokeness as a phenomenon that can be defeated in the short or medium term is unrealistic. They compare it to religious faith, which, unlike a political view, is usually seen as much deeper and more powerful.[1] I'd argue that the definition of religion has two key pieces, and both are necessary to consider. Religions are of course distinguished by a metaphysical belief system that inspires individual passion. But another important aspect of religions, and the one that many of those who make the comparison to wokeness ignore, is that they are distinguished from other belief systems by their proven ability to survive across generations under a wide variety of conditions.

Christianity, Judaism, Islam, Hinduism, and the rest of the world religions are, to use the phrase popularized by Nassim Nicholas Taleb, Lindy, meaning that because they have been around for a long time we can expect them to be around in the future.[2] They have survived through historical eras in which they have been supported by the state, oppressed by it, or treated with indifference. As they have remained strong after an endless number of trials, we can conclude that something very deep in human nature causes many to find each of the major world religions appealing.

Compare this to modern ideologies. Nazism and communism have survived as major forces in the world as long as there have been Nazi and communist governments. Government officials who believed in Jewish conspiracies and the importance of race science under Hitler, or who at least said they did, became democrats after the Second World War. According to a report commissioned by the government, as of 1957, 77 percent of senior officials in the West German Justice Ministry were former Nazi Party members.[3] The Soviet government wasn't conquered by a foreign army but stopped believing in communism in the late 1980s and then disbanded, while in China the state remains communist in name only. The CCP deals with protests for democracy in Hong Kong by closing some publications and arresting a few individuals, while to root out conservative Islam in Xinjiang it has to operate on a more industrialized scale.

Baathism emerged in the Arab world as a modernizing faith that opposed sectarianism and Muslim extremism. It took power in two Middle Eastern countries but now exists only as a zombie doctrine in one of them, while Islam remains both a political force and a fundamental guide determining how hundreds of millions live across the Arab world.

Nationalism is something in between a religion and a twentieth-century ideology. Its rise has historically been tied to the modern state, which usually finds it useful. But sometimes nationalism emerges in opposition to existing power, as happened near the end of the Austro-Hungarian, Ottoman, and Soviet empires. At the same time, people can assimilate into a new country pretty quickly and forget their old attachments. Populations changing their national loyalties is more common than the adoption of new religious faiths; it has been noted that when Russia moved into eastern Ukraine in early 2022 it found much less support among the local population than it had only eight years before.

The key thing to realize about wokeness in this context is that it has never faced a real stress test. Its fundamental tenets have been law in the United States for over half a century. Practically every major nonreligious institution in the country is forced to be conscious of race and sex, censor the speech of its employees in the name of sensitivity, act as if disparate outcomes are a sign of discrimination, and employ an internal bureaucracy to enforce these rules. Wokeness thus has no history of surviving without state support. In fact, even with state support, and with practically unlimited rhetorical backing from elite institutions, it still struggles to win hearts and minds. Wokeness remains mostly a political loser for the left, which is why it obfuscates on issues like critical race theory and the fact that civil rights law in its current form all but requires speech restrictions and racial quotas. Wokeness does not appear to be able to motivate its adherents to make the extreme kinds of sacrifices that are the hallmarks of true religious faith. It can't even convince liberals to keep their kids in inner-city public schools.

Wokeness may end up not as a religion but something analogous to liberal democracy.[4] That is, an ideology that contains a blueprint for the organization of political life and is taken for granted by much of the world. There is a possibility that in future generations color-blindness or not changing an institution to accommodate the feelings of hypersensitive employees and government neutrality in matters of culture will be seen as outdated—like the divine right of kings. People will think that of course society cannot tolerate massive differences in outcomes between groups, and that it is the job of governments to do something about them. While free speech was fine in the past, protecting certain classes from indignity, particularly women as they become better represented in influential institutions, will be seen as requiring compromise on that principle. Alternatively, people might come to no such conclusions, but the laws of political gravity might be such that interest groups organized around gender, race, and sexuality naturally constitute themselves in developed states and begin pushing for greater representation, which governments have a natural tendency to give in to as this development has downstream cultural effects.

Tyler Cowen believes that the world is getting more "woke" and that this is a good thing, but he takes the term to mean something akin to tolerance in the classic liberal sense. In that formulation, 1950s America would be considered more woke than the antebellum South, and Saudi Arabia became more woke when it began to let women drive in recent years.[5] By this standard, there appears to be a greater shift to what we can call more left-wing attitudes on race and sexuality relative to the historical norm.[6] But if wokeness is defined as an obsession with racial and gender disparities, the restriction of speech to overcome them, and government programs and private- and public-sector bureaucracies meant to undo them, then there is not yet much evidence that wokeness can be a major force in society without government backing.

France provides a counterexample to the American model of the management of race and gender issues. Its laws generally ban the state from collecting data on the race, religion, and ethnicity of individuals.[7] This means that, much to the chagrin of some American liberals, France cannot have disparate impact standards, state-enforced affirmative action, or even programs targeted at a group with a particular ancestry. It is perhaps not a coincidence that in a country that bans the kind of data collection necessary to enforce woke policies, we see much more resistance to wokeness as a cultural force among the political elite. In late 2020, the French education minister warned that "there's a battle to wage against an intellectual matrix from American universities."[8]

President Emmanuel Macron has spoken in similar terms, and he is something of a moderate on cultural issues. Suppose his nation is unable to hold wokeness at bay. In that case, this will provide evidence either that developed societies naturally drift toward wokeness or, alternatively, that American elite culture is so strong that it can overcome resistance even on the most difficult terrain. It must be said, of course, that in some ways wokeness in France appears stronger than in the US, mainly due to the existence of hate speech laws. Yet one of the main arguments of this book is that while Americans may have more freedoms than those in other countries in theory, in reality their speech and behavior are regulated to an unusual degree.

As pointed out in chapter 3, the US resembles the French state in not collecting religious data, and we are not nearly as woke on religion as we are on matters of race and sex, giving little thought to economic or arrest disparities between those of differing faiths. We do not care about achievement gaps between various "white" or "Latino" subgroups, once again because we do not have the numbers necessary to even begin to care. This argues that the degree of wokeness in a country and what form it takes are contingent on whether and how certain kinds of data is collected.

Outside of the West, the case for a universal move toward wokeness seems even weaker. Part of the reason it is difficult to draw conclusions about such things is that countries do not make up an independent set of observations, since ideas travel across borders and the US has such a globally powerful cultural influence. Thus if we see homosexuality becoming more acceptable in most or all countries, is this a natural consequence of modernity, or just a sign that Hollywood and the State Department are everywhere? Nonetheless, there is evidence of growing right-wing cultural populism across most of the major countries of the world over the last decade, including Brazil, China, India, Russia, and Turkey. Even though in most states there does tend to be a move toward greater liberalization on matters related to sexuality, the vast majority of the nations of the world are still far from an American-style war on sex stereotypes and the public celebration of new sexual orientations.[9]

That said, it is still possible that once you undo the excesses of civil rights law, wokeness will remain as strong as ever and eventually show itself to be just as capable as major world religions of long-term viability and the intergenerational transfer of belief. There are few reasons to think this will be true so far, but regardless, the possibility cannot be dismissed with certainty. No matter what they think about the arguments presented here, the path for opponents of wokeness is still clear. They need to run the experiment of eliminating disparate impact, affirmative action, and similar policies, and find out what happens.

Imagining a Non-Woke America, and World

Wokeness as a cultural phenomenon seems permanent because it is all-encompassing. A single intense news cycle can be disorienting and make people question whether things will ever go back to normal. Wokeness can be understood as a series of recurring moral panics backed up by state power. Their cumulative effect can make them seem a natural part of our social world. That effect is even stronger when the moral panics represent an entire worldview that permeates everything from entertainment reporting to how children are taught math and science. I want to end this book by providing an outline of what a move away from wokeness would look like, and how its triumph can come to be seen as less natural and inevitable over time.

Charting the path forward can provide hope to critics of the phenomenon and political activists who want to believe that their work can make a difference. It can also serve to create a guide to what incremental developments will look like throughout the process. There will be no V-day celebrating the end of wokeness; rather, its defeat, like its victory, will have involved a series of steps in the same direction, each seemingly small in its own right but ultimately contributing to a social revolution.

In the approach to fighting wokeness argued for in this book, politics comes first. A Republican president at some point comes into office, and his administration goes to war with disparate impact, affirmative action, and the current interpretation of Title IX, starting with executive orders. Not only that, but Republican appointees in various agencies start to be on the lookout for race- and gender-conscious programs, which they will no longer see as mere annoyances or policies they disagree with but as part of a larger structure that in the aggregate has contributed to the destruction of what they hold dear. While judges are in theory apolitical, no reasonable person doubts that they are influenced by the same intellectual trends as the rest of us, which means that conservative jurists will likewise take a harder line toward policies that many of them already oppose.

The backlash will be limited for the same reason that the creation of woke policies drew so little attention in the first place. Concepts like whether anti-discrimination laws authorize class action lawsuits, who is entitled to attorney's fees, the existence of punitive damages, and whether corporations must engage in extensive record keeping have never inspired much passion among the general public or even drawn its attention. This demonstrates that there is not always a strong correlation between how much energy surrounds a public policy debate and how important it ends up being. Just as how civil rights law, in terms of reach and scope, expanded in executive agencies and the courts without much public pressure, it can contract in the same way. Of course, the analogy is not perfect. When civil rights law expanded, it did so with the support of a well-organized lobby, a bipartisan consensus in Washington, and the sympathy of the media. This may make rolling it back more difficult, but in a world where conservatives recognize the importance of the issues involved, they will form their own lobbies that seek to influence the government and help level the playing field. Greater polarization in the media and the general public relative to decades past ensures that the backlash to any changes to civil rights law is muted.

Changes made through the courts will be permanent, for all practical purposes, while those that stem from executive orders or agency decisions will always be under threat as soon as a Democrat comes into office. Some of them certainly will be overturned, which means that in civil rights law, like much else, policy shifts in predictable ways depending on who is in power. At the same time, raising the profile of racial debates in which Republicans have an advantage will result in Democratic presidents thinking twice about taking bold action in the face of hostile public opinion. Courts find it easier to overturn new actions than to invalidate established programs and procedures, and the public is more likely to draw its attention to departures from current policies than to continuations of them. This means that supporters and opponents of Title IX as social engineering, affirmative action, and the disparate impact standard face special obstacles when they try to change the status quo. Conservatives at least have public opinion on their side, and—given the clear legislative history of the Civil Rights Act and the absurd degree of executive branch overreach on issues such as Title IX—they also have the correct legal arguments and, more importantly, a majority of the Supreme Court.

As they focus on the excesses of civil rights law, conservatives not only scale it back when needed, but they will lean in to fight explicit discrimination against whites, men, Asians, and whoever else may find themselves on the wrong side of government preferences. They begin to sue to stop explicit and thinly veiled discrimination against what are now referred to as "unprotected groups." The Supreme Court has for decades explicitly rejected the idea that anti-white discrimination is more legally acceptable than anti-minority discrimination. It starts paying attention to whether lower courts have actually followed this principle, and more lawyers and plaintiffs are willing to file lawsuits to give it practical effect. Not only is this the legally correct position, but it prevents an outcome in which, having rolled back affirmative action and disparate impact, Republicans find that institutions nevertheless continue to operate as before. The law can change, and the threat of costly lawsuits may still come only from one side. If anti-discrimination laws are not going to be repealed, then a world where everyone is protected is necessary to prevent institutions from becoming woke to protect themselves.

Getting conservatives to focus on civil rights law also has an effect at the state level, which forms another source of pressure pushing back on woke institutions. Republicans outside of Washington begin to notice more local instances of racial preferences in contracting, college admissions, and other areas of government work. They begin rolling back such policies. Leverage is used not only to stop woke policies but to mandate race- and color-blindness as a precondition for having government business.

While running for president in 2016, Jeb Bush bragged to Republicans that he ended affirmative action by executive order in Florida.[10] This had little effect on primary voters, who had forgotten about what used to be a hot-button issue in the decade and a half since he accomplished this policy objective. Now, with the conservative movement focusing on civil rights law as the ultimate source of wokeness, ambitious politicians compete to get ahead on relevant issues in order to portray themselves as true champions of the anti-woke cause. Eventually, it becomes as unthinkable for a red state to support race or sex preferences through taxpayer money as it would be to fund abortion.

The movement does not simply depend on politicians taking certain actions because it is the right thing to do. Conservatives form activist organizations focused on civil rights law that are analogous to the National Rifle Association, the National Right to Life Committee, and Club for Growth. Such lobbying groups ensure uniformity within the party, even in cases where taking the conservative position might potentially cost a politician support with the wider public. Elected officials are rated and judged according to how strongly they stand for an anti-woke agenda, and positions advocated for by the anti-woke lobby become standard for Republican politicians. Once in office, they work to satisfy this lobby like any other, seeking policy victories they can promote and appointing their people to government positions. Of course, the anti-woke lobby will not be called the anti-woke lobby any more than the pro-woke lobby clearly articulates its implicit vision. Rather, groups that oppose affirmative action, disparate impact, and other harmful policies will in all earnestness continue to call themselves things like the Center for Individual Rights and the Center for Equal Opportunity, and for good reason.

After only one Republican administration, with the help of the Supreme Court, most of the high-level policy work against wokeness has already been done. Affirmative action executive orders are modified to have an effect opposite to the one they had previously, the federal government no longer adopts a disparate impact standard, the concept of a hostile work environment is all but defined out of existence, and bureaucrats begin to seek out and fight explicit anti-white and anti-male discrimination in accordance with a correct interpretation of the law.

The Supreme Court, whose current makeup represents decades of conservative electoral victories, has ruled the right way on these issues, creating synergy between the efforts of the executive and judicial branches. A new status quo has been created, and conservatives have set up the activist groups and lobbying organizations necessary to keep up the pressure and ensure no backsliding.

Government policy conscious of race and sex is not yet completely eliminated. That may or may not come with time. Yet one focused Republican administration and a united conservative movement have used their power to significantly reduce the level of government social engineering. The effects on the wider culture are not felt right away. In fact, things may temporarily go in the opposite direction, as the attack on civil rights law mobilizes the identity left and its media supporters to pressure institutions to swear fealty to the old order.

Yet this doesn't last long. Within a decade of the start of the war on wokeness, it begins to decline as a cultural force. As it turns out, moral panics only become a permanent part of life when they are backed up by state power and lead to the creation of new laws and bureaucracies. Corporations realize that although they get some temporary good press when they announce that they are sticking with their affirmative action programs, doing so puts them in jeopardy of facing lawsuits from groups discriminated against—while doing little to protect them, given that lawsuits based on disparate impact or creating a hostile work environment are becoming less common and lucrative.

The human resources industry, originally expanded to manage personnel under a regulatory system with vague mandates surrounding race and sex, begins to shrink. Likewise, with fewer regulatory requirements from OCR and more pressure coming from conservative state legislators, universities scale back their DEI bureaucracies. There is, of course, inertia, and HR does more than enforce civil rights law, so the effects of all this will not be immediate. In times of cost-cutting in state budgets and corporate austerity, however, woke commissars start to look much less necessary than they used to. The same is true within government entities, including primary and secondary schools. Since going back to the original meaning of the Civil Rights Act also means more legal skepticism toward the permissibility of intentional discrimination against whites and males, a few high-profile legal cases make affirmative action programs look riskier than before. Government scaling back the vague standards of affirmative action and disparate impact as it goes after intentional discrimination consistently reduces the need for ideologically driven HR departments and DEI staff.

After the first ten years or so, we start to see downstream cultural effects that people no longer connect to the original policy discussions surrounding civil rights law. Hiring standards start to change. There begins to be a turn toward the greater use of written tests as the doctrine of disparate impact is weakened or abolished. Corporations and institutions that embrace standardized tests in general do better than those that don't. Selection occurs both within and across firms; companies notice that departments that rely on more objective criteria are more productive, and businesses that reject testing completely lose out to those that do not. Slowly but surely, each firm, industry, and profession moves toward more efficient hiring and promotion standards.

Economic growth begins to pick up as more competent individuals are put in the most lucrative and prestigious jobs and there is better matching between individual skill sets and occupational attainment. GDP growth, which had hovered around 2 to 3 percent a year for decades, begins to tick up by a point or two, an effect that compounds and makes Americans much wealthier in the long run. Given the complexity inherent in trying to understand real-world data, analysts are unable to pinpoint exactly why, but build various theories related to directions in globalization and wise management of the economy by the Federal Reserve. Rolling back anti-discrimination law having made practically every profession and industry slightly more competent and efficient will not be considered, because the proposition is difficult to test and goes against ideological commitments that analysts still hold on to. Those who fought to change anti-discrimination laws do not receive credit for any of this; given the ideological makeup of academia, history may in fact remember them as having ushered in a new era of intolerance when faced with social progress.

Outside of the increasingly intolerant academy, however, a few moderate and conservative writers present evidence that the recent move toward meritocracy has strengthened the economy. Not that anyone much cares what professors think anyway; with incomes rising, fewer young people go to college and fewer intelligent adults seek to become academics, which, along with a cultural shift to the right, contributes to a decline in the prestige of the profession. Business leaders, who had gotten used to one status quo and learned to live with anti-discrimination law as it used to exist, now adapt to a new reality and find it much more profitable. They again become ardent defenders of the status quo, this time on the side of justice, merit, and truth.

At established institutions and businesses, people begin to laugh, socialize, speak, and date in greater freedom. Corporate cultures begin to diverge. Of course, feelings are hurt along the way. Many individuals select out of environments that accept crude jokes or aggressive flirting, while others are excited by the possibility of being in a work environment in which they can meet new and interesting people who can eventually become close friends and maybe even partners and spouses. No one can predict what the end result of this sorting will be, but a free market in labor, like a free market in anything else, reveals itself to be the only realistic way to aggregate preferences. As individuals can pick environments that suit themselves during work hours, just as they are already allowed to do in their personal lives, rates of depression and anxiety decline. Fewer people are going to psychiatrists and taking mind-altering medications, facts that in some corners of the press are discussed in the context of a rise in "untreated mental health issues." Eventually people will watch, with curiosity, TV shows and movies from the 1990s and 2000s about the soul-crushing dreariness and boredom of corporate life after it had been sanitized by HR, all the while wondering how and why Americans once made work so miserable. Workers actually liking their jobs makes them more productive, which is yet another driver of GDP growth.

After some years, the changes we first started to see in limited form accelerate and take off. If the first decade of the war on wokeness involved societal changes that at least a few observers could trace to developments in the law, the second decade moves us toward a complete

forgetting of the connection. The chain of causation is no less real, but
it becomes harder to prove. The acceleration comes in part due to economic developments that include the rise of new firms and industries.
Established institutions can only change so much. HR departments and
diversity bureaucrats are not all immediately fired after they are no longer needed, and executives and managers retain old habits and promote
old norms regarding personnel management. The true change comes
when enough time has passed that more of the largest and most powerful firms in the economy are those that did not develop their procedures and internal cultures while under the boot of an expansive and
arbitrary system of civil rights law. These upstarts not only outcompete
established businesses by relying more on meritocratic procedures and
systems and making work life more tolerable, but force old companies
to either adapt to stay competitive or, if they cannot, get left behind.

New businesses and social arrangements that seem unusual but meet
human needs begin to emerge. All throughout history, religions, families,
and other private institutions have created norms, practices, and institutions that facilitate young people meeting so that they can eventually
get married and form families. Under civil rights law, women started
to enter a workplace that became increasingly sanitized to respond to
the wishes of the most sensitive and brittle among them. Careers became more important relative to other areas of life at the same time it
was made illegal to mix work with love or sexual desire. Unsurprisingly,
fewer and fewer people ended up getting married or having children.

In the post-woke world, some corporations start encouraging dating and forming close personal bonds among their employees. This can
take many forms, from Christian matchmaking to promoting a party-
like atmosphere. These pro-relationship corporations will come in conservative and liberal forms. Other firms explicitly market themselves
as providing a more "professional" or "classic" work experience. They
may draw people who are already happily married, those currently not
looking for a relationship, and those who simply dislike mixing work
and love. No law will prevent companies from adopting old EEOC regulations from previous decades as their model of personnel management. We will see a period of wild experimentation, with some forms of

corporate organization drawing a great deal of media coverage. People will criticize many of these experiments, and they will become the subject of public outrage. After civil rights law has been defanged, however, government no longer has the ability to easily shut such efforts down. Eventually public anger subsides, and the idea of the media attacking a firm because it dislikes its internal culture will seem as intolerant as attacking a religious community for its doctrines, or homosexuals for what they do together as consenting adults.

Politics starts to dominate less of our public discourse. Now that the law no longer forces corporations to take a side on hot-button issues like racial preferences and what defines a "woman," more and more firms opt for political neutrality. Before civil rights law was rolled back, left-wing institutions that celebrated racial diversity and LGBT identity were allowed, but conservative corporations were all but illegal. Now, there are still more liberal firms than conservative ones due to factors such as the political leanings of young white-collar employees. Nonetheless, some businesses become aligned with the right on culture war issues, and large institutions are no longer seen as hyperpoliticized and monolithically liberal, which takes some of the anger out of our public life.

Rates of mental illness begin to decline even further. Young people no longer grow up in a world in which they are told that they are fragile, that things have never been more unjust, and that being a woman or non-white is a major burden that makes an individual subject to an endless stream of belittling insults and large and small acts of discrimination. The culture undergoes a subtle shift, as individuals focus more on the things they can control and less on those they can't. Tried-and-true paths to meaning—family, personal accomplishments, religion, community—play a larger role in people's lives, and politics and government-certified minority status matter less. As the premium on being a "victim" decreases, we see a large drop-off in the number of teenagers and young adults identifying as sexual minorities, which had become a way to gain status in a more confused previous era.

Moral panics still exist. But with weaker civil rights laws in place, they do not overwhelm and destroy institutions and have little lasting effect on how society functions. Before, an unarmed black man would be killed by police, or a prominent woman would talk about being sexually harassed, and human resources departments in practically every major institution would try to get on the right side of the issue. This was due to the political leanings of HR professionals and the threat of lawsuits and government intervention aimed at those showing themselves insufficiently sensitive to which way the political winds were blowing. This effect remains; even in a world without civil rights laws, companies would still try to avoid bad press. But less is expected from major corporations, since they are no longer seen as allies for one side in the culture war, and when they do promise to take a more activist role in the midst of a moral panic, they rarely follow up or make lasting changes.

Few people think too deeply about the connection between law and popular culture—music, art, and TV shows. Yet even in the freest societies, law shapes culture, which means that it cannot help but drive popular entertainment. In the late 2010s and early 2020s, there was a realization that popular culture had become decadent, as Hollywood came to produce less compelling original material and rely more on remakes of classic works.[11] Few at the time realized that this was because demands for artificial kinds of gender and racial equality in cultural products had made original and compelling art much more difficult to create. This is why many of the most critically acclaimed TV shows of recent years have been set in either the distant past, fantasy universes, or the criminal underworld, where there is less pressure for politically correct stories that obviate natural differences between men and women and insert unrealistic levels of ethnic diversity that distract from the ability to find inspiration in a work. When the excesses of civil rights law are rolled back, Americans return to being comfortable with human nature and are ready to appreciate more interesting and novel art.

The downstream effects of the American move back toward freedom and merit are felt abroad. Given the US role in the world, other countries often follow its lead in cultural matters. Americans winning their own battle against wokeness at home weakens it everywhere else. The amount of freedom in the world increases, and countries on every continent see fewer moral panics and faster economic growth. As the US becomes less woke at home, cultural imperialism plays less of a role in its foreign policy. While at one time elites in Washington demanded that other nations adhere to ideas about race and sexuality that were in many cases new and still widely controversial even at home, now they deal with foreign nations in a more respectful manner and look for ways to cooperate based on mutual self-interest. Alongside the booming global economy that has resulted from the return of merit hiring and creative destruction across and within firms, we move toward world peace and the preservation of true cultural diversity.

Getting the state out of the business of social engineering does not take us back to the 1950s. One can't unring a bell, and there are many aspects of life at that time that we should not want to return to. But the idea that we would go back to Jim Crow–type laws in the South, or even that public opinion would tolerate any jurisdiction of notable size doing so, is absurd, even if we might expect those who support the legal status quo to warn us about a slippery slope leading to that ultimate end.

All of this probably won't happen. But some of it might. And although we should have little confidence that we can accurately predict what kind of world will result once we eliminate certain aspects of anti-discrimination law and make others more consistent, one of the aims of this book is to convince the reader that there would be downstream influences on practically all areas of life. In the 1960s, the federal government got into the business of social engineering. It is impossible to know exactly which ideas associated with wokeness required civil rights law to triumph and which ones would have gained prominence anyway. It is also impossible to quantify the harm done to economic growth and human flourishing caused by the path the federal government took.

While the above portrait presented an optimistic—almost certainly too optimistic—view of what the world would look like with weaker and more consistent civil rights laws, one can also conjure up nightmare scenarios. Nonetheless, the case for being more optimistic about the result relies on a few basic principles that most reasonable people share: that freedom, including freedom of speech, is good for individuals and institutions; that arbitrary state power is bad; that businesses know more than the government about how to create a more productive and harmonious workforce; and that the state should not be in the business of social engineering, including the regulation of humor and dating.

We have never had an honest discussion about how the modern idea of civil rights—based on usually vague affirmative action standards, disparate impact, the elimination of sex stereotypes, and anti-harassment law—clashes with basically all other rights Americans hold dear and with our assumptions about what makes for a free and prosperous society. Rather, supporters of the current system pretend that the conflict does not exist. Bringing attention to what civil rights law actually does beyond supposedly prohibiting race and sex discrimination is the first step toward helping people understand what freedoms have been lost, and what the world might be like if we could regain them.

In the relationship between culture and law, the arrow of causation does not flow in one direction. It is impossible to imagine either a society in which the dominant ideas of a nation do not affect its laws and regulations, or one in which government power does not influence how people think and act and what they believe. To even ask which causal arrow has greater weight is likely asking too much of social scientists. At the same time, historical research, by looking at the order of events, can make the case that many of the ideas fundamental to wokeness were part of law before they were part of American culture. In other words, there is a striking resemblance between assumptions of civil rights laws that go back to the 1970s and cultural ideas and forces that have come to ascendance much more recently.

One does not have to squint to see the connections between the disparate impact legal standard and theories of "structural discrimination"; affirmative action as required by government and race-consciousness in the private and public sectors; anti-harassment laws and sterilized HR-compliant corporate environments; best practices standards in civil rights law and diversity trainings; Title IX regulations and harassment policies on college campuses; and how the government classifies people according to race and how the wider culture divides them.

No one alive in the 1960s could have imagined where government getting into the business of social engineering would eventually take us. After all, those paying attention at the time were thinking in terms of a static economic system in which the spoils of a heavily regulated but nonetheless successful postwar American capitalism would be divided more equally across groups. In contrast, allowing for more freedom, experimentation, and creative destruction almost by definition leads to more uncertain outcomes. Those who want to move us away from the current civil rights regime will, if they succeed, put us down a path that is even more unpredictable than that taken in the 1960s. Their efforts will likely have impacts that are only slightly noticeable in the short run, which means that it will be easy to believe nothing very important has happened even after political victories. A historical perspective can help guard against disillusionment.

The story of how America became woke reveals that the most important legal and regulatory decisions often get little to no attention. The Civil Rights Act was debated out in the open by elected representatives, but the revolutionary innovations of the decades after its signing were mostly ignored by the general public. Attempts to undo them would probably get more attention; the left has shown great ability to mobilize on issues related to identity. But in this case, a mobilized right and public opinion can serve to check its excesses.

Federal contracting regulations and which standards to use to prove discrimination are simply not very compelling topics to most casual followers of the news. Even those inclined to liberally throw around the epithets "racist" and "sexist" against their political opponents always have more tempting targets than those who speak in the boring language of court decisions and the Code of Federal Regulations.

Among its many other goals, this book argues against our tendency to mistake salience for importance. Wokeness inspires passions on both sides. While debates over hot-button issues are often dismissed as insignificant by those who have an aesthetic or ideological commitment to the idea that politics should mostly be about economic issues, Americans, just like other people, have made clear that they care deeply about what kind of culture they live in. Yet for half a century now the culture war has been an asymmetric fight, with one side able to inspire a critical mass of bureaucrats and activists who do their work far from public attention, and the other doing little more than encouraging and reflecting mass discontent without much impact. The anti-woke movement may never be able to inspire as many bureaucrats and lawyers as its opponents, but through the judicious use of power it can help eventually reverse much of the damage that has been done to our economy, politics, and ability to organize and live our lives free from government control. The effort to roll back civil rights law will not be the final battle in the war on wokeness but the beginning, allowing those who want to build a society based on the ideals of freedom and progress a fair chance in the struggle.

Acknowledgments

Given that this book is the culmination of over a decade of study and thought on these topics, there are too many people who have influenced my thinking and helped me on this journey to list here. I will mostly focus on thanking those who helped most in the years immediately before publication, as the chain of causation becomes less certain the further one goes back. The idea for the book originally came from a reading group on woke institutions that included Patrick Brown, Connor Harris, Zach Goldberg, Charles Fain Lehman, Megan McArdle, Gabriel Rossman, and Aaron Sibarium. The readings we discussed originally motivated me to write the article "Woke Institutions Is Just Civil Rights Law," which contained incipient versions of many of the arguments made here. Seeing the reaction to it convinced me that there was widespread interest in hearing more about how we got here and how opponents of wokeness can do more than just complain about what they find distasteful.

I've also had important discussions on the topics covered in this work with Bryan Caplan, Gail Heriot, Eric Kaufmann, Michael Lachanski, Dan Morenoff, Steven Pinker, Philippe Lemoine, Vivek Ramaswamy, Sarah Rogers, Alex Nowrasteh, and Chris Rufo. Jonah Davids has done all that I can ask from a research assistant. Tyler Cowen has been perhaps the most influential public supporter of my work, and I will always be grateful for that. The Alan Rupe Foundation provided a grant to help write this book. Michael Howard helped track down data on the rise of human resources. Finally, social media and comments on my Substack have, for better or worse, greatly influenced my thinking on political issues. I thank all the anons and real names out there who have been part of the never-ending discussion that this book represents a continuation of. My sincerest hope is that it will help move us beyond that discussion and ultimately reshape laws and institutions, away from adherence to ideas and practices that are ultimately poisonous for humanity.

Notes

Introduction

1.   Hayek, Friedrich von. 1944. *The Road to Serfdom*. George Routledge & Sons: p. v.

Chapter 1. How to Understand Wokeness

1.   "Transcript: Ezra Klein Interviews Ramesh Ponnuru." Mar 2, 2021. *The New York Times*. https://www.nytimes.com/2021/03/02/podcasts/ezra-klein-podcast-ramesh-ponnuru-transcript.html.
2.   Caldwell, Christopher. 2020. *The Age of Entitlement: America Since the Sixties*. Simon & Schuster: ch. 8.
3.   Rufo, Christopher F. Oct 14, 2021. "Walmart vs. Whiteness." *City Journal*. https://www.city-journal.org/walmart-critical-race-theory-training-program; Xiu, Meimei. Jun 29, 2022. "Harvard Prof. John Comaroff Faces New Allegations of Misconduct in Amended Suit." *The Harvard Crimson*. https://www.thecrimson.com/article/2022/6/29/comaroff-amended-complaint/. Notably, a premise of this lawsuit and related coverage was revealed to be false and fabricated, as detailed in Sibarium, Aaron. Aug 19, 2022. "This Harvard Professor Was Found Guilty in the Press. Court Records Tell a Different Story." *The Washington Free Beacon*. https://freebeacon.com/campus/this-harvard-professor-was-found-guilty-in-the-press-court-records-tell-a-different-story/.
4.   D'Agostino, Tom. May 5, 2022. "Linkedin Is on the Hook for $1.8 Million for Alleged Gender Bias." *HR Morning*. https://www.hrmorning.com/news/linkedin-is-on-the-hook-for-1-8-million-for-alleged-gender-bias/; "B&H Foto Resolves Allegations of Discrimination, Bias, and Harassment with OFCCP." Oct 13, 2017. Carla Irwin & Associates. https://carlairwininc.com/blog/bh-foto-resolves-allegations-of-discrimination-bias-and-harassment-with-ofccp/.
5.   Eilperin, Juliet. Dec 30, 2014. "Harvard Settles Title IX Case with Administration, Agrees to Revise Sexual Assault Policies." *The Washington Post*. https://www.washingtonpost.com/news/post-politics/wp/2014/12/30/harvard-settles-title-ix-case-with-administration-agrees-to-revise-sexual-assault-policies/.
6.   Pluckrose, Helen, and James Lindsay. 2020. *Cynical Theories: How Activist Scholarship Made Everything About Race, Gender, and Identity—and Why This Harms Everybody*. Pitchstone Publishing: Introduction and ch. 2.
7.   Gottfried, Paul. 2022. *Multiculturalism and the Politics of Guilt: Toward a Secular Theocracy*. University of Missouri Press: Introduction.
8.   Thernstrom, Abigail M. 1987. *Whose Votes Count?: Affirmative Action and Minority Voting Rights*. Harvard University Press.
9.   Seabury, Paul. Feb 1, 1972. "HEW & the Universities." *Commentary Magazine*: pp. 38–44.
10. Skrentny, John David. 1996. *The Ironies of Affirmative Action: Politics, Culture, and Justice in America*. University of Chicago Press: ch. 5.

11. Graham, Hugh David. 1990. *The Civil Rights Era: Origins and Development of National Policy, 1960–1972.* Oxford University Press: p. 340.

12. Wood, Peter. 2003. *Diversity: The Invention of a Concept.* Encounter Books: pp. 143–56.

13. Graham, *Civil Rights Era*, pp. 34–35.

14. Ibid., ch. 10, conclusion.

15. Skrentny, *Ironies of Affirmative Action*, ch. 4.

16. Wood, *Diversity*, pp. 169–90.

17. Pinker, Steven. 2003. *The Blank Slate: The Modern Denial of Human Nature.* Penguin Books: ch. 18.

18. Pfeiffer, Alex. Sep 8, 2016. "Black Democratic Lawmakers Don't See Sexism in the Justice System." *The Daily Caller.* https://dailycaller.com/2016/09/08/black-democrat-lawmakers-dont-see-sexism-in-the-justice-system/.

19. Havel, Vaclav. 1978. "The Power of the Powerless," in Keane, John. 1985. *The Power of the Powerless: Citizens Against the State in Central-Eastern Europe.* M. E. Sharp.

20. Reilly, Wilfred. Sep 15, 2020. "A Fragile Argument." *Commentary Magazine.* https://www.commentary.org/articles/wilfred-reilly/white-fragility-fragile-racism-argument/.

21. As David Azerrad notes in his review of Kendi's *Stamped from the Beginning*, "Nowhere in his 500-page tome does he ever see racial disparities between Asians and whites. If he did, he would have to conclude that America is in fact an Asian supremacist nation which, based on income and educational attainment, discriminates against whites—unless they are Ashkenazi Jews—and blacks—unless they are Nigerians." Azerrad, David. Spring 2020. "The Social Justice Endgame." *Claremont Review of Books.* https://claremontreviewofbooks.com/the-social-justice-endgame/.

22. Goldberg, Zach. Aug 4, 2020. "How the Media Led the Great Racial Awakening." *Tablet Magazine.* https://www.tabletmag.com/sections/news/articles/media-great-racial-awakening.

23. Paul, James D., and Robert Maranto. Nov 8, 2021. "Other Than Merit: The Prevalence of Diversity, Equity, and Inclusion Statements in University Hiring." American Enterprise Institute. https://www.aei.org/research-products/report/other-than-merit-the-prevalence-of-diversity-equity-and-inclusion-statements-in-university-hiring/.

24. Parloff, Roger. Dec 9, 2015. "Big Business Asks Supreme Court to Save Affirmative Action." *Fortune.* https://fortune.com/2015/12/09/supreme-court-affirmative-action/.

25. Strauss, Valerie. Feb 4, 2020. "University of California Should Keep Requiring SAT or ACT Scores for Admissions, Task Force Says." *The Washington Post.* https://www.washingtonpost.com/education/2020/02/04/university-california-should-keep-requiring-sat-or-act-scores-admissions-task-force-says/.

26. Rasmussen, Leif. Nov 16, 2021. "Increasing Politicization and Homogeneity in Scientific Funding: An Analysis of NSF Grants, 1990–2020." *Center for the Study of Partisanship and Ideology.* https://www.cspicenter.com/p/increasing-politicization-and-homogeneity-in-scientific-funding-an-analysis-of-nsf-grants-1990-2020.

27. Myers, Steven Lee. Oct 24, 2021. "She Is Breaking Glass Ceilings in Space, but Facing Sexism on Earth." *The New York Times.* https://www.nytimes.com/2021/10/23/world/asia/china-space-women-wang-yaping.html.

28. Holder, Josh, and Amy Schoenfeld Walker. Aug 24, 2021. "Many Older Americans Still Aren't Vaccinated, Making the Delta Wave Deadlier." *The New York Times.* https://www.nytimes.com/interactive/2021/08/24/world/vaccines-seniors.html.

29. Gramlich, Josh. Oct 27, 2021. "What We Know About the Increase in US Murders in 2020." Pew Research Center. https://www.pewresearch.org/fact-tank/2021/10/27/what-we-know-about-the-increase-in-u-s-murders-in-2020/.

30. Bohman, John H., and Thomas J. Mowan. 2021. "Global Crime Trends During COVID-19." *Nature Human Behaviour* 5: 821–22; Lehman, Charles Fain. Sep 27, 2021. "Denying the Crime Spike." *City Journal.* https://www.city-journal.org/third-ways-misdirection-on-violent-crime.

31. Sowell, Thomas. 2009. *Black Rednecks and White Liberals.* Encounter Books; Sowell, Thomas. 2019. *Discrimination and Disparities.* Hachette UK.

32. Skrentny, John David. 2001. "Republican Efforts to End Affirmative Action: Walking a Fine Line," in Levin, Martin A., Marc Landy, and Martin Shapiro. *Seeking the Center: Politics and Policymaking at the New Century.* Georgetown University Press: 132–71, p. 140.

33. Kiley, Kevin, and Stephen Vaisey. 2020. "Measuring Stability and Change in Personal Culture Using Panel Data." *American Sociological Review* 85(3): 477–506.

34. Perry, Mark J. Dec 13, 2016. "Fortune 500 Firms 1955 v. 2016: Only 12% Remain, Thanks to the Creative Destruction That Fuels Economic Prosperity." American Enterprise Institute. https://www.aei.org/carpe-diem/fortune-500-firms-1955-v-2016-only-12-remain-thanks -to-the-creative-destruction-that-fuels-economic-prosperity/.

35. Greer, Tanner. Jul 3, 2021. "Culture Wars Are Long Wars." The Scholar's Stage. https:// scholars-stage.org/culture-wars-are-long-wars/.

Chapter 2. Lies, Damned Lies, and Civil Rights Law

1. Gold, Michael Evan. 1980. "A Tale of Two Amendments: The Reasons Congress Added Sex to Title VII and Their Implication for the Issue of Comparable Worth." *Duquesne Law Review* 19(3): 453–77, pp. 457–60.

2. Freeman, Jo. 2000. *The Politics of Women's Liberation: A Case Study of an Emerging Social Movement and Its Relation to the Policy Process.* iUniverse: p. 54.

3. Skrentny, John David. 2004. *The Minority Rights Revolution.* Harvard University Press: pp. 112–13.

4. Burstein, Paul. 1998. *Discrimination, Jobs, and Politics: The Struggle for Equal Employment Opportunity in the United States Since the New Deal.* University of Chicago Press: pp. 73–74.

5. Skrentny, *Minority Rights Revolution*, p. 93.

6. Ibid., p. 101.

7. Napolitano, Steven. 1987. "Interpreting the Legislative History of Section 706(g) of Title VII." *Boston College Third World Law Journal* 7(2): 263–76, p. 271.

8. Bovard, James. Mar 1994. "Job-Breakers: The EEOC's Assault on the Workplace." *The American Spectator* 27(3): 32–37, p. 32.

9. Belz, Herman. 1991. *Equality Transformed.* Transaction Publishers: p. 31.

10. Ekins, Emily. Oct 31, 2017. "The State of Free Speech and Tolerance in America." Cato Institute. https://www.cato.org/survey-reports/state-free-speech-tolerance-america.

11. "Number of TV Households in America: 1950–1978." 2014. *The American Century.* https:// americancentury.omeka.wlu.edu/items/show/136.

12. Perlstein, Rick. 2009. *Nixonland: The Rise of a President and the Fracturing of America.* Scribner: p. 334.

13. Glazer, Nathan. 1987. *Affirmative Discrimination: Ethnic Inequality and Public Policy.* Harvard University Press: p. 4.

14. Graham, *Civil Rights Era*, pp. 412–13.

15. Ibid., pp. 333–34.

16. *Chrysler Corp. v. Brown*, 441 US 281, 99 S. Ct. 1705 (1979): pp. 303–07.

17. Lorenzetti, Laura. Feb 10, 2016. "Fortune 500 Companies Are Getting Billions from Federal Small Business Contracts." *Fortune.* https://fortune.com/2016/02/10/small-business -contract-problems/.

18. "US Department of Labor Announces Best Year for Compliance Assistance by Office of Federal Contract Compliance Programs." Oct 19, 2020. US Department of Labor. https:// www.dol.gov/newsroom/releases/ofccp/ofccp20201019-0.

19. This discussion is based on regulations found in 41 CFR § 60–1 and 41 CFR § 60–2.

20. "General Affirmative Action Programs Frequently Asked Questions." Last accessed Aug 29, 2022. Office of Federal Contract Compliance Programs. https://www.dol.gov/agen cies/ofccp/faqs/general-aaps#Q1.

21. Anderson, Terry H. 2005. *The Pursuit of Fairness: A History of Affirmative Action.* Oxford University Press: p. 103.

22. Kotlowski, Dean J. 2001. *Nixon's Civil Rights: Politics, Principle, and Policy*. Harvard University Press: p. 123.

23. Havel, Vaclav. 1978. "The Power of the Powerless," in Keane, John, ed. 1985. *The Power of the Powerless: Citizens Against the State in Central-Eastern Europe*. M. E. Sharp.

24. Text of the CRA of 1964 can be found at https://www.ourdocuments.gov/doc.php?flash=false&doc=97&page=transcript.

25. Belz, *Equality Transformed*, pp. 46–48.

26. This discussion is taken from Graham, *Civil Rights Era*, pp. 149–51.

27. Glazer, *Affirmative Discrimination*, p. 45.

28. Belz, *Equality Transformed*, pp. 28–29.

29. Ibid., pp. 125–28.

30. Graham, *Civil Rights Era*, pp. 384–89.

31. Rivers, Richard R. 1973. "In America, What You Do Is What You Are: The Equal Employment Opportunity Act of 1972." *Catholic University Law Review* 22(2): 455–66, pp. 462–63.

32. Blumrosen, Alfred W. 1971. *Black Employment and the Law*. Rutgers University Press: pp. 58–59.

33. Heriot, Gail, and Alison Somin. 2018. "The Department of Education's Obama-Era Initiative on Racial Disparities in School Discipline: Wrong for Students and Teachers, Wrong on the Law." *Texas Review of Law & Policy* 22: 471–566.

34. Moran, Rachel F. 2005. "Undone by Law: The Uncertain Legacy of *Lau v. Nichols*." *Berkeley La Raza Law Journal* 16(1): 1–10.

35. *Gulino v. Board of Education of the City School District of N.Y.*, 907 F. Supp. 2d 492 (S.D.N.Y. 2013).

36. Heriot, Gail L. 2020. "Title VII Disparate Impact Liability Makes Almost Everything Presumptively Illegal." *NYU Journal of Law & Liberty* 14(1): p. 37.

37. Pierce, Michelle Ridgeway. 1989. "Sexual Harassment and Title VII—A Better Solution." *Boston College Law Review* 4(4): 1071–1101, pp. 1072–74.

38. Volokh, Eugene. 1997. "What Speech Does 'Hostile Work Environment' Harassment Law Restrict?" *Georgetown Law Journal* 85(3): 627–48.

39. "Harassment." Accessed Aug 29, 2022. US Equal Employment Opportunity Commission. https://www.eeoc.gov/harassment.

40. Matsakis, Louise. Feb 16, 2018. "Labor Board Rules Google's Firing of James Damore Was Legal." *WIRED*. https://www.wired.com/story/labor-board-rules-google-firing-james-damore-was-legal/.

41. Melnick, R. Shep. 2018. *The Transformation of Title IX: Regulating Gender Equality in Education*. Brookings Institution Press: pp. 40–41.

42. For example, the NBA has over one hundred times the revenue of the WNBA, with the latter having never even generated a profit. The very existence of women's professional basketball is something of an economic mystery. Faria, Zachary. Dec 8, 2022. "The 'Pay Gap' Debate Between the NBA and WNBA Is a Joke." *Washington Examiner*. https://www.washingtonexaminer.com/opinion/the-pay-gap-debate-between-the-nba-and-wnba-is-a-joke.

43. Melnick, *Transformation of Title IX*, pp. 87–89.

44. Ibid., p. 43.

45. Ibid., pp. 15–16.

46. Ibid., pp. 7–12.

47. Ibid., p. 85.

48. Ibid., p. 78.

49. Ibid., pp. 132–33; Gray, Gary R., and John A. Pelzer. 1995. "The Impact of Title IX on the Discontinuation of NCAA Division I Wrestling Programs." *Journal of Legal Aspects of Sports* 5(2): 117–22.

50. Eisenburg, Jeff. 2022. "Counting Men as Women?: Inside the Fuzzy Math of Title IX

Compliance." *Yahoo! News.* https://sports.yahoo.com/counting-men-as-women-inside-the-fuzzy-math-of-title-ix-compliance-132707743.html.

51. Ibid.
52. Melnick, *Transformation of Title IX*, pp. 187–91.
53. Gersen, Jacob, and Jeannie Suk. 2016. "The Sex Bureaucracy." *California Law Review* 104(4): 881–948, pp. 897–902.
54. Melnick, *Transformation of Title IX*, pp. 191–96.
55. Gersen and Suk, "The Sex Bureaucracy."
56. Ibid., p. 907.
57. Ibid., pp. 918–22.
58. Melnick, *Transformation of Title IX*, pp. 206–10.
59. "Questions and Answers on Title IX and Sexual Violence." Apr 29, 2014. U.S. Department of Education. https://www2.ed.gov/about/offices/list/ocr/docs/qa-201404-title-ix.pdf.
60. "Notice of Language Assistance: Dear Colleague Letter on Title IX Coordinators." Apr 24, 2015. U.S. Department of Education. https://www2.ed.gov/about/offices/list/ocr/letters/colleague-201504-title-ix-coordinators.pdf.
61. Ibid.
62. The Violence Against Women Reauthorization Act of 2013, Pub. L. 113–4, 127 Stat. 54, 90 (2013) (codified at 20 USC § 1092(f)(8)).
63. Gersen and Suk, "The Sex Bureaucracy," p. 912.
64. Ibid., p. 928.
65. Gersen and Suk, "The Sex Bureaucracy," pp. 909–10; 20 US Code § 1682.
66. Johnson, KC. Oct. 2017. "The Campus Sex-Crime Tribunals Are Losing." *Commentary Magazine.* https://www.commentary.org/articles/kc-johnson/campus-sex-crime-tribunals-losing/.
67. Sapir, Lior. 2020. "Regulate Now, Explain Later: Understanding the Civil Rights State's Redefinition of 'Sex.'" PhD dissertation: ch. 1.
68. Reilly, Kate. Sep 7, 2017. "Betsy DeVos Moves to End Obama's Guidelines for Campus Sexual Assault Investigations." *TIME.* https://time.com/4931796/betsy-devos-title-ix-sexual-assault/.
69. "Rescinded Policy Guidance." Last accessed Aug 29, 2022. US Department of Education. https://www2.ed.gov/about/offices/list/ocr/frontpage/faq/rr/policyguidance/respolicy.html.
70. Melnick, *Transformation of Title IX*, pp. 221–22.
71. "The US Department of Education Releases Proposed Changes to Title IX Regulations, Invites Public Comment." Jun 23, 2022. US Department of Education. https://www.ed.gov/news/press-releases/us-department-education-releases-proposed-changes-title-ix-regulations-invites-public-comment.
72. *Buettner-Hartsoe v. Baltimore Lutheran High School Association*, No. RDB-20–3132, 2022 BL 255532 (D. Md., Jul 21, 2022).
73. *Richmond v. J. A. Croson Co.*, 488 US 469, 109 S. Ct. 706 (1989): part III.
74. Unz, Ron. Dec 3, 2013. "Statistics Indicate an Ivy League Asian Quota." *The New York Times.* https://www.nytimes.com/roomfordebate/2012/12/19/fears-of-an-asian-quota-in-the-ivy-league/statistics-indicate-an-ivy-league-asian-quota. It appears that more Asians were admitted after public awareness of the quota issue grew starting around 2012: see VerBruggen, Robert. Apr 28, 2022. "Racial Preferences on Campus: Trends in Asian Enrollment at US Colleges." Manhattan Institute. https://www.manhattan-institute.org/verbruggen-racial-preferences-trends-in-asian-enrollment-at-us-colleges.
75. Wong, Alia. 2018. "Harvard's Impossible Personality Test." *The Atlantic.* https://www.theatlantic.com/education/archive/2018/06/harvard-admissions-personality/563198/.
76. Wax, Amy L. 2011. "Disparate Impact Realism." *William & Mary Law Review* 53: 621–712.
77. Dorn, Emma, Bryan Hancock, Jimmy Sarakatsannis, and Ellen Viruleg. Dec 8, 2020.

"COVID-19 and Learning Loss—Disparities Grow and Students Need Help." McKinsey & Company. https://www.mckinsey.com/industries/public-and-social-sector/our-insights /covid-19-and-learning-loss-disparities-grow-and-students-need-help.

78. Stolberg, Sheryl Gay, and Erica L. Green. Aug 18, 2021. "The Biden Administration Will Use a Federal Civil Rights Office to Deter States from Banning Universal Masking in Classrooms." *The New York Times.* https://www.nytimes.com/2021/08/18/us/politics/biden -masks-schools-civil-rights.html.

79. Bovard, "Job-Breakers."

80. Thernstrom, Abigail M. 1987. *Whose Votes Count?: Affirmative Action and Minority Voting Rights.* Harvard University Press.

81. Bernstein, David E. 2019. "Antidiscrimination Law and the Administrative State: A Skeptic's Look at Administrative Constitutionalism." *Notre Dame Law Review* 94(3): 1381–1415, pp. 1392–94.

82. Bernstein, David E. 2003. *You Can't Say That!: The Growing Threat to Civil Liberties from Antidiscrimination Laws.* Cato Institute: Introduction; Thorsby, Devon. 2015. "What Your Real Estate Agent Can't Tell You." *U.S. News & World Report.* https://realestate.usnews .com/real-estate/articles/what-your-real-estate-agent-cant-tell-you.

83. Claburn, Thomas. May 9, 2019. "Oracle's Legal Woes Deepen: Big Red Sued (Again) for Age and Medical 'Discrimination.'" *The Register.* https://www.theregister.com/2019/05/09 /oracle_sued_age_discrimination/; Scheiber, Noam. Feb 12, 2022. "Making 'Dinobabies' Extinct: IBM's Push for a Younger Work Force." *The New York Times.* https://www.ny times.com/2022/02/12/business/economy/ibm-age-discrimination.html; Baron, Ethan. Jul 23, 2019. "Google Settles 'Age-Discrimination' Class-Action Lawsuit with More than 200 Workers for $11 Million." *The Seattle Times.* https://www.seattletimes.com/business /google-settles-age-discrimination-class-action-lawsuit-with-more-than-200-workers -for-11-million/.

84. Johnson, Judith J. 2006. "Rescue the Americans with Disabilities Act from Restrictive Interpretations: Alcoholism as an Illustration." *Northern Illinois University Law Review* 27: 169–246, pp. 212–37.

85. "Charge Statistics (Charges filed with EEOC) FY 1997 Through FY 2021." Accessed Aug 29, 2022. US Equal Employment Opportunity Commission. https://www.eeoc.gov /statistics/charge-statistics-charges-filed-eeoc-fy-1997-through-fy-2021.

86. *PGA Tour, Inc. v. Martin*, 532 US 661, 121 S. Ct. 1879 (2001).

87. *Jones v. Mayer Co.*, 392 US 409, 88 S. Ct. 2186 (1968).

Chapter 3. The Standardization of the American Workplace and University

1. Mousavizadeh, Philip. Nov 10, 2021. "A 'Proliferation of Administrators': Faculty Reflect on Two Decades of Rapid Expansion." *Yale Daily News.* https://yaledailynews.com /blog/2021/11/10/reluctance-on-the-part-of-its-leadership-to-lead-yales-administration -increases-by-nearly-50-percent/.

2. Kundla, Alek. Dec 28, 2021. "Ohio's Wasteful and Divisive Commitment to 'Equity, Diversity and Inclusion.'" *National Review.* https://www.nationalreview.com/2021/12/ohio -states-wasteful-and-divisive-commitment-to-diversity-equity-and-inclusion/.

3. E. S. and William McGill. 1972. "Universities in Danger: The United States Office for Civil Rights *Contra* Columbia University." *Minerva* 10(2): 319–22.

4. Melnick, *Transformation of Title IX*, p. 21.

5. Dobbin, Frank. 2009. *Inventing Equal Opportunity.* Princeton University Press: p. 169.

6. *Meritor Sav. Bank v. Vinson*, 477 US 57, 106 S. Ct. 2399 (1986).

7. "Best Practices and Tips for Employees." Last accessed Aug 29, 2022. US Equal Employment Opportunity Commission. https://www.eeoc.gov/initiatives/e-race/best-practices -and-tips-employees.

8. Dobbin, Frank, and John R. Sutton. 1998. "The Strength of a Weak State: The Rights Revolution and the Rise of Human Resources Management Divisions." *American Journal of Sociology* 104(2): 441–76.
9. For the growth in private enforcement regimes in the American system and the history of civil rights law in that context, see Farhang, Sean. 2010. *The Litigation State: Public Regulation and Private Lawsuits in the U.S.* Princeton University Press.
10. Heriot, Gail L. 2022. "The Roots of Wokeness: Title VII Damage Remedies as Potential Drivers of Attitudes Toward Identity Politics and Free Expression." San Diego Legal Studies Paper 22–001, *Texas Review of Law & Politics*, forthcoming: pp. 19–21.
11. Farhang, *The Litigation State*, pp. 147–49.
12. Resnick, Jordan L. 1995. "Beyond Mastrobuono: A Practitioners' Guide to Arbitration, Employment Disputes, Punitive Damages, and the Implications of the Civil Rights Act of 1991." *Hofstra Law Review* 23(4): pp. 913–73, p. 917, fn 16; The Americans with Disabilities Act of 1991 states that the remedies available to plaintiffs are the same as under the Civil Rights Act of 1964, for which the Civil Rights Act of 1991 creates punitive damages. For discussion and references to the law, see *Kramer v. Banc of America Securities, LLC*, 355 F.3d 961 (7th Cir., 2004).
13. Belz, *Equality Transformed*, pp. 44–45.
14. Mattera, Philip. January 2019. "Big Business Bias: Employment Discrimination and Sexual Harassment at Large Corporations." Good Jobs First. https://www.goodjobsfirst.org/wp-content/uploads/docs/pdfs/BigBusinessBias.pdf.
15. For a discussion of this case, see Hanania, Richard. Oct 12, 2021. "Wokeness as Saddam Statues: The Case of the Tesla Elevator Operator." https://richardhanania.substack.com/p/wokeness-as-saddam-statues-the-case.
16. Torchinsky, Rina. Apr 14, 2021. "Judge Cuts the Payout in a Black Former Tesla Contractor's Racial Discrimination Suit." NPR. https://www.npr.org/2022/04/14/1092804493/telsa-racial-discrimination-lawsuit-15-million; *Diaz v. Tesla, Inc.*, 3:17-cv-06748-WHO (N.D. Cal. Oct. 1, 2021).
17. "Justice Department Reaches Settlement with Bank of America to Resolve Claims of Disability Discrimination and Compensate Victims." Jul 23, 2020. U.S. Department of Justice. https://www.justice.gov/opa/pr/justice-department-reaches-settlement-bank-america-resolve-claims-disability-discrimination.
18. Fitzpatrick, Brian T. "An Empirical Study of Class Action Settlements and Their Fee Awards." *Journal of Empirical Legal Studies* 7(4): 811–46, p. 824.
19. Brimelow, Peter, and Leslie Spencer. Feb 15, 1993. "When Quotas Replace Merit, Everybody Suffers." *Forbes*: pp. 80–102.
20. "Coca-Cola Settles Race Suit." Nov 16, 2021. CNN Money. https://money.cnn.com/2000/11/16/companies/coke/.
21. Koenig, Andy. Aug 28, 2016. "Look Who's Getting That Bank Settlement Cash." *The Wall Street Journal*. https://www.wsj.com/articles/look-whos-getting-that-bank-settlement-cash-1472421204.
22. See Hersch, Joni, and Jennifer Bennett Shinall. 2015. "Fifty Years Later: The Legacy of the Civil Rights Act of 1964." *Journal of Policy Analysis and Management* 34(2): 424–56, pp. 441–46.
23. "Charge Statistics (Charges filed with EEOC) FY 1997 Through FY 2021." Accessed Aug 29, 2022. US Equal Employment Opportunity Commission. https://www.eeoc.gov/statistics/charge-statistics-charges-filed-eeoc-fy-1997-through-fy-2021.
24. In fig. 3.3, civil case totals are from the Statistical Tables of the Federal Judiciary for 1976–2020. For 1965–1975, see Shughart II, William F., and Gokhan R. Karahan. 2004. "Study of the Determinants of Case Growth in US Federal District Courts, Final Report." https://www.ojp.gov/pdffiles1/nij/grants/204010.pdf. Civil rights case totals are from the Statistical Tables of the Federal Judiciary for 1976–2020. For the period 1970–1975, they are found at the website of the Federal Judicial Center. For the period 1967–1969, they

are estimated from the same source based on how many cases are closed beginning in 1970. The same methodology is used for calculating employment cases and ADA cases in fig. 3.4.

25. Heriot, "The Roots of Wokeness," pp. 36–37.
26. The possibility that this could happen was brought up by Gail Heriot in an interview for the *Institutionalized* podcast that can be found at https://podbay.fm/p/institutiona lized/e/1649839500.
27. Farhang, *The Litigation State*, pp. 173–99.
28. See Miller, Benjamin P. n.d. "Title VII Affirmative Defense in the Real World: Recent Application of *Ellerth/Faragher* and What They Require": p. 7. https://web.archive.org /web/20160327223342id_/http://www.miller-attorney.com:80/articles/MillerTitleVII .pdf.
29. Ibid.
30. "Best Practices and Resources." Last accessed Aug 29, 2022. Office of Federal Contract Compliance Programs. https://www.dol.gov/agencies/ofccp/compliance-assistance/out reach/resources.
31. "Best Practices for Fostering Diversity & Inclusion" Last accessed Aug 29, 2022. *Office of Federal Contract Compliance Programs*. https://www.dol.gov/agencies/ofccp/compliance -assistance/outreach/hbcu-initiative/best-practices.
32. "Promising Practices for Preventing Harassment." Last accessed Aug 29, 2022. US Equal Employment Opportunity Commission. https://www.eeoc.gov/laws/guidance/promising -practices-preventing-harassment.
33. Kalev, Alexandra, Frank Dobbin, and Erin Kelly. 2006. "Best Practices or Best Guesses?: Assessing the Efficacy of Corporate Affirmative Action and Diversity Policies." *American Sociological Review* 71(4): 589–617, p. 90.
34. Heriot, "The Roots of Wokeness," pp. 42–44.
35. Ibid., p. 42, fn 117.
36. Lynch, Frederick R. 2017. *The Diversity Machine: The Drive to Change the "White Male Work-place."* Routledge: pp. 25–27.
37. Al-Gharbi, Musa. Sep 16, 2020. "Diversity-Related Training: What Is It Good For?" *Het-erodox: The Blog.* https://heterodoxacademy.org/blog/diversity-related-training-what-is -it-good-for/.
38. Ibid.
39. Dobbin, *Inventing Equal Opportunity*, p. 87.
40. Ibid., pp. 95, 115, 122.
41. Ibid., pp. 96, 112–24.
42. I first heard Gabriel Rossman use the term "force multiplier" in this context.
43. Pompeo, Joe. Jun 4, 2020. "*New York Times* Employees Rebel Against Tom Cotton's Send-in-the-Troops Op-Ed." *Vanity Fair.* https://www.vanityfair.com/news/2020/06/new-york -times-employees-rebel-against-tom-cotton-send-in-the-troops-op-ed.
44. Yoffe, Emily. Oct. 2019. "'I'm Radioactive.'" *Reason.* https://reason.com/2019/08/23/im -radioactive/.
45. Oliver Darcy. Jun 10, 2022. "The *Washington Post* Fires Reporter Felicia Sonmez after a Week of [Her] Feuding Publicly with Her Colleagues." CNN. https://www.cnn.com /2022/06/09/media/felicia-sonmez-washington-post/index.html.
46. Wax, "Disparate Impact Realism"; Singal, Jesse. 2021. *The Quick Fix: Why Fad Psychology Can't Cure Our Social Ills.* Farrar, Straus and Giroux.
47. Epstein, Richard. 1992. *Forbidden Grounds*. University of Chicago Press: p. 289.
48. Graham, Hugh Davis. 2000. "The Civil Rights Act and the American Regulatory State," in Grofman, Bernard, ed. *Legacies of the 1964 Civil Rights Act*. University of Virginia Press: 43–64, pp. 46–52.
49. Clegg, Roger. Dec 1, 2001. "Disparate Impact in the Private Sector: A Theory Going Hay-

wire." American Enterprise Institute: pp. 4–5. https://www.aei.org/research-products /report/disparate-impact-in-the-private-sector/.

50. Stoll, Ira. Summer 2022. "Growth in Administrative Staff, Assistant Principals Far Out-paces Teacher Hiring." Education Next. https://www.educationnext.org/growth-admin istrative-staff-assistant-principals-far-outpaces-teacher-hiring/.

51. Leslie, Larry L., and Gary Rhoades. 1995. "Rising Administrative Costs: Seeking Explana-tions." *The Journal of Higher Education* 66(2): 187–212, p. 187.

52. Zywicki, Todd J., and Christopher Koopman. 2017. "The Changing of the Guard: The Po-litical Economy of Administrative Bloat in American Higher Education." George Mason Law & Economics Research Paper No. 17–12: pp. 14–15.

53. Leslie and Rhoades, "Rising Administrative Costs," p. 194.

54. Hartocollis, Anemona. Mar 29, 2016. "Colleges Spending Millions to Deal with Sexual Misconduct Complaints." *The New York Times*. https://www.nytimes.com/2016/03/30/us /colleges-beef-up-bureaucracies-to-deal-with-sexual-misconduct.html.

55. Ibid.

Chapter 4. Government as the Creator of New Races and Genders

1. Mora, G. Cristina. 2014. *Making Hispanics: How Activists, Bureaucrats, and Media Con-structed a New American.* University of Chicago Press: p. 99.

2. Petri, Alexander E., and Daniel E. Slotnik. Oct 15, 2021. "Attacks on Asian-Americans in New York Stoke Fear, Anxiety and Anger." *The New York Times*. https://www.nytimes .com/2021/02/26/nyregion/asian-hate-crimes-attacks-ny.html.

3. VerBruggen, "Racial Preferences on Campus."

4. Unz, Ron. Dec 2012. "The Myth of American Meritocracy." *The American Conservative*. https://www.unz.com/wp-content/uploads/2013/09/AmericanMeritocracy.pdf.

5. "Revisions to the Standards for the Classification of Federal Data on Race and Ethnicity." Oct 30, 1997. Office of Management and Budget. https://obamawhitehouse.archives.gov /omb/fedreg_1997standards.

6. "DIRECTIVE NO. 15: Race and Ethnic Standards for Federal Statistics and Administra-tive Reporting." May 12, 1977. Office of Management and Budget. https://wonder.cdc.gov /wonder/help/populations/bridged-race/directive15.html.

7. "Arrests by Race and Ethnicity, 2018." 2018. FBI: UCR. https://ucr.fbi.gov/crime-in-the -u.s/2018/crime-in-the-u.s.-2018/tables/table-43; "Annual Demographic Report: Fiscal Year 2018." 2018. Office of the Director of National Intelligence. https://www.dni.gov/files /documents/EEOD/FY18_IC_Annual_Demographic_Report_V6_ExecSec.pdf.

8. "Admissions Statistics." Last accessed Aug 29, 2022. Harvard College. https://college.har vard.edu/admissions/admissions-statistics.

9. "Undergraduate Student Profile." Last accessed Aug 29, 2022. Stanford University. https://facts.stanford.edu/academics/undergraduate-profile/.

10. "Fast Facts: SAT Scores." Last accessed Aug 29, 2022. National Center for Education Sta-tistics. https://nces.ed.gov/fastfacts/display.asp?id=171; "2021 Annual Diversity Report." 2021. Google. https://static.googleusercontent.com/media/diversity.google/en//annual-re port/static/pdfs/google_2021_diversity_annual_report.pdf?cachebust=2e13d07.

11. Masci, David. Oct 11, 2016. "How Income Varies Among US Religious Groups." Pew Research Center. https://www.pewresearch.org/fact-tank/2016/10/11/how-income-varies -among-u-s-religious-groups/.

12. Discussion in this part of the chapter is based on Skrentny, *Minority Rights Revolution*, ch. 4. See also Graham, Hugh Davis. 2003. *Collision Course: The Strange Convergence of Affirmative Action and Immigration Policy in America.* Oxford University Press: pp. 137–43.

13. Pearson, Henry G. 1966. "Title VII: Reporting and Record Keeping." *Boston College Law Review* 7: 549–60, p. 552; Anderson, *Pursuit of Fairness*, p. 99.

14. Skrentny, *Ironies of Affirmative Action*, p. 127

15. Skrentny, *Minority Rights Revolution*, p. 86.

16. Hammerman, Herbert. 1988. "'Affirmative Action Stalemate': A Second Perspective." *Public Interest* 93: 130–34, p. 131.

17. "1970 Census." n.d. U.S. Census Bureau. https://www.census.gov/history/pdf/1970_questionnaire.pdf.

18. Mora, *Making Hispanics*, p. 3.

19. Ibid., pp. 25–26.

20. Ibid., pp. 31–36.

21. Ibid., p. 35.

22. Ibid., p. 39.

23. Ibid., pp. 44–45.

24. Ibid., pp. 159–60.

25. Ibid., pp. 50–51.

26. Ibid., pp. 69–74.

27. Ibid., ch. 3.

28. "Census Questions on Race Assailed as Political by Population Experts." May 14, 1978. *The New York Times*. https://www.nytimes.com/1978/05/14/archives/census-questions-on-race-assailed-as-political-by-population.html.

29. Mora, *Making Hispanics*, p. 101.

30. Taylor, Paul, Mark Hugo Lopez, Jessica Martínez, and Gabriel Velasco. Apr 4, 2012. "When Labels Don't Fit: Hispanics and Their Views of Identity." Pew Research Center. https://www.pewresearch.org/hispanic/2012/04/04/when-labels-dont-fit-hispanics-and-their-views-of-identity/.

31. Lopez, Mark Hugo. Oct 22, 2013. "Three-Fourths of Hispanics Say Their Community Needs a Leader." Pew Research Center. https://www.pewresearch.org/hispanic/2013/10/22/three-fourths-of-hispanics-say-their-community-needs-a-leader/.

32. "The Use of 'LatinX' Among Hispanic Voters." n.d. Bendixen & Amandi International. https://www.politico.com/f/?id=0000017d-81be-dee4-a5ff-efbe74ec0000.

33. Sowell, Thomas, 1983. *The Economics and Politics of Race: An International Perspective*. William Morrow: p. 187.

34. Bernstein, David E. 2022. *Classified: The Untold Story of Racial Classification in America*. Simon & Schuster: p. 9.

35. Orlans, Harold. 1989. "The Politics of Minority Statistics." *Society* 26(4): 24–25.

36. "The Population of Hawai'i by Race/Ethnicity: US Census 1900–2010." Jun 16, 2011. Native Hawaiian Data Book. http://www.ohadatabook.com/T01-03-11u.pdf.

37. Skrentny, *Minority Rights Revolution*, ch. 5.

38. Graham, *Collision Course*, pp. 146–49.

39. "SBA Releases FY 2020 Disaggregated Contracting Data." Dec 1, 2021. US Small Business Administration. https://www.sba.gov/blog/sba-releases-fy-2020-disaggregated-contracting-data.

40. "Counting in the Dark: Michael Omi Shows That the Census Has Become a Critical Racial Battleground." Apr 30, 2001. *Colorlines* 12; Bernstein, *Classified*, pp. 23–24.

41. For a discussion of the political activity of white ethnics, see Skrentny, *Minority Rights Revolution*, ch. 9.

42. Ibid., pp. 281–82.

43. Ibid., pp. 287–89.

44. Ibid., pp. 294–95.

45. Bernstein, *Classified*, p. 73.

46. Hanania, Richard. 2021. "Cui Bono?: Partisanship and Attitudes Toward Refugees." *Social Science Quarterly* 102(1): 166–178.

47. Cohn, D'Vera, Eileen Patten, and Mark Hugo Lopez. Aug 11, 2014. "Puerto Rican Population Declines on Island, Grows on US Mainland." Pew Research Center. https://

www.pewresearch.org/hispanic/2014/08/11/puerto-rican-population-declines-on-island -grows-on-u-s-mainland/; Gonzalez-Barrera, Ana, and Mark Hugo Lopez. May 1, 2013. "A Demographic Portrait of Mexican-Origin Hispanics in the United States." Pew Research Center. https://www.pewresearch.org/hispanic/2013/05/01/a-demographic-portrait-of-mex ican-origin-hispanics-in-the-united-states/.

48. See Schultz, Vicki. 2002. "The Sanitized Workplace." *Yale Law Journal* 112(8): 2061–193: p. 2075, fn 20.

49. Discussion of government policy with regard to discrimination against women in the years after the Civil Rights Act relies on Skrentny, *Minority Rights Revolution*, pp. 111–19.

50. Ibid., p. 117.

51. *Peltier v. Charter Day Schools*, No. 20–1001 (4th Cir., Jun 14, 2022).

52. Ibid., Wynn concurrence, fn 6.

53. Kaufmann, Eric. May 30, 2022. "Born This Way?: The Rise of LGBT as a Social and Polit- ical Identity." Center for the Study of Partisanship and Ideology. https://www.cspicenter .com/p/born-this-way-the-rise-of-lgbt-as-a-social-and-political-identity; Stevenson, Bet- sey, and Justin Wolfers. 2009. "The Paradox of Declining Female Happiness." *American Economic Journal: Economic Policy* 1(2): 190–225. https://www.nber.org/papers/w14969.

54. Melnick, *Transformation of Title IX*, pp. 85–86.

55. *Parker v. Franklin County Community School Corp.*, 667 F.3d 910 (7th Cir., 2012); Melnick, *Transformation of Title IX*, p. 287.

56. Melnick, *Transformation of Title IX*, pp. 114–15.

57. *Wilson v. Southwest Airlines Co.*, 517 F. Supp. 292 (N.D. Tex. 1981).

58. Campbell, Alexia Fernández. Jun 20, 2019. "These News Anchors Say Their Bosses Are Grooming Younger Women Who Look Like Them to Take Their Jobs." *Vox*. https://www .vox.com/2019/6/20/18691881/ny1-anchors-sue-age-discrimination.

59. Schultz, "The Sanitized Workplace."

60. Melnick, *Transformation of Title IX*, ch. 11.

61. Brenan, Megan. Oct 24, 2019. "Record-High 56% of US Women Prefer Working to Home- making." Gallup. https://news.gallup.com/poll/267737/record-high-women-prefer-work ing-homemaking.aspx.

62. Rosenfeld, Michael, Rueben J. Thomas, and Sonia Hausen. 2019. "Disintermediating Your Friends: How Online Dating in the United States Displaces Other Ways of Meeting." *PNAS* 116(36): 17753–58, fig. 1.

63. Ortiz-Ospina, Esteban, and Sandra Tzvetkova. Oct 16, 2017. "Working Women: Key Facts and Trends in Female Labor Force Participation." Our World in Data. https://ourworldin data.org/female-labor-force-participation-key-facts.

64. Liptak, Adam. Jun 15, 2020. "Civil Rights Law Protects Gay and Transgender Workers, Supreme Court Rules." *The New York Times*. https://www.nytimes.com/2020/06/15/us /gay-transgender-workers-supreme-court.html.

65. Kaufmann, "Born This Way?"

66. Sailer, Steve. Jul 8, 2012. "Diversity Before Diversity: James Jesus Angleton." *iSteve*. https:// isteve.blogspot.com/2012/07/diversity-before-diversity-james-jesus.html; Sailer, Steve. Jan 19, 2014. "Diversity Before Diversity: Oklahoma's 1907 Senators." *The Unz Review*. https://www.unz.com/isteve/diversity-before-diversity-oklahomas/; Sailer, Steve. Jul 6, 2012. "Diversity Before Diversity: Duke Kahanamoku." *iSteve*. https://isteve.blogspot.com /2012/07/diversity-before-diversity-duke.html.

67. Fuller, Thomas. Feb 27, 2021. "He Came from Thailand to Care for Family. Then Came a Brutal Attack." *The New York Times*. https://www.nytimes.com/2021/02/27/us/asian -american-hate-crimes.html.

68. Naylor, Brian. Nov 23, 2020. "Alejandro Mayorkas, Biden's Pick for DHS Head, Would Be 1st Latino in Post." NPR. https://www.npr.org/sections/biden-transition-updates /2020/11/23/938027626/alejandro-mayorkas-bidens-pick-for-dhs-head-would-be-first -latino-in-post.

69. "Best Practices for Fostering Diversity & Inclusion." Last accessed Aug 29, 2022. Office of Federal Contract Compliance Programs. https://www.dol.gov/agencies/ofccp/compliance-assistance/outreach/hbcu-initiative/best-practices.

Chapter 5. Social Engineering as a Cause of Stagnation, Ennui, and Social Strife

1. On the ubiquity and universality of ethnic differences in outcomes, see Sowell, *Discrimination and Disparities*.
2. Ibid., pp. 179–245.
3. Farron, "Prejudice Is Free," 231–38.
4. Ibid.
5. Fukuyama, Francis. 2011. *The Origins of Political Order: From Prehuman Times to the French Revolution*. Farrar, Straus and Giroux.
6. Hoogenboom, Ari. 1959. "The Pendleton Act and the Civil Service." *The American Historical Review* 64(2): 301–18, p. 302.
7. Jenckes, Thomas E. 1868. "The Civil Service Report of Mr. Jenckes, of Rhode Island, from the Joint Select Committee on Retrenchment, Made to the House of Representative of the United States, May 14, 1868." US Government Printing Office: p. 13.
8. The text of the Pendleton Act is available on the website of the National Archives, at https://www.archives.gov/milestone-documents/pendleton-act.
9. Hoogenboom, "The Pendleton Act," p. 303.
10. Ibid., p. 304.
11. Ibid., p. 317.
12. For discussion of this point, see Wax, "Disparate Impact Realism," pp. 637–44.
13. Ibid., pp. 644–64.
14. Belz, *Equality Transformed*, p. 28.
15. Berns, Walter. May 1, 1981. "Let Me Call You Quota, Sweetheart." American Enterprise Institute. https://www.aei.org/articles/let-me-call-you-quota-sweetheart/.
16. Belz, *Equality Transformed*, p. 119.
17. "Federal Civil Rights Enforcement: A Report of the United States Commission on Civil Rights." Sep 1970. US Commission on Civil Rights: p. 81–84. https://static.ewg.org/reports/2021/BlackFarmerDiscriminationTimeline/cr12en2.pdf.
18. Belz, *Equality Transformed*, pp. 124–26.
19. Malbin, Michael J. Sep 29, 1973. "Employment Report/Proposed Federal Guidelines on Hiring Could Have Far-reaching Impact." *National Journal*: 1429–34.
20. Belz, *Equality Transformed*, p. 127.
21. Quoted in Glazer, *Affirmative Discrimination*, p. 55.
22. Belz, *Equality Transformed*, pp. 127–28.
23. Berns, "Let Me Call You Quota."
24. Rein, Lisa. Apr 2, 2015. "For Federal-Worker Hopefuls, the Civil Service Exam Is Making a Comeback." *The Washington Post*. https://www.washingtonpost.com/news/federal-eye/wp/2015/04/02/for-federal-worker-hopefuls-the-civil-service-exam-is-making-a-comeback/.
25. Bovard, James. Mar 1994. "Job-Breakers: The EEOC's Assault on the Workplace." *The American Spectator*: pp. 32–37.
26. Greenlaw, Paul S., and Sanne S. Jensen. 1996. "Race-Norming and the Civil Rights Act of 1991." *Public Personnel Management* 25(1): 13–24.
27. Lasley, James. 2012. *Los Angeles Police Department Meltdown: The Fall of the Professional-Reform Model of Policing*. CRC Press: pp. 109–10.
28. Associated Press. Mar 23, 2022. "Army Eases Fitness Test Standards for Women, Older Troops." *U.S. News & World Report*. https://www.usnews.com/news/politics/articles/2022-03-23/army-eases-fitness-test-standards-for-women-older-troops.

29. Belz, *Equality Transformed*, p. 123.
30. Wayt, Theo. Mar 15, 2022. "Silicon Valley Firm Apologizes After Asking Job Applicants for IQ Scores." *New York Post*. https://nypost.com/2022/03/15/silicon-valley-firm-apologizes-after-asking-applicants-for-iq-scores/.
31. Wax, "Disparate Impact Realism," pp. 648–50, 672.
32. Ibid., pp. 642–44, 655–56.
33. Ramey, Garey, and Valerie A. Ramey. Mar 2010. "The Rug Rat Race." Brookings Institution. https://www.brookings.edu/wp-content/uploads/2010/03/2010a_bpea_ramey.pdf.
34. The discussion on happiness research in this paragraph is based on the discussion in Stephens-Davidowitz, Seth. 2022. *Don't Trust Your Gut: Using Data to Get What You Really Want in Life*. Dey Street Books: ch. 8 and ch. 9.
35. *Dobbs v. Jackson Women's Health Organization*, No. 19–1392, 597 US ___ (2022). See Part II.D.3 of the opinion.
36. Leiter, Brian. 2012. *Why Tolerate Religion?* Princeton University Press.
37. Graf, Nikki. Feb 25, 2019. "Most Americans Say Colleges Should Not Consider Race or Ethnicity in Admissions." Pew Research Center. https://www.pewresearch.org/fact-tank/2019/02/25/most-americans-say-colleges-should-not-consider-race-or-ethnicity-in-admissions/.
38. *Davis v. Monsanto Chemical Co.*, 858 F.2d 345 (6th Cir., 1988).
39. Dunbar, Robin I. M. 1998. "The Social Brain Hypothesis." *Evolutionary Anthropology* 6(5): 178–190.
40. Schumpeter, Joseph A. 1942. *Capitalism, Socialism and Democracy*. Harper Torchbooks: p. 83.
41. Becker, Gary S. 2010. *The Economics of Discrimination*. University of Chicago Press.
42. Jeste, Dilip V., Ellen E. Lee, and Stephanie Cacioppo. 2020. "Battling the Modern Behavioral Epidemic of Loneliness: Suggestions for Research and Interventions." *JAMA Psychiatry* 77(6): 553–54.
43. Wee, Sui-Lee, and Raymond Zhong. Sep 1, 2021. "After Proudly Celebrating Women, Alibaba Faces Reckoning Over Harassment." *The New York Times*. https://www.nytimes.com/2021/09/01/technology/china-alibaba-rape-metoo.html.
44. Cheng, J. Yo-Jud, and Boris Groysberg. Jan 8, 2020. "How Corporate Cultures Differ Around the World." *Harvard Business Review*. https://hbr.org/2020/01/how-corporate-cultures-differ-around-the-world.
45. Boxell, Levi, Matthew Gentzkow, and Jesse M. Shapiro. 2022. "Cross-Country Trends in Affective Polarization." *The Review of Economics and Statistics* 1(60).
46. Klein, Ezra. 2020. *Why We're Polarized*. Simon & Schuster.
47. Abramowitz, Alan, and Jennifer McCoy. 2019. "United States: Racial Resentment, Negative Partisanship, and Polarization in Trump's America." *The Annals of the American Academy of Political and Social Science* 681(1): 137–56.
48. Perlstein, *Nixonland*, Preface and ch. 1.
49. See, e.g., Gilens, Martin. 1995. "Racial Attitudes and Opposition to Welfare." *The Journal of Politics* 57(4): 994–1014; Sears, David O., Richard R. Lau, Tom R. Tyler, and Harris M. Allen Jr. 1980. "Self-interest vs. Symbolic Politics in Policy Attitudes and Presidential Voting." *American Political Science Review* 74(3): 670–84; Gilens, Martin. 1996. "'Race Coding' and White Opposition to Welfare." *American Political Science Review* 90(3): 593–604; Hawley, George, and Richard Hanania. Nov 29, 2020. "The National Populist Illusion: Why Culture, Not Economics, Drives American Politics." Center for the Study of Partisanship and Ideology. https://www.cspicenter.com/p/the-national-populist-illusion-why-culture-not-economics-drives-american-politics.
50. Enders, Adam M. 2021. "A Matter of Principle?: On the Relationship Between Racial Resentment and Ideology." *Political Behavior* 43(2): 561–84.
51. For a less biased take on the data, see Hawley and Hanania, "The National Populist Illusion."

52. Anderson, *Pursuit of Fairness*, pp. 116–27.

53. See "Affirmative Action on the Ballot." Last accessed Aug 30, 2022. Ballotpedia. https://ballotpedia.org/Affirmative_action_on_the_ballot. This analysis excludes two referenda listed on the page as of February 2021 because they did not deal with affirmative action. One was a successful Colorado 1992 initiative that rejected sexual orientation as a protected class in the state, and the other a failed 2003 California initiative to completely do away with all racial classification in public education, public employment, and government contracting.

54. "'EEO Is the Law' Poster." Last accessed Aug 30, 2022. US Equal Employment Opportunity Commission. https://www.eeoc.gov/employers/eeo-law-poster.

55. Chait, Jonathan. Feb 8, 2022. "The Left Is Gaslighting Asian Americans About College Admissions." *New York Magazine*. https://nymag.com/intelligencer/2022/02/the-left-is-gaslighting-asian-americans-on-school-admissions.html.

56. Goldberg, Jonah. Apr 2, 2016. "Trump's Lies Are a Loyalty Test for His Followers." *National Review*. https://www.nationalreview.com/g-file/donald-trump-michelle-fields-corey-lewandowski-lies-followers/; Parker, Ashley, and Marianna Sotomayor. May 2, 2021. "For Republicans, Fealty to Trump's Election Falsehood Becomes Defining Test." *The Washington Post*. https://www.washingtonpost.com/politics/republicans-trump-election-falsehood/2021/05/01/7bd380a0-a921-11eb-8c1a-56f0cb4ff3b5_story.html.

57. Anderson, *Pursuit of Fairness*, pp. 105–6.

58. Kotlowski, *Nixon's Civil Rights*, pp. 127–30.

59. Sowell, Thomas. 2005. *Affirmative Action Around the World: An Empirical Study*. Yale University Press.

Chapter 6. Republicans and Civil Rights Law

1. Hanson, Robin. Mar 13, 2019. "To Oppose Polarization, Tug Sideways." *Overcoming Bias*. https://www.overcomingbias.com/2019/03/tug-sideways.html.

2. For a summary, see Bazelon, Simon, and Matthew Yglesias. Jun 21, 2021. "The Rise and Importance of Secret Congress." *Slow Boring*. https://www.slowboring.com/p/the-rise-and-importance-of-secret.

3. Ahmari, Sohrab. May 29, 2019. "Against David French-ism." *First Things*. https://www.firstthings.com/web-exclusives/2019/05/against-david-french-ism.

4. Soave, Robbie. Apr 21, 2021. "Why the Conservative War on Woke Capital Is Doomed to Fail." *Reason*. https://reason.com/2021/04/21/woke-capital-conservatives-regulate-richard-hanania/.

5. Hanania, Richard. Winter 2021. "The Weakness of Conservative Anti-Wokeness." *American Affairs*. https://americanaffairsjournal.org/2021/11/the-weakness-of-conservative-anti-wokeness/; Hanania, Richard. Feb 23, 2022. "Conservatives Are Walking into a Trap on Antitrust." *Newsweek*. https://www.newsweek.com/conservatives-are-walking-trap-antitrust-opinion-1681927.

6. "Text of Goldwater Speech on Rights." Jun 19, 1964. *The New York Times*. https://www.nytimes.com/1964/06/19/archives/text-of-goldwater-speech-on-rights.html.

7. Har, Janie. Nov 4, 2020. "Politically Liberal California Rejects Affirmative Action." *AP News*. https://apnews.com/article/race-and-ethnicity-campaigns-san-francisco-college-admissions-california-4c56c600c86f37289e435be85695872a.

8. Bazelon, Simon, and David Shor. Sep 28, 2021. "A Permanent CTC Expansion with a Sharper Means-Test Would Protect Poor Kids Better and Be More Popular." *Slow Boring*. https://www.slowboring.com/p/a-permanent-ctc-expansion-with-a.

9. Greenberg, Stanley B. Mar 25, 2022. "The Real Lesson for All Factions of the Democratic Party." *The American Prospect*. https://prospect.org/politics/real-lesson-for-all-factions-of-the-democratic-party/.

10. Saad, Lydia. Jul 30, 2021. "Americans' Confidence in Racial Fairness Waning." Gallup. https://news.gallup.com/poll/352832/americans-confidence-racial-fairness-waning.aspx.

11. Cited in Wolters, Raymond. 1996. *Right Turn: William Bradford Reynolds, the Reagan Administration, and Black Civil Rights.* Routledge: Introduction.

12. Lochhead, Carolyn. Nov 4, 2004. "Gay Marriage: Did Issue Help Re-Elect Bush?" *SFGate.* https://www.sfgate.com/news/article/GAY-MARRIAGE-Did-issue-help-re-elect-Bush-26 77003.php.

13. Block, M., and S. Twist. 1994. "Report Card on Crime and Punishment." US Department of Justice. https://www.ojp.gov/ncjrs/virtual-library/abstracts/report-card-crime-and-pun ishment.

14. Eskridge, William N., Jr. 1991. "Reneging on History?: Playing the Court/Congress/President Civil Rights Game." *California Law Review* 79(3): 613–84, pp. 618–23.

15. Perlstein, *Nixonland*, ch. 6.

16. Kotlowski, *Nixon's Civil Rights*, p. 7.

17. See Teles, Steven M. 2012. *The Rise of the Conservative Legal Movement.* Princeton University Press.

18. Yalof, David Alistair. 2001. *Pursuit of Justices: Presidential Politics and the Selection of Supreme Court Nominees.* University of Chicago Press: pp. 97–99.

19. Melnick, *Transformation of Title IX*, pp. 39–41.

20. Graham, *Civil Rights Era*, p. 340; Skrentny, *Ironies of Affirmative Action*, ch. 7.

21. Skrentny, *Ironies of Affirmative Action*, ch. 3, ch. 5.

22. Cohen, Alex, and John F. Kowal. Mar 19, 2019. "Is the GOP Warming Up to the Equal Rights Amendment?" https://www.brennancenter.org/our-work/analysis-opinion/gop-warm ing-equal-rights-amendment.

23. Teles, *Rise of the Conservative Legal Movement.*

24. Wolters, *Right Turn*, ch. 1.

25. Dobbin, *Inventing Equal Opportunity*, pp. 136–37; DuRivage, Virginia. 1985. "The OFCCP Under the Reagan Administration: Affirmative-Action in Retreat." *Labor Law Journal* 36(6): 360–68, pp. 364–65.

26. DuRivage, "The OFCCP Under the Reagan Administration," p. 364.

27. On Reagan's second term, see Wolters, *Right Turn*, ch. 13.

28. "Son of Bob Jones." Feb 19, 1986. *The Washington Post.* https://www.washingtonpost .com/archive/politics/1986/02/19/son-of-bob-jones/c5fe1e76-d6d9-40b4-8fc1-f3f909f 402fc/.

29. Melnick, *Transformation of Title IX*, p. 254.

30. Graham, Hugh Davis. 1998. "The Storm Over Grove City College: Civil Rights Regulation, Higher Education, and the Reagan Administration." *History of Education Quarterly* 38(4): 407–29, pp. 408–9, 422.

31. See, e.g., Walker, Dana. Jan 15, 1986. "Meese Says Affirmative Action Agreement Near." UPI. https://www.upi.com/Archives/1986/01/15/Meese-says-affirmative-action-agreement -near/8154506149200/; "Son of Bob Jones."

32. Eskridge, Jr., "Reneging on History?" p. 633.

33. Holmes, Steven A. Oct 23, 1990. "President Vetoes Bill on Job Rights; Showdown Is Set." *The New York Times.* https://www.nytimes.com/1990/10/23/us/president-vetoes-bill-on -job-rights-showdown-is-set.html.

34. Heriot, "The Roots of Wokeness," p. 32.

35. Anderson, *Pursuit of Fairness*, pp. 211–12.

36. "Foes Pledge to End 'Affirmative Racism.'" Feb 13, 1997. *Deseret News.* https://www.de seret.com/1997/2/13/19294912/foes-pledge-to-end-affirmative-racism.

37. Merida, Kevin. Jul 29, 1995. "Within GOP, Conflicts on Affirmative Action." *The Washington Post.* https://www.washingtonpost.com/archive/politics/1995/07/29/within-gop-con flicts-on-affirmative-action/56168550-bad7-42bb-b973-02387af26e10/.

38. Merida, Kevin. Jul 21, 1995. "Senate Rejects Gramm Bid to Bar Affirmation [*sic*] Action Set-Asides." *The Washington Post*. https://www.washingtonpost.com/archive/politics /1995/07/21/senate-rejects-gramm-bid-to-bar-affirmation-action-set-asides/f66a37 55-21ba-44e3-b4dd-e1a0c7819013/.

39. "Report on the Activities of the Committee on the Judiciary of the House of Representatives During the One Hundred Fourth Congress Pursuant to Clause 1(D) Rule XI of the Rules of the House of Representatives." Jan 2, 1997. GovInfo. https://www.govinfo.gov /content/pkg/CRPT-104hrpt879/html/CRPT-104hrpt879.htm.

40. Broder, David S. Jul 22, 1995. "Kemp Says GOP Candidates Wrong on Affirmative Action." *The Washington Post*. https://www.washingtonpost.com/archive/politics/1995/07/22 /kemp-says-gop-candidates-wrong-on-affirmative-action/72820c28-397c-4cb1-bd8d -5292065ff2e4/.

41. "Bush's Statement on Affirmative Action." Jan 15, 2003. *The New York Times*. https://www .nytimes.com/2003/01/15/politics/bushs-statement-on-affirmative-action.html.

42. Songer, Michael J. 2005. "Decline of Title VII Disparate Impact: The Role of the 1991 Civil Rights Act and the Ideologies of Federal Judges." *Michigan Journal of Race & Law* 11: 247–73.

43. The version passed by the Senate was then adopted by voice vote in the House.

44. Hare, Christopher, Keith T. Poole, and Howard Rosen. Feb 13, 2014. "Polarization in Congress Has Risen Sharply. Where Is It Going Next?" *The Washington Post*. https://www .washingtonpost.com/news/monkey-cage/wp/2014/02/13/polarization-in-congress-has -risen-sharply-where-is-it-going-next/; Khazatsky, Andrei. 2022. "The Rise of Political Polarization and Partisanship in the US." *The UNISVerse*. https://theunisverse.com/2031 /features/the-rise-of-political-polarization-and-partisanship-in-the-u-s/.

45. Andris, Clio, et al. 2015. "The Rise of Partisanship and Super-Cooperators in the US House of Representatives." *PLOS ONE* 10(4).

46. For this trend in the U.S. as part of a global phenomenon, see Gethin, Amory, Clara Martínez-Toledano, and Thomas Piketty. 2022. "Brahmin Left Versus Merchant Right: Changing Political Cleavages in 21 Western Democracies, 1948–2020." *The Quarterly Journal of Economics* 137(1): 1–48.

47. See Hanania, Richard. Nov 1, 2021. "Liberals Read, Conservatives Watch TV." https:// richardhanania.substack.com/p/liberals-read-conservatives-watch; Hanania, Richard. Oct 22, 2022. "A Psychological Theory of the Culture War." https://richardhanania.sub stack.com/p/a-psychological-theory-of-the-culture.

48. Melnick, *Transformation of Title IX*, ch. 2, figs. 2–2, 2–4.

49. Steinhauer, Jennifer. Dec 4, 2012. "Despite Bob Dole's Wish, Republicans Reject Disabilities Treaty." *The New York Times*. https://www.nytimes.com/2012/12/05/us/despite-doles -wish-gop-rejects-disabilities-treaty.html.

50. 117th Congress (2021–2022). n.d. "H.R.5—Equality Act." Congress.gov. https://www.con gress.gov/bill/117th-congress/house-bill/5?q=%7B%22search%22%3A%5B%22equality+act %22%5D%7D&s=1&r=3.

51. Melnick, *Transformation of Title IX*, pp. 247–51.

52. Wolters, *Right Turn*, ch. 5.

53. Hawley and Hanania, "The National Populist Illusion."

54. See Thoreson, Ryan. Jan 8, 2021. "Trump Administration Again Weakens LGBT Protections." Human Rights Watch. https://www.hrw.org/news/2021/01/08/trump-administ ration-again-weakens-lgbt-protections.

55. See Gersen, Jeanie Suk. May 16, 2020. "How Concerning Are the Trump Administration's New Title IX Regulations?" *The New Yorker*. https://www.newyorker.com/news/our -columnists/how-concerning-are-the-trump-administrations-new-title-ix-regulations.

56. See Dorman, Sam. Sep 2, 2020. "Chris Rufo Calls on Trump to End Critical Race Theory 'Cult Indoctrination' in Federal Government." Fox News. https://www.foxnews.com/poli tics/chris-rufo-race-theory-cult-federal-government; Meckler, Laura, and Josh Dawsey.

Jun 21, 2021. "Activist Christopher Rufo Fuels GOP's Critical Race Theory Fight." *The Washington Post*. https://www.washingtonpost.com/education/2021/06/19/critical-race -theory-rufo-republicans/.

57. Meckler, Laura, and Devlin Barrett. Jan 5, 2021. "Trump Administration Seeks to Undo Decades-Long Rules on Discrimination." *The Washington Post*. https://www.washington post.com/education/civil-rights-act-disparate-impact-discrimination/2021/01/05/4f570 01a-4fc1-11eb-bda4-615aaefd0555_story.html.

58. Skrentny, "Republican Efforts to End Affirmative Action," p. 148.

59. Reilly, Wilfred. 2019. *Hate Crime Hoax: How the Left Is Selling a Fake Race War*. Simon & Schuster.

60. See "How Popular Is Joe Biden?" *FiveThirtyEight*. https://projects.fivethirtyeight.com /biden-approval-rating/.

Chapter 7. What Is to Be Done?

1. Link, Devon. Jul 9, 2020. "Fact Check: Sex Between Police Officers and Their Detainees Isn't Illegal in Many States." *USA Today*. https://www.usatoday.com/story/news/fact check/2020/07/09/fact-check-police-detainee-sex-not-illegal-many-states/5383769002/.

2. "Statistics and Historical Comparison." Accessed Sep 2, 2022. GovTrack. https://www .govtrack.us/congress/bills/statistics; "Executive Orders." Accessed Sep 2, 2022. The American Presidency Project. https://www.presidency.ucsb.edu/statistics/data/executive -orders.

3. "About the Supreme Court." Accessed Sep 2, 2022. U.S. Courts. https://www.uscourts.gov /about-federal-courts/educational-resources/about-educational-outreach/activity-re sources/about.

4. Caldwell, Christopher. 2020. *The Age of Entitlement: America Since the Sixties*. Simon & Schuster: ch. 8.

5. Heriot, "Title VII Disparate Impact Liability," pp. 42–43.

6. Gerstein, Josh, and Ximena Bustillo. Sep 24, 2021. "DOJ Forgoes Appeal of Order Blocking Money for Minority Farmers." *Politico*. https://www.politico.com/news/2021/08/24 /doj-appeal-minority-farmers-506820.

7. Teles, Steven M. 2012. *The Rise of the Conservative Legal Movement*. Princeton University Press: ch. 1.

8. Meckler, Laura, and Devlin Barrett. Jan 3, 2019. "Trump Administration Considers Rollback of Anti-Discrimination Rules." *The Washington Post*. https://www.washingtonpost .com/local/education/trump-administration-considers-rollback-of-anti-discrimination -rules/2019/01/02/f96347ea-046d-11e9-b5df-5d3874f1ac36_story.html.

9. Heriot, "Title VII Disparate Impact Liability," pp. 99–103.

10. Sullivan, Charles A. 2003. "The World Turned Upside Down: Disparate Impact Claims by White Males." *Northwest University Law Review* 98(4): 1505–66, p. 1546.

11. For arguments regarding the unconstitutionality of disparate impact based on discrimination against whites and the broad delegation of authority, see Heriot, "Title VII Disparate Impact Liability," pp. 143–69.

12. "The US Department of Education Releases Proposed Changes to Title IX Regulations, Invites Public Comment." Jun 23, 2022. US Department of Education. https://www .ed.gov/news/press-releases/us-department-education-releases-proposed-changes-title -ix-regulations-invites-public-comment.

13. See "US Department of Labor Announces Best Year for Compliance Assistance by Office of Federal Contract Compliance Programs." Oct 19, 2021. US Department of Labor. https://www.dol.gov/newsroom/releases/ofccp/ofccp20201019-0; "Federal Civilian Employment." Sep 2017. U.S. Office of Personnel Management. https://www.opm.gov /policy-data-oversight/data-analysis-documentation/federal-employment-reports/re ports-publications/federal-civilian-employment/; Hill, Fiona. May 27, 2020. "Public Ser-

vice and the Federal Government." Brookings Institution. https://www.brookings.edu/policy2020/votervital/public-service-and-the-federal-government/.

14. *Texas Department of Housing and Community Affairs v. Inclusive Communities Project, Inc.*, 576 US ___ (2015).

15. Wolter, *Right Turn*, ch. 14; Anderson, *Pursuit of Fairness*, p. 272.

16. Anderson, *Pursuit of Fairness*, pp. 252–53.

17. Wiggins, Bradford J., and Cody D. Christopherson. 2019. "The Replication Crisis in Psychology: An Overview for Theoretical and Philosophical Psychology." *Journal of Theoretical and Philosophical Psychology* 39(4): 202–17.

18. Melnick, *Transformation of Title IX*, ch. 12.

19. *Comcast Corp. v. National Association of African American–Owned Media*, 589 US ___ (2020): II.A.

20. "*Gratz v. Bollinger; Grutter v. Bollinger.*" n.d. The Center for Individual Rights. https://www.cir-usa.org/case/gratz-v-bollinger-grutter-v-bollinger/.

21. Storm, Roy. Nov 20, 2019. "Snubbing Trump, Lawyers Doling More Cash to Democrats." *Bloomberg Law*. https://news.bloomberglaw.com/us-law-week/snubbing-trump-lawyers-doling-more-cash-to-democrats.

22. Epstein, Richard A. 1995. *Forbidden Grounds: The Case Against Employment Discrimination Laws*. Harvard University Press: pp. 415–16.

23. Gray, C. Boyden. Apr 27, 2021. "Re: Coca-Cola's Racially Discriminatory Outside Counsel Policy." Boyden Gray & Associates PLLC. https://mma.prnewswire.com/media/1498756/POFR_COKE_Boyden_Gray__21_4_27_Letter_to_Coca_Cola_FINAL.pdf?p=pdf.

24. Heriot, "Title VII Disparate Impact Liability," p. 139.

25. DuRivage, "The OFCCP Under the Reagan Administration," p. 364.

26. See "Diversity on Boards." Accessed Mar 18, 2022. California Secretary of State. https://www.sos.ca.gov/business-programs/diversity-boards.

27. Skrentny, "Republican Efforts to End Affirmative Action," p. 140.

28. Heriot, Gail L. Apr 17, 2018. "It's Time for the Executive Branch to Conduct a 'Disparate Impact Inventory': Remarks at the Federalist Society's Sixth Annual Executive Branch Review." Washington, DC. San Diego Legal Studies Paper No. 18–347.

29. Farhang, *The Litigation State*.

30. Atterbury, Andrew. Dec 16, 2021. "DeSantis Pushes Bill That Allows Parent to Sue Schools Over Critical Race Theory." *Politico*. https://www.politico.com/news/2021/12/16/desantis-bill-critical-race-theory-525118; see Sen. Diaz. 2022. "Florida Senate—2022: SB 148." The Florida Senate. https://www.flsenate.gov/Session/Bill/2022/148/BillText/Filed/HTML.

31. Temple-West, Patrick, and Joshua Franklin. Aug 7, 2022. "US Banks Tout Fossil Fuel Credentials After Republican ESG Backlash." *Financial Times*. https://www.ft.com/content/a35dc7ce-defb-4181-b528-c0b1e34e1d07?shareType=nongift.

32. I'd like to thank Jonathan Mitchell for bringing the idea of using state contracting to go after wokeness to my attention.

33. Claburn, Thomas. May 9, 2019. "Oracle's Legal Woes Deepen: Big Red Sued (Again) for Age and Medical 'Discrimination.'" *The Register*. https://www.theregister.com/2019/05/09/oracle_sued_age_discrimination/; Scheiber, "Making 'Dinobabies' Extinct"; Baron, "Google Settles 'Age-Discrimination' Class-Action."

34. Hochman, Nate. Mar 7, 2022. "Another Republican Drops Support for the Pro-Trans Fairness for All Act." *National Review*. https://www.nationalreview.com/corner/another-republican-drops-support-for-the-pro-trans-fairness-for-all-act/.

35. "Booker Applauds Bipartisan Vote in House to Pass CROWN Act." Mar 18, 2022. https://www.booker.senate.gov/news/press/booker-applauds-bipartisan-vote-in-house-to-pass-crown-act. For the text of the bill: https://www.congress.gov/bill/117th-congress/house-bill/2116/text.

36. Rovner, Julie. Dec 14, 2009. "Abortion Funding Ban Has Evolved Over the Years." NPR. https://www.npr.org/templates/story/story.php?storyId=121402281?storyId=121402281.

37. Rovner, Julie. Mar 21, 2018. "Clash Over Abortion Stalls Health Bill, Again." NPR. https://www.npr.org/sections/health-shots/2018/03/21/595191785/clash-over-abortion-hobbles-a-health-bill-again-here-s-how.

Conclusion. Unleashing American Freedom and Creativity

1. See Lyons, N. S. Jan 18, 2022. "No, the Revolution Isn't Over." *The Upheaval*. https://theupheaval.substack.com/p/no-the-revolution-isnt-over?s=r.

2. See Marcus, Ezra. Jun 17, 2021. "The Lindy Way of Living." *The New York Times*. https://www.nytimes.com/2021/06/17/style/lindy.html.

3. "Most of Post-War Justice Ministry Were Nazis: Report." Oct 10, 2016. *The Local*. https://www.thelocal.de/20161010/most-of-post-war-justice-ministry-were-nazis-study/.

4. I thank a commentator who goes by the name "Mark" on my Substack for making this point. https://twitter.com/RichardHanania/status/1507451105092939777?s=20&t=aQp_vnl-CAyLY1zjEo6LKQ.

5. Cowen, Tyler. Sep 19, 2021. "Why Wokism Will Rule the World." *Bloomberg*. https://www.bloomberg.com/opinion/articles/2021-09-19/woke-movement-is-global-and-america-should-be-mostly-proud.

6. Pinker, Steven. 2018. *Enlightenment Now: The Case for Reason, Science, Humanism, and Progress*. Penguin Books: ch. 17.

7. McAuley, James. Jun 26, 2020. "How France's Aversion to Collecting Data on Race Affects Its Coronavirus Response." *The Washington Post*. https://www.washingtonpost.com/world/europe/coronavirus-france-race-data/2020/06/25/e5b4d0a6-b58d-11ea-9a1d-d3db1cbe07ce_story.html.

8. Onishi, Norimitsu. Feb 9, 2021. "Will American Ideas Tear France Apart?: Some of Its Leaders Think So." *The New York Times*. https://www.nytimes.com/2021/02/09/world/europe/france-threat-american-universities.html.

9. Poushter, Jacob, and Nicholas Kent. Jun 25, 2020. "The Global Divide on Homosexuality Persists." Pew Research Center. https://www.pewresearch.org/global/2020/06/25/global-divide-on-homosexuality-persists/.

10. Neely, Tucker. Jan 7, 2016. "He Got His Way. Then He Got a Mess." *The Washington Post*. https://www.washingtonpost.com/sf/national/2016/01/07/decidersbush/.

11. Douthat, Ross. 2020. *The Decadent Society: How We Became the Victims of Our Own Success*. Simon & Schuster: ch. 4; Douthat, Ross. Mar 7, 2018. "The Autumn of the Oscars." *The New York Times*. https://www.nytimes.com/2018/03/07/opinion/oscars-irrelevant-decline-ratings.html.

Index

Page references in *italics* refer to figures and tables.

Melnick, R. Shep, 50–51, 53, 172,
194
merit
concept of, 20
Pendleton Act, 123, 125, 127
vs. representation, 125, 126
war on, 122–130
Meritor Savings Bank v. Vinson, 47
Merit Systems Protection Board,
126
Mexican Americans, 97–98,
105–106
Microsoft, 25
minorities
"minority rights revolution,"
159
official classifications of,
116–118
recognition of, 104–105
sexual, 115–116
Mitchell, John, 34
Mora, G. Christina, 97–98
moral panics, 229–230
Morgan Stanley, 72
Motorola, 40
Musk, Elon, 3, 136
Muslims, 18, 91, 117, 217

NAACP, 42
NASA, 20
National Center for Education
Statistics, 95
National Council of La Raza, 99
nationalism, 218
National Labor Relations Board,
49
National Organization for
Women, 109
National Review (periodical), 159,
210
National Rifle Association, 224
National Right to Life Committee,
224
National Science Foundation, 20
Native Americans, 57, 95–97,
102–103
Native Hawaiians, 95, 101, 102–103
Nazi Party, 122, 217

neoconservatives, 19
nepotism, 122–123
new right, 154–158
New Yorker (periodical), 88
New York Times (periodical), 20,
29, 84, 92, 99, 142
Ninth Circuit Court of Appeals,
71, 111
Nixon, Richard, 6, 11, 34, 37, 49,
98, 148, 160, 161–162, 168,
178, 191
Nixon administration, 86, 104,
127, 151, 159, 162
nondiscrimination, 39, 57, 109–110
non-retaliation principle, 80–81,
84
Novartis, 72

Obama, Barack, 34, 177
Obama administration, 44, 53–54,
74, 87, 104, 113, 178, 194, 211
Obergefell v. Hodges, 118, 134
O'Connor, Sandra Day, 196–197,
203
OCR. *see* Office for Civil Rights
(OCR)
OFCCP. *see* Office of Federal
Contract Compliance
Programs (OFCCP)
Office, The (TV show), 142
Office for Civil Rights (OCR), 44,
165, 175, 187, 194
limiting power of via courts,
198–199
Title IX guidance, 49–56
Office of Federal Contract
Compliance Programs
(OFCCP), 34, 37, 57, 60, 63,
74, 80, 118, 162, 164, 205–206,
209
Office of Management and Budget
(OMB), 94–95, 99, 102–103
Office of Personnel Management
(OPM), 126, 127
Office of the Director of National
Intelligence, 95
Office Space (film), 142
Ohio State University, 64

About the Author

RICHARD HANANIA is a research fellow at the University of Texas and the president and founder of the Center for the Study of Partisanship and Ideology. He was previously a research fellow at the Saltzman Institute of War and Peace Studies at Columbia University. He is also the author of *Public Choice Theory and the Illusion of Grand Strategy*. Hanania earned his PhD in political science from UCLA and is a graduate of the University of Chicago Law School.